A
LOANWORD
APPROACH

A LOANWORD APPROACH

to the

Teaching of English as a Foreign Language in Korea

Exploring the Effectiveness of a Multimedia Curriculum

David Kent

National Library of Australia Cataloguing-in-Publication entry:
Kent, David Bradley, author.
A loanword approach : to the teaching of English as a foreign language in Korea : exploring the effectiveness of a multimedia curriculum /
David Kent.

ISBN: 978-1-925555-02-8 (paperback)
Includes bibliographical references.
English language—Study and teaching—Korean speakers.
Language and languages—Foreign words and phrases.
Applied linguistics.
428.24957

Pedagogy Press. Sydney, Australia.
www.pedagogypress.com

First Edition.

DEDICATION

For Shirley May.

CONTENTS

ACKNOWLEDGMENTS

I extend my sincere and deepest appreciation to:

The *first-year Korean university students* who participated in the research for this book, as their involvement was invaluable, and made the book possible.

I also extend a great debt of gratitude to *Noel David* for his continued encouragement and support in all matters, and to *Matthew Hathaway* for being a valuable sounding board.

Special appreciation needs also to be attributed to my wife, *HyunHee*, for without her love, tolerance, sacrifice, and unyielding support, this book would not exist.

PREFACE

The native language of South Korea has come to contain a linguistic subset consisting of English and European loanwords and pseudo-loanwords. The notion that the English as a foreign language (EFL) learner is immersed in such a lexicon, and that this terminology could be utilized to effectively assist target language (Standard American English) vocabulary acquisition by the false-beginner through computer assisted language learning (CALL), was evaluated and examined.

The empirical investigation employed a within-methods (i.e. experiment and survey) design. To this end, multimedia-based learning environments were developed and deployed to empirically test investigative suppositions, in particular, to examine how the students' knowledge of English words adapted for use in the South Korean vernacular – loanwords – was affected by their attitudes towards computerized instruction, their preference for certain methods of learning and teaching, and also by the attributes of computerized instructional packages. Ultimately, a method of instruction grounded in both CALL and linguistic theory was developed, and its effectiveness for use with South Korean EFL learners in a university English program setting during the mid 2000s was assayed. Scholarly accounts of the South Korean cultural learning style were also taken into consideration, and the implications such accounts held for the implementation of CALL initiatives at the time scrutinized.

The findings of this study are significant at the administrative, practitioner, and field level. Research outcomes indicate (a) computer use did not bias results obtained through CALL; (b) use of the L1 (first language) to assist foreign language acquisition produced positive learning gains, albeit marginal and limited, as evidenced by the persistent difficulty that learners had in building new form-meaning connections between pseudo-loanwords in South Korean and English equivalents; and, (c) multimedia-based learning developed on cultural and classroom expectations of learners, as found in the literature, was not as successful as that it was contrasted against. Consequently, results of the research came to support usability of CALL and multimedia content in the tertiary education sector, the existence of a 'stabilized interlanguage' in South Korea, and the need to re-profile the South Korean cultural learning style and student classroom expectations pertaining to EFL.

Organization of the Text

This book has been reworked from a doctoral dissertation. It is intended to be read as a whole or in part, and by those members of the general public, or academia, who are interested in the topic.

It commences by providing a context for what will be explored throughout the text, by laying out a background and rationale in *Part One*. The core concepts from this background are then expanded upon within *Part Two* and *Part Three* of the book.

Part Two focuses on the place of EFL in the Korean education system and the implementation of computer technology for teaching and learning, while also examining the cultural influences on computer assisted learning and the use of English loanwords in the Korean context. Support from language learning and teaching theory then emerges to allow for the development of a loanword approach to the teaching of English as a foreign language. Focus is specifically placed on the decades of the 1990s and 2000s.

Part Three then focuses on developing a means to effectively implement this approach, from a multimedia context during the mid 2000s, along with a means to examine its efficacy. The method, refinement, findings and discussion of results are detailed.

The final chapter of the book, encompassing *Part Four*, comes to highlight the implications emerging from the text, and the potential significance of these to the field. Areas of future research are also underscored here.

Part One
INTRODUCTION

Part One
INTRODUCTION

BACKGROUND AND RATIONALE

The current education system of South Korea, hereafter Korea, was shaped around the middle of last century, tied specifically to national development goals, and came to see universal secondary and primary education provided to the population in just over a generation. To date, the grade school education system has been shaped by seven national curriculums (the seventh having a number of revisions), with each stressing importance on one aspect of education or another. This includes, more recently, focusing heavily on languages such as English and the use of educational technology in the learning process.

Regardless of the changes made to the teaching of English in Korea, and perhaps due to the cultural context of the local learning environment, Korean tertiary level students are still largely false-beginners of English. A false-beginner can be described as a person who has studied a second or foreign language for some time, has a limited knowledge of the language, but is unable to functionally communicate beyond the level of a beginner. Primarily, this book envisions that the linguistic competence of the Korean English as a foreign language (EFL) student can be effectively stimulated through the use of loan terminology, or more precisely, the English that forms a part of the learners' native vernacular (Shim, 1994; Baik & Shim 1998; J. J. Lee, 2004). Such terminology is intrinsically tied to the original culture (Taylor & Taylor, 1995), and it is believed that such nativized lexical elements could function as cross-linguistic mnemonic keys for phrases and vocabulary learned in the target language (Daulton, 1999a). Korean learners, even at advanced levels, inappropriately and continually misuse these terms in English conversation (Kent, 2000; Lee, 2004). The use and misuse of this terminology also leads to misunderstanding and confusion in the language learning process (Shepherd, 1996). Further, students are unaware of the contextual use of such vocabulary, and the differences in meaning in Korean from the English language source (Shaffer, 1999).

Although usefulness of the English inherent within the native vernacular is recognized as a learning resource for Japanese English as a foreign language (EFL) students (Daulton, 1998, 1999a, 1999b, 2003; Shepherd, 1996; Simon-Maeda, 1997) and their Korean counterparts (Shaffer, 1999), examination of the effectiveness of the practical application of such terminology for foreign language acquisition is extremely limited in Korea. Daulton (1998) highlights the scant research and empirical studies available, illustrating the positive effect of loanwords on English vocabulary acquisition for Japanese EFL students at all levels. Unfortunately, no substantial literature is available involving Korean learners.

In the past, extensive use of the native language in EFL has occurred through such largely criticized methodologies as grammar-translation, and this has since given way to approaches like the English-only policy of the communicative language teaching (CLT) approach. Where the theoretical basis underlying the communicative approach derives from the view that second/foreign languages are learned in a similar fashion to first languages, and that language is a system for expression of meaning, then the primary function of language is for interaction and communication, and the structure of language reflects its functional and appropriate communicative use (Richards & Rogers, 2001). As a result, the ability to be understood is more important than the grammatical correctness of the linguistic message. CLT also brought with it a shift from teacher-centered classrooms, as found in the application of methodologies like grammar-translation, to that of emphasis on creating student-centered classrooms.

Further, in the EFL arena, first language use by students has, among other things, traditionally been viewed as a crutch, but as Weschler (1997) argues, it can provide scaffolding and act as a building block for second language acquisition. Daulton (1998) agrees with this and, along with Canagarajah (1999), views the native language as a resource rather than a problem. Meanwhile, Danhua (1995) views it as a means of reference for adjusting to the target language. However, use of the first language with the target language has been seen as a hindrance, providing 'interference' which learners should try to avoid. Although Corder (in Ellis, 1992, p. 37) does suggest that such interference can be recast as a learner "strategy", from which the learner's native language may facilitate the developmental process of foreign language acquisition by assisting the learner to progress more rapidly along the universal route when the first language is similar to the one being acquired. Aspects of the native language in such cases can be used as a resource providing a strategy of communication. However, as Wigglesworth (2002, p. 22) cautions, even though native language use within EFL instructional settings can be defended, it must be introduced with "great care and attention".

Development of a loanword approach in the EFL teaching context seeks to emphasize vocabulary development by considering the first language loanword bank as a useful store of knowledge. This target language knowledge kernel can then promote aspects of positive transfer, lighten the burden of learning throughout the foreign language acquisition process, and provide scaffolding by acting as a building block for foreign language acquisition and using the native language as a resource and a means of reference for adjusting to the target language.

In this regard, loan terminology found in the first language of Korean EFL learners can be applied judiciously in that its use can be for support and scaffolding of lexical content for vocabulary acquisition in the target language (Standard American English). In fact, such an approach could go one step further than CLT, by not just using English to learn English, but applying the English inherent within the native vernacular to assist in the foreign language acquisition process of the false-beginner by stimulating positive language transfer. Nation (1990) provides support for such use of the first language in that it can assist in lightening the burden of learning. A bridge of linguistic commonality between Korean and English, and a bridge between the initial learning gap of these two languages, could then be provided. Further, Cook (1993, p. 92) affirms that "the multi-competence viewpoint that the foreign language learner's mind contains a double system in which two languages are used" should be considered within EFL environments, as opposed to forcing L2 (second language) learners to concentrate solely on use of the target language.

Taking the above into account, constructing an appropriate EFL framework for the use of loanwords for vocabulary acquisition in the EFL Korean context first required determining useful linguistic data that could assist false-beginners with their English vocabulary acquisition. This stemmed from previous research (see Kent, 1996). Development of such a framework also needed to center on an approach, or model, that provides the learner with an intellectual toolbox from which they can develop appropriate vocabulary acquisition and construct foreign language knowledge. This approach was then extended to include a variety of language activities, comprising those already familiar to the learner, from which the Korean EFL student could utilize their existing target language competence. This competence takes the form of a 'loanword bank' and was utilized in order to facilitate learning and to guide students along the foreign language acquisition and development pathway through one of two instructional strategies. These instructional strategies were packaged in multimedia-based computer assisted language learning (CALL) formats, and were specifically created to be applied during the course of research for this book.

The first format, used in Module One and being a traditional teaching oriented module, was behavioristic CALL phase focused (see Warschauer & Healey, 1998) and based on a restricted CALL approach (refer to Bax, 2003). The design matches closely with what the literature presents as a traditional view of Korean education, a behaviorist based transmission model or "learning as knowledge-absorption model" (Chun & Plass, 2000, p. 160), and with learner expectations (Cortazzi, 1990; Eastmond, 2000; Finch, 2000; Hofstede, 1986; Joo, 1997; Min, Kim & Jung, 2000; Park & Oxford, 1998). As such, this module maintains a focus on 'computer as expert', and is thereby perhaps more culturally compliant than the second module. Such learning systems are seen to take on the role of drill master (Backer, 1995), tutor (Taylor, 1980), or magister (Higgins, 1986). "The computer-magister knows the truth, intervenes to guide the student toward the truth, and then judges the student's performance" (Backer, 1995, p. 3). As Deubel (2003) highlights, assumptions of the behavioristic pedagogue, found within the restricted CALL approach, see students learn by doing, experiencing, and engaging in trial and error.

Module Two, an edutainment based module, was communicative CALL phase based (as presented by Warschauer & Healey, 1998) and takes on an open CALL approach (see Bax, 2003), which allows for cognitive theories of discovery/development, and hence the rationale behind the use of a puzzle/game type format for the exercises included in the module. This learning model maintains a focus on the 'computer as pedagogue', contrasts a number of Korean learner expectations and the cultural learning style as presented in the literature, and relies upon an active processor "learning-as-knowledge-construction model" (Chun & Plass, 2000, p. 160). In the 'computer-as-pedagogue' model (Higgens, 1986, 1988), the computer "waits until summoned, responds to requests and serves", and although knowing the truth (as does the 'behavioristic magister'), the communicative CALL pedagogue, found within the open CALL approach, patiently provides only requested activities or information so that the student engages in exploration and discovery (Backer, 1995, p. 3). Successful learning here, using a cognitive model, depends on the quality of processing that occurs while actively engaging with the subject matter (Atkins, 1993; Duffy & Cunningham, 1996).

The following sections of the book will now expand upon the central concepts so far presented. Part Two details those aspects of the Korean education system, the implementation of technology, aspects of culture, and usage of language that come to support the theoretical use of a loanword approach to the teaching of English as a foreign language in the country. Part Three then illustrates the means applied to effectively implement and test the efficacy of just such an approach from within a multimedia context, and provides in-depth discussion of the results of implementation. The final section of the book, Part Four, then details the significance of these findings along with the implications that emerge.

Part Two
EDUCATION, TECHNOLOGY, CULTURE, AND LANGUAGE

Part Two
EDUCATION, TECHNOLOGY, CULTURE, AND LANGUAGE

Overview

This part of the book highlights the complex relationship between the Korean cultural context and the implementation of educational technology by looking closely at the local English as a foreign language (EFL) environment, particularly that which emerged in the 1990s and 2000s. This is achieved by providing an outline of the state of EFL and information communication technology (ICT) in the Korean education system in those times, and by briefly highlighting the means by which computer assisted language learning (CALL) systems were applied in the nation's EFL classrooms. The Confucian consciousness is considered, and the possible impact of the local cultural context on CALL of the era illustrated. An approach that takes into account aspects of the Korean cultural learning style as it relates to the local educational environment, and one that aims to incorporate first language (L1) use to assist in foreign language (Standard American English) vocabulary acquisition, is then envisioned.

Introduction

The need to educate an increasing number of people within Korea in the digital era has led to both bold reforms and experimentation with advanced technologies (I. Jung, 2000). Reforms include the widespread development and integration of ICT, restructuring of the college scholastic ability test (CSAT), a focus on student-centered education, and increased English language teaching (Seth, 2002). However, as Park and Oxford (1998) state, Korea is predominantly racially homogenous and primarily monolingual, and this is still primarily the case today even though the legal immigrant non-Korean population of 1.1% (Koehler, 2006) has tripled over the last ten years to 3.4% (Eum, 2015). Consequently students have had little opportunity to use English outside classrooms, and although technology increases access to English learning contexts, it has not been as interactive as students have required. Although Jeon and Kim (2001) have pointed out that Korean education has undergone historic changes, and that communicative competence is gaining focus in English classrooms, "students have little access to authentic language input and limited opportunities to interact with native speakers" (S. Y. Kim, 2002b, p. 132). Communicative competence, as Hymes (1972) defines it, refers to the ability to use speech appropriately in varying social contexts and seeing competent speakers of a language know what to say, who to say it to, and how to say it. The constant obstacle for English as a foreign language (EFL) educators is that English is employed as a foreign language and restricted largely to classroom settings. In addition, Korean students approach teachers who are first language (L1) speakers of English through Korean cultural perspectives (Windle, 2003), and remnants of the Confucian consciousness in terms of education and learning culture (see Seth, 2002) can strongly impinge upon learning styles and teaching methods (Gray, 1998; Lim & Griffith, 2003; Min, Kim, & Jung, 2000; Shaffer, 2001). The impact that such perspectives have had on the implementation of initiatives, such as computer assisted language learning (CALL), is important to consider. While such cultural paradigms may be instructive as well as proffering ways for the effective use and development of educational technology across a variety of settings (including that of vocabulary development), consideration also needs to be given to student attitudes toward EFL, instructional methods and how these elements shape approaches to learning (see Troudi, 2005).

There has been limited examination of any influence of the Korean cultural learning style on the application of CALL initiatives within the nation. Moreover, the English vocabulary existing within the native vernacular of Korean EFL students, through borrowing, has largely been ignored as a viable and rich source of linguistic data from which language use and the promotion of foreign language vocabulary acquisition could be fostered.

This vocabulary consists of direct loanwords, hybrid terms, substitution, and a pseudo loanword category that includes truncated terminology, false cognates (or false friends), and fabricated loans. Direct loanwords are those that contain the same denotational meaning in both the original and borrowing language (e.g. *juice*), but at times these words may carry more semantic weight or typically cover more narrow semantic territory (e.g. *burberry* for any *long coat*). Hybrid terms are words formed by a mixture of the original and borrowing languages (e.g. *com-maeng* for *computer illiterate*). Substitution terms are words that are now commonly used in place of the native term in the borrowing language (e.g. *a-reu bai-teu*, from the German *arbeit*, for *part-time job*). Truncated terminology includes words that are shortened from an existing foreign language term (e.g. *remote control* to *remocon*). False cognates are words that generally maintain the original pronunciation, sometimes slightly phonologically altered, but possess a different denotational meaning in the borrowing language, for example, *cunning* refers to being *deceptive* or *exhibiting ingenuity* in English but to the concept of *cheating on an exam* in Korean. Finally, fabricated loan terms are those that sound like English words but are not used by first language (L1) speakers of English in the same way (e.g. *open car* for *convertible* in Korean). These categories and terms will be discussed in detail throughout Section D, English loanwords in the Korean Context, found later in this part of the book.

Several resources have been made available in Korea acknowledging that this linguistic terminology (loanwords), in which the learner is immersed, can assist with (Standard American) English language learning and vocabulary acquisition (see Campbell, Kim, & Campbell, 2002; Flattery, 2007; Kosofsky, 1986; Shaffer, 1999; Vercoe, 2007). Particular assistance can be gained through 'positive transfer', which is defined as "the facilitating influence of cognate vocabulary or any other similarities between the native and target languages" (Odlin, 1989, p. 26).

Further, it has been emphasized when using loanwords to assist in vocabulary acquisition that students should be made aware of loanword cognates that can assist in learning additional similar words (Daulton, 1999; Yoshida, 1978), and since loanwords often undergo phonetic changes when being borrowed, students also need to be made aware of the English pronunciation of these words (Chujo & Nishigaki, 2004). Truncated loanword terminology could also be used in the Korean classroom to illustrate the difference between native and target language use by focusing on expanded forms, and such approaches are considered in Flattery (2007). Examples of these truncated forms are: *a-pa-teu* for *apartment*, *remicon* for *ready-mixed concrete*, and *remocon* for *remote control*. The use of English loans found in the L1, but not commonly heard in the English language, can also be introduced, along with more common vocabulary via recontextualization tasks. (For sources discussing such an approach, see Flattery, 2007). For example, the English terms *various* or *comprehensive* can be taught along with the loanword use of *omnibus*, as this term in both English and Korean refers to *including many things* or *having a variety of purposes or uses* (e.g. *omnibus CD* in Korean for *a compact disc (CD) of various artists* in English). Other borrowed terms, such as *meeting* for *blind date*, can be introduced in usage context – that is, introduced to students through dialogue (also see citations in Flattery, 2007). Loanword vocabulary has also been taught using associative tasks (see Shaffer, 1999). Examples from Korean include: *o-ba-i-teu* (*overeat* meaning *vomit*) used in conjunction with English verbs with the prefix *over* to make new terms that show an action has been done to too great an extent such as: *overactive*, *overcharge*, *overconfident*, and *overwork*; and *skinship* (meaning *close physical contact, usually between mother and child* in English but *close physical contact among people in general* in Korean) used in conjunction with English nouns with the suffix *ship* to teach terms such as *friendship, partnership, membership,* and *relationship.* Shaffer (1999) also highlights mnemonic techniques for illustrating differences in meaning between borrowed terms in Korean and their English equivalents (false cognates) by having students conceptualize an image of the term and drawing this on the board next to a conceptual drawing of the same term by an instructor who is an L1 speaker of English. This may see the student draw a large luxury apartment complex (or condominium) where many people live, while the instructor draws a large house for a single family after being presented with the vocabulary item *mansion* (an English term borrowed into Japanese, and entering Korean from there).

Techniques, such as those just outlined, could assist learners in acquiring target language denotational and connotational meanings for loanword vocabulary found in the Korean vernacular and variety of English, develop a morphosyntactic understanding of the use of such vocabulary in (Standard American) English, and perceive how this vocabulary is related to other words by rules in the target language. This is important since the borrowed vocabulary, when entering Korean and spoken in the local vernacular and variety, is sometimes abbreviated, and often the original grammar associated with the term is disregarded. Individual terms that were once "prepositions become nouns, nouns become verbs, and conjunctions and suffixes just disappear" (Sheperd, 1996, p. 2).

A. EFL IN THE KOREAN EDUCATION SYSTEM

The Grade School Sector

Throughout the 1990s, education policy changes were significantly historic in Korea, especially "… in the area of English teaching, where the decade of the 1990s experienced more changes than the century that had preceded it" (Kwon, 2000, p. 47). During the mid 1990s, the English Program in Korea (EPIK) was introduced into middle schools, and it specified that first language (L1) speakers of English provide education alongside Korean co-teachers to enhance instructional competence. Also in 1997, English was introduced as a regular subject within elementary schools. In addition, video and audiocassettes supplemented authorized texts for Third and Fourth grades, while for Fourth and Fifth grades, computer-based materials were made available. This curriculum not only made English language education a compulsory subject for ten years of consecutive schooling (H. J. Lee, 2001), but affirmed Korea's place in Kachru's Expanding Circle (Kachru, 1998, 2005).

In terms of language education, the Seventh National Curriculum was introduced to elementary and middle schools in 2001 and extended to high schools in 2003, reaffirming the need for English instruction at all levels of schooling. This curriculum also gave specific emphasis to communicative competence and fluency through a grammatical-functional syllabus (Kwon, 2000), based upon a rationale concerning the need to understand Western culture. There have since been further revisions, with the 2007 and 2009 revisions being made available online (NCiC, 2015).

Since March 2001, elementary and middle school teachers have been required to teach English by communicating in English (S. Y. Kim, 2002b) where input and interaction are encouraged with English as the primary means by which teachers and students engage in communication. There is also an important difference between the use of classroom English and teaching English through communicating in English. As S. Y. Kim (2002b) reminds us, classroom English is functional and is used for greetings, starting and ending sections of lessons, and general management. Teaching English by communicating in English requires the use of English as often as possible, both in and out of class time. Historically, the most frequent problems encountered by teachers trying to implement such an approach centered upon a lack of teacher English language proficiency and also a lack of training in the use of communicative language teaching approaches (Li, 1998). These problems have been exacerbated by low student motivation, limited student oral proficiency and, in the secondary school setting, large class sizes, lack of teacher preparation time, and pressure to prepare students for the CSAT (S. Y. Kim, 2002a).

The University Sector

During the 1990s, "globalization became one of the most popular words in Korean society" (S. O. Park, 1998, p. 123) and was much discussed, particularly in relation to the learning of foreign languages (Shin, 2003). The impact of globalization on Korean education led to increased importance being placed on the learning of Standard American English (Kwon, 2000), so consequently, the employment of L1 speakers of English was advanced as the main means to provide English as a foreign language (EFL) education in the tertiary education sector. H. J. Lee (2001, ¶. 11) commented: "Educational administrators as well as our students are often misdirected to believe that native speakers are ... their only resource for improving their English proficiency". Today, there has been a slight shift away from this, with acceptance of a wider base of accents with citizens of America, Australia, Canada, Ireland, New Zealand, the Republic of South Africa, and the United Kingdom eligible to obtain an E-2 Foreign Language Instructor Visa (MOJ, 2015).

Ahn (2002) also draws our attention to the fact that in general university English classes, learners have low motivation. Further, it was noted that textbooks were lacking, and this "combined with a delivery of instruction largely devoid of learner involvement has led to a situation in which college English is largely viewed with criticism" (Ahn, 2002, pp. 196-197). Additionally Pak (1999) comments that it is not easy to find any first language culture within college level English language teaching texts, as most of these textbooks are generally imported (H. J. Lee, 2001). That said, there has been a series of EFL textbooks published in Korea that aims to impart English linguistic knowledge through the extensive use of Korean culture along with limited L1 use (Finch & Hyun, 2000). It is proposed that such material needs to be incorporated within university English classes taught by L1 speakers of English and/or the homework process, and this should stimulate Korean EFL student engagement with English language activities through the specific and controlled use of their first language as well as using the cultural familiarity of the learner.

Nevertheless, and regardless of what textbooks are employed, a number of universities came to require certain pass grades on standardized English language tests. Along with this, a number of universities required proficiency in computer literacy before undergraduate students were granted graduate status. English language skills, and later information communication technology (ICT) skills, were then viewed as essential within the Korean educational environment during this time.

B. APPLICATION OF COMPUTER TECHNOLOGY IN THE KOREAN EDUCATION SYSTEM

ICT Implementation in Schools and Universities for Language Learning

In Korea since the early 1990s, "the introduction of cutting-edge information and communication technologies has come to be seen as a barometer of national competitiveness and quality of life, and is being specifically pursued as part of a national development strategy" (Ministry of Information and Communication, in I. Jung, 2000, p. 2). Korea, in terms of information communication technology (ICT) use, has had one of the most advanced educational strategies in Asia (UNESCO, 2002), and has long been considered one of the most wired countries on Earth (Hachigian, 2002).

Computer education classes for at least an hour per week became mandatory in 2001 for Grades One and Two, and in 2003, mandatory for Grades Three to Six. This was in addition to the use of computers for more general instructional purposes to which most students were already exposed three to four hours each week. The importance of computer-based instruction was further strengthened by another mandate that required that at least ten percent of class time should involve computer use (Korean Education and Research Information Service [KERIS], 2001).

The high priority assigned to computer use in Korean grade schools, and its extensive use, was criticized. For example, M. Lee (2001) asserted that it could reduce the attention given other educational needs, and may eventually adversely impact upon the intellectual development of children. Similarly, the educational psychologist Jane Healy (cited in Cuban, 2001, p. 60) stated that prior to the age of seven, spending time with computers "not only subtracts from important developmental tasks but may also entrench bad learning habits, leading to poor motivation and even symptoms of learning disability".

With regard to ICT instruction replacing previously used video and audio instructional technologies, H. Chun (2002) highlighted the need to question how useful and effective these computer assisted language learning, or CALL-based, methods were in comparison to earlier technologies. Chun's concerns were particularly important since in Korea, eventually, "30 percent of the regular [grade school] curriculum will be conducted employing multimedia instructional and learning methods" (MEHRD, 2002, p. 147).

Yet, in contrast to the grade school setting where computer-based initiatives were being used to assist learning, government reforms for the development of ICT utilization within higher education focused firmly on administrative use, infrastructure development, and the promotion of research (KERIS, 2001). At the time, this also saw a lack of focus on the development of e-learning initiatives in the Korean tertiary education sector compared with other nations such as China and Japan. Increasingly too, tertiary education providers globally have been increasing online instruction of traditionally taught courses over the last decade (Elgort, Marshall, & Mitchell, 2003; Palloff & Pratt, 2001). Even though cyber-class systems existed in Korea, there was minimal CALL use within university EFL classes. Systems generally lacked the e-learning capacity of more advanced software and were designed largely for classroom management support and administrative duties. These systems were predominantly web-based, with most first language (L1) English speaking faculty members locked out due to lack of administrative support or problems in dealing with the Korean language interface. Subsequently, there was no complete alignment among universities regarding CALL with the ICT instructional initiatives set in place at the grade school level. Further, textbooks were favored in university-level curriculums and despite the access to, and the availability of, "computers and the internet, the integration of web technology into the curriculums of Korean universities has not found widespread acceptance" (Min, et al, 2000, p. 120). Multimedia and ICT use within university classes, especially for English language learning taught by L1 English speaking instructors, is therefore minimal or non-existent. This is still largely the case a decade later.

Alternatively, the Korea National Open University (KNOU) was extensively utilizing ICT as a means to deliver instruction. KNOU joined with eight traditional universities to form the Korea Virtual University Consortium and was collaborating with those universities to design web-based courses. A number of traditional universities also began to offer credit and non-credit web-based courses, and the college consortium forming the Open Cyber University (OCU) operated web-based courses for students of member schools. However, as Eastmond (2000) states,

> Asia has more enrolments in open and distance education than anywhere else in the world ... Using the United Kingdom's Open University (UKOU) completion rate of 49% as a baseline, completion rates in Asia are much lower: 28% at Indira Gandhi National Open University (OU), 17% at Sukhotai Thammathirat, and only 10% at the Korean National OU (p. 103).

Eastmond (2000) then cautioned that attempts to import courses from other nations have failed when transplanted into Asian learning contexts, predominantly due to the local cultural and learning environments. Ellis (1994) also highlighted problems associated with the transfer of Western teaching styles to Asia, particularly those relating to English language teaching. Oka (2004) and Weschler (1997) have questioned the applicability and appropriateness of universal English language teaching assumptions and approaches when viewed in relation to the Asian context. Critchley (1998) provided support for this notion by observing that most language learning theories and theories of language were developed in contexts where English was taught as a second language, and have largely been transplanted without modification into the Asian EFL context.

Considering such views, it was considered that aspects of the cultural learning style and Confucian consciousness of Korean EFL students might hold important implications for the application of ICT and the design of CALL systems for effective use with these learners. The term 'Confucian consciousness' (Kent, 2004) was adopted to encompass the traditional patterns of social behavior, especially those involving learner interaction, based on recent interpretations of East Asian cultural traits (as presented in Cortazzi, 1990; Finch, 2000; Hofstede, 1986; Hyun, 2001; and, Joo 1997). The term has also been extended to include the learning culture unique to Korea (see Seth, 2001), particularly as it relates to its conceptualization of proper teaching methods, lesson design, learner expectations, and classroom management (outlined in Finch, 2000; Gray, 1998; Lim & Griffith, 2003; Min, Kim & Jung, 2000; Park & Oxford, 1998; Robertson, 2002a, 2002b, 2003; Shaffer, 2001; Windle, 2003). It is therefore suggested that any design or use of such CALL systems would also need to take into account both cultural and learning factors. As O'Hagan (1999), Healey (1999) and Warschauer (1996) highlight, CALL effectiveness relies on instructional design methodologies and implementation techniques and does not result from use of the medium itself. As such, CALL needs to be made more congruent with Korean EFL student levels and expectations and the local cultural learning context, and address the learning style and 'hidden assumptions' associated with the Confucian consciousness. It is envisioned that CALL initiatives in the Korean educational landscape could only then, and as Ahn (2002) and I. O. Kim (2000) mention, be more directed to assist in transitioning students from roles of dependent and passive learners to more active and autonomous learners.

CALL Software and Courseware in Grade School and University Settings

Although ICT is highly developed and widespread in Korea today, the implementation of multimedia use within the Korean education system has in the past suffered from a number of deficiencies. These include a lack of available software for education, lack of training for teachers in the use of computer equipment, and lack of planning for the use of existing media and associated classroom facilities (KERIS, 2001).

Furthermore, much research on the use of CALL and the application of computer-based learning within Korean EFL classes has essentially only centered on the use of Computer Mediated Communication (CMC) as well as use of the internet for in-class instruction. Limited research has existed concerning the impact of software packages and courseware. This can be explained by the fact that in-class use of CMC and internet-based activities cost much less than EFL software packages and courseware initiatives (even free ones like Moodle) and require less time-consuming and less expensive development. As Min, et al (2000) highlight, "costs of the packages and the installation of them on the main server is too high for Korean university level institutions, where English is a requisite course for thousands of students" (p. 124).

Nonetheless, a vast number of domestically and internationally produced commercial software packages did exist and were readily available to both Korean EFL students and their teachers. However, "many creative commercial software packages may not be effectively used in classes if they're not restructured before their use" (Pusack & Otto in Min, et al, 2000, p. 120). Also commercial packages effective in one setting may fail in another (Pankuch, 1998). Indeed, reorganization, using PowerPoint, of Ministry of Education disc-based English language learning content designed for use with third and fourth year students has been utilized "to reduce the instructor's burden of administering a class entirely in English" (J. Kang, 2002, p. 295).

At this time, educators also had access to a number of programs for multimedia creation and media editing from which they could and did produce and develop materials for students to study with outside of class. Yang (2002) recognized that songs could provide children with motivation, spur their interest, and assist them in remembering linguistic information with ease. As a result, the notation program *Finale 2002* was applied in middle school EFL classes "to help children learn the rhythm and lyrics of a song in accordance to their level" (Yang, 2002, p. 299). This was an effective use of multimedia to assist Korean "stress deaf" (Kenstowicz, 2005, p. 13) students, whose L1 is syllable timed, to develop familiarity and mastery of stress-timed English. Such a task can be daunting (Bell in Thompson & Gaddes, 2005) as Korean syllables are of approximately the same duration and do not exhibit alternations in degree of stress (de Jong, 1994; Jun, 1996; Lim 2001), while in English, stressed syllables are significantly longer than unstressed ones with most vowels in unstressed syllables reducing to a schwa (Bolinger, 1965), with the rhythm of English "characterized by alternations in degree of stress" (Trofimovich & Baker, 2006, p. 11). The value of audio with middle school children studying English was also recognized by S. G. Hong (2002), who suggested several methods through the use of *Cool Edit* for sound file creation, and *Cdex 120* for the conversion of audio. Files were then integrated into PowerPoint to teach elements of popular music, providing lyrics along with audio, to generate interactive exercises for in-class use. I. S. Im (2002) also emphasized the use of flash cards along with picture and sound dictionaries for use with middle school students for vocabulary learning, and adapted use of the *Quia puzzle maker* for this function. In addition, C. H. Lee (2000) stressed the use of information gaps and simulations as a means to provide EFL students with language practice. He referred to programs such as *Storyboard* and the use of authoring tools as a means for educators to construct learner material.

Nonetheless, C. H. Lee (2000) has warned that, although teacher-created CALL software allows learners to gain control over the learning environment, teachers still need to remind Korean students to participate actively in the educational process. It was also determined that Korean "elementary school students were passive when directing their language learning" (Y. S. Jung, 2000, p. 43).

Even so, Korean academics conducting studies into the use of courseware within the secondary school system during this time found that students in experimental groups utilizing software were able to achieve higher scores, indicating better proficiency, than students on national standardized listening tests. These students also gained confidence in listening to and speaking with L1 speakers of English (Choi, Kim, Lee, & Sol, 1999). So too, when utilizing multimedia courseware collaboratively with children, Y. S. Jung (2000) found that interaction features believed to foster language learning were 25% higher in the experimental group than in the control group. There were also significant differences in listening comprehension and attitudes when friend and non-friend groups were formed. However, the type of group formation did not appear to lead to any significant differences in oral proficiency development and in vocabulary learning. Both friend and non-friend groups performed similarly in this regard.

Additionally, H. J. Lee (2001) highlighted a study conducted by Park and Kim concerning English language education at the grade school level that put forth a compelling finding. Achievement test scores from students taught by Korean teachers with the assistance of multimedia devices were similar to scores of students taught by L1 speakers of English, with both scores higher than those obtained by team taught students. This highlighted an interesting area for further research, especially since the Korean perception was, and to some degree still is, "native English speaking teachers are much valued to preserve the authenticity of the foreign language in the classroom" (H. J. Lee, 2001, ¶. 2).

In fact, it is the teacher who is crucial to the instructional use of multimedia within classroom environments (Cunningham, 2000; Y. S. Jung, 2001). Teacher knowledge concerning technology, as well as their preparation, combined with their ability to "integrate and refine the lesson with technology, were the key to whether it was effective or not" (Stepp-

Greany, 2002, p. 170). However, in Korea at the time, there were very few studies that focused on the use of training in technology, and little research concerning teachers' beliefs and the effect of those beliefs on technology oriented language instruction (Y. S. Jung, 2001). W. K. Choi (2002, p. 236) also noted that although CALL was gaining widespread acceptance, it was "not yet well conceptualized in the minds of learners as an effective teaching and learning tool, particularly in teaching and learning environments of Korea". Like teacher studies, research examining learner responses, as well as their degree of satisfaction with CALL material, was limited in scope, focusing only on CMC or web-based instruction (see H. K. Choi, 2004; Hwang, 2002; C. J. Kwon, 2004; O, 2005; Oh, 2003a, 2003b).

Notwithstanding, disc-based multimedia content for grade school classroom use was officially deployed with integration of computer assisted instruction (CAI) alongside the textbooks published by the Ministry of Education, and put into nationwide practice through the Seventh Elementary English curricula in 2001. Use of these textbooks was required by the National Curriculum. Consequently, items of English language education including the "number of new words, grammatical patterns, language functions, [and] cultural items" were dictated. English language skills were then largely taught in lower grades with a focus on speaking, while higher grades focused on reading and writing (M. Lee, 2001).

The newly introduced multimedia discs used in conjunction with grade school textbooks for English language learning at the turn of the 21st century provided four kinds of instructional models: presentation, tutorial, simulation, and edutainment/courseware (Pang, 2002). As a result of examining the practical use of these materials, Choi and Shin (2002) inform that: (a) more detailed teacher guidebooks would lead to more effective use of the system; (b) that teachers need to develop innovative methods to encourage active use of the materials, rather than passive watching of the media; and (c) teachers need to manipulate the programs in conjunction with other English curriculum content. They additionally called for more teaching modules to be introduced within the system. The Korean government also recognized that the quality and quantity of educational content was not completely satisfactory, and that effort should be put into this as well as in construction of a multimedia service system to support every subject available within school curriculums (KERIS, 2001).

To a very limited extent, disc-based resources were also being used within university EFL classrooms, and in this case, Keem (2000) found, by examining levels of student achievement at course end, students conducting self-study with multimedia, as well as engaging in multimedia instruction within the classroom, were able to outperform students who engaged in the self-study of multimedia materials alone. W. K. Choi (2002) also found that Korean university students with higher grades were more responsive to CAI, and therefore able to gain benefits from such instruction, while those with lower grades preferred traditional classroom lectures to CALL. Moreover, it has also been shown that individual variables such as gender, computer ownership and computer ability did impact on the effectiveness of university level English reading classes conducted with technology (H. S. Kang, 2000). Additionally, Lee and Kastner (1999) stated that although CAI activities eventually led to a sense of empowerment and independence, and students became more accountable for their own learning, they were in fact "very challenging for most [Korean university] students because they perceive themselves as dependent language learners and expect to be told what to do and how to do it" (Lee & Kastner, 1999, p. 29).

Traditionally, Korean teachers provided learners with teacher-centered classrooms, adopting a method of one-way instruction over two-way interaction (Jeon & Hahn, 2006). Significantly, Ahn (2002) considered that the use of CAI could provide Korean instructors of English at the college level a way to provide a student-centered classroom which would allow students to engage in autonomous, independent, and interactive learning while providing motivation and language skills development. While I. O. Kim (2000, p. 39) stressed that "Korean students have been accustomed to lecture-oriented rote learning", but the use of CAI and multimedia-based materials can accommodate various learning styles simultaneously, and that optimal results can be achieved by the use of multimedia, specifically with communicative activities, targeting specific language skills.

There was, unfortunately, a significant lack of research available on the development of Korean university student EFL skills through the use of technology during this period. As Lee and Yang (2002) note, there were indeed "very few cases of using CALL in regular [university] English programs" pre-millennium. Korean researchers who did focus on the use of CALL within university English programs included C. I. Lee (2000) as well as Lee and Pyo (2002), and they have since revealed that the impact of educational computer use within these programs have largely generated less than satisfactory results.

The CALL initiatives for university students that did exist during the 2000s typically consisted of resource lists for student access outside of class time, which provided limited activities for individual study and language practice. Yet there were some other initiatives; for example, Lee and Yang (2002) refer to the homepage project of the Foreign Language Education Centre of Paichai University; and similarly, Lee and Pyo (2002) highlight the use of web-based instruction within English language courses at Woosong University and the development of a program to study the effectiveness of both on- and off-line delivery of instruction. In this study, significant differences were found between scores from online and offline students, with the offline classes performing significantly higher than online ones, and in a very consistent manner (Lee & Pyo, 2002). Lee and Yang (2002) also indicated that such results stemmed from a student lack of minimum levels of functional English and learner independence. This further highlights the importance of ICT teacher training to redress such deficiencies, and a particular need for establishing a meaningful learning environment when employing CAI and multimedia-based CALL materials in this era, and also in the cultural context of Korea. With this in mind, even today, it can still be noted that "… online systems are not being used properly in an integrated and standardized form within the regular university curriculum" (Hoh, 2005, p. 341), as there is still a need "… to promote and develop multimedia-assisted teaching methods in university education" (C. J. Kwon, 2005, p. 169).

C. CULTURAL INFLUENCES ON COMPUTER ASSISTED LANGUAGE LEARNING OF ENGLISH AS A FOREIGN LANGAUGE

Computer assisted language learning (CALL) initiatives in the Korean educational environment were employed, with varying degrees of success, during the decades of the 1990s and 2000s. Yet one important aspect appears to have been consistently underemphasized during this era: the impact of the local cultural context and learning environment on the development and implementation of CALL. This is a particularly critical concern as cultural contexts and coping with cultural differences in the learning process of students, and the impact of this on teaching and learning styles in Korea, is considered to be significant. As a result, this section of the book examines the issues surrounding the local cultural context during this period of time, including the disposition of students towards computer assisted instruction (CAI), the Korean learning style, and English as a foreign language (EFL) learning styles. It then presents a focused approach to CALL that involves first language (L1) usage in the Korean context, and a means to assess it.

The Confucian Consciousness in Korea

Soper (1997) observed that students who come from teaching backgrounds of a traditional nature believe that "a teacher should dictate knowledge to them" (p. 18). Similarly Min, et al (2000) have illustrated that Korean students strongly agree with the attitude that the teacher is responsible for the learning of students. Importantly, these factors hold implications for the implementation of CALL within Confucian-based societies like Korea. As Hofstede (cited in Joo, 1997) states, the Confucian mindset sees the role of the teacher as 'an authoritative figure', where learning effectiveness relates to teacher excellence, and so students expect that their teacher will have and provide them with all of the answers that they need. So too, Eastmond (2000) notes that in many Asian countries, the teacher is a *sensei* who conveys wisdom and knowledge, and the student role is one of listening carefully, learning deeply, and applying that wisdom – an empty vessel theory of teaching and learning.

Within Korea, Park and Oxford (1998) have come to illustrate that language learning is perceived by students as teacher-centered, and that most "EFL teachers in Korea remain the primary source of action and linguistic input – the main 'actors' in the classroom" (p. 107). Such a 'teacher as expert' paradigm relies on transfer rather than the creation of knowledge, and sees students regard themselves as dependent learners who engage in individualistic memorization and rote learning, rather than as participants in the collectivist creation of knowledge that leads to learning. Yet, Kubota (2001) has noted that different pedagogies are at play in the EFL classrooms of Japan, and that individualism and independence can take on different meanings in different cultural contexts (Fujita & Sano, 1988), allowing for "multiple meanings of cultural constructs such as individualism, independence, and creativity" (Kubota, 2001, p. 30). In the Korean context though, Rhee, Uleman, and Lee (in Windle, 2003, p. 7) also remind us that the "individualism-collectivism construct is not so straightforward". Still, the Confucian tradition encourages master-apprentice relationships and a culture of learning that "promotes teacher dependency for passive students, a tradition hard to reverse" (Eastmond, 2000, p. 104). As such, in Korea, the 'empty-vessel' argument of teaching and learning has been and still is, perhaps, predominant, and "in many respects, English-teaching and language learning methods in Korea have not yet caught up with the times. Centuries-old methods of dealing with both teaching and learning languages are still closely adhered to" (Shaffer, 2001, p. 1).

The Korean Cultural Learning Style

Antecedent research shows that "each culture has its own distinctive value systems and orientations which illuminate what is of significance within that society" (Hyun, 2001, p. 205). In Korea, Confucianism thrives more than in any other Asian nation including China and Japan (Crowder Han, 1995), and pervades everyday Korean life (Hyun, 2001; Koh, 1996). Breen also notes that Koreans have adopted Confucianism in a more extreme manner than the Chinese (Breen, 1999, p. 12) and have outdone their elder brother in the application of Confucian tradition (Breen, 1999, p. 43). These precepts generate a cultural learning style that would likely come to strongly influence the means of acquiring knowledge. As Joyce and Weil (1986) highlight, a people's culture strongly influences their personalities and ways of communication. However, according to Hyun (2001), it is also vital to realize that an individual's values can vary greatly within a culture, and that it is essential to see people both as individuals as well as a cultural group (Kalaboukas, 1997, cited in Armitage, 2001).

Nonetheless, the cultural notions that Korean EFL students maintain can affect their classroom behavior, educational development, and use of English language skills, as well as guide their interaction with L1 speakers of English (see Armitage, 2001; Breen, 1999; Cronin, 1995; Gray, 1998; Lim & Griffith, 2003; Min, Kim, & Jung, 2000; Robertson, 2002a, 2002b, 2003; Shaffer, 2001; Windle, 2003). Such behavior may then also be seen to impact upon the use of CALL, both in self-access and collaborative modes, and would result from the means by which students would expect to acquire knowledge, and as such would need to be considered in the design and application of such material. However, scant research exists regarding these notions, with few researchers alluding to such issues (for example, C. H. Lee, 2000; Y. J. Lee, 2000; Pankuch, 1998). Keeping these factors in mind, it was considered that by effectively taking the local cultural and learning context into consideration, this would allow even greater promise for the efficacy of CALL initiatives in Korea. Accordingly, further explanation of the cultural background and Confucian mindset is warranted.

The Confucian consciousness, examined by Cortazzi (1990), is responsible for many of the 'hidden assumptions' concerning teaching methods, lesson content, and learner expectations that students, particularly Koreans, come to exhibit within classrooms. Finch (2000) lists Korean classroom expectations, and also refers to Hofstede (1986), as does Hyun (2001) and Joo (1997), who focus on cultural differences in learner-teacher interactions throughout the world. Hofstede, reporting on the Confucian consciousness, sees problematic situations between a teacher and student arise from: differences in social position; differing student perceptions of curriculum relevance between two societies; profiles of cognitive abilities; and expected patterns of interaction. Among fifty countries that Hofstede (1986) placed on a 1 to 100 point scale, Korea ranked 18 for individualism, denoting a 'collectivist' society; 61 for large power-distance in social positions; 85 for strong uncertainty avoidance; and 40 denoting Korea as a 'feminine' class society.

While it is important to recognize the interaction characteristics of Koreans, and those based on Hofstede by Finch (2000) do come to represent the typical schema found in the literature, they also come to help polarize the Asian (Korean) versus Western (American) teaching and learning contexts into dichotomous differences (see Kubota, 2001). It is also important to note that this view is not intended to define one as superior over the other, but to illustrate that there is a common perception perpetuated by the literature for each. These dichotomies have been widely criticized (see Holliday, 1999; Littlewood, 1999; Pennycook, 1994, 1996), and aspects of each side of the dichotomy have been observed in various contexts within the Asian and Western educational spheres, "raising the question of whether educational practices in the United States are distinct from those in Asia" (Kubota, 2001, p. 23). Nonetheless, it is recognized that cultural differences do exist, and that each cultural group has a set of certain shared views and social practices that can impact upon the educational process, and influence approaches to learning (see Atkinson, 1999; Littlewood, 1999). As such, dichotomy can help to inform us of the impact of Confucianism as an imported dynamic on Korean EFL learners, and can serve as a base from which to extend study of the Korean educational context.

In addition, although much research linking the Confucian consciousness and Korean classroom interactions has been undertaken (refer to Gray, 1998; Lim & Griffith, 2003; Robertson, 2002a, 2002b, 2003; Shaffer, 2001; Windle, 2003), there is still limited research detailing specifically how such notions of interaction in the Korean EFL classroom can come to affect the use of media and computer systems for learning. Although Y. J. Lee (2000) has indicated that rather than being forums of communication and discussion, English Educational TV programs tend to be language lessons, and they "are merely promoting the Korean identity as in the dependent second language [learner] mode", and laments that their "content and presentation clearly portray the audience as helpless and dependent learners" (pp. 107-108).

EFL and the Korean Cultural Learning Style

"Though some Korean students may express complete disinterest in Confucianism, they still remain bound by its approach to disciplinary habits of work and study, life and play" (Korean Overseas Information Service, 1993, cited in Cronin, 1995, ¶. 9). Cronin (1995), from her teaching of Korean students, discovered that learners would respond to certain class activities with statements like "the professor is the expert" and "we have never before been given a choice". Breen (1999) also states that questioning, even by students at the university level, is viewed as an insult and challenge to the instructor. This kind of student outlook may also impact upon the L1 English speaking teacher by leading to cultural misunderstandings and interaction problems in the classroom (see Lim & Griffith, 2003; Kolarik, 2004; Robertson, 2003), and combat efforts to implement a learner-centered approach to education (O'Donnell, 2006).

Teacher-student interactions, as studied by Armitage (2001) and by Choi (cited in Armitage), have come to examine Korean EFL students living and studying abroad, and the difficulties experienced in relationships with lecturers/tutors and peer students during class discussions. Although the Korean students in the study did recognize their lack of competence in spoken English, they also perceived Australian students as selfish, talking without recognizing the needs of others, nor allowing others like themselves an opportunity to speak, and they also viewed lecturers/tutors as unable to manage classes to allow all students an equal voice. Further, Lee (cited in Armitage, 2001) highlighted the Korean lack of confidence in communicative English in university English classes taught by L1 speakers of English, and determined that such lack of confidence stems from an inordinate focus on reading and writing as well as the limited opportunities Korean students have had to speak English. Lee also mentions that differences arising from the teacher-student relationship may affect the development of student confidence when speaking in English with L1 speakers of the language. Additionally, as Windle (2003) points out, after surveying 104 university English students, Confucian traditions, such as allowing men to speak before women can in a group, no longer influence classroom behavior. However, Korean EFL learners do perceive classroom environments of L1 English speaking teachers to be very different from that of Korean teachers. If given a choice, half of those surveyed would not speak to a foreign teacher; students were culture-bound and interpreted actions of foreign teachers in terms of Korean cultural perspectives; and learners tended not to use specific English expressions since the Korean equivalents would be impolite (Windle, 2003). This last point implies that the native language produces an affective cultural barrier over the foreign language linguistic use of Korean EFL students, at least initially, by dictating what is contextually appropriate or inappropriate (see Troudi, 2005) stemming from Confucian consciousness, and in this case relating to politeness strategies.

Armitage (2001) further indicates that, for those studying abroad, Koreans disregard other cultures and their teachers' experiences. It is unclear how this relates to the reaction of Korean EFL students to the in-country L1 English speaking teacher. This behavior may relate to Confucian consciousness which demands splits in society to form groups that are generally at superior or subordinate levels. Such a construct also extends to the definition of self and others where Koreans view themselves as one group and others collectively as those who are non-Korean (Breen, 1999; Kosofsky, 1990). In relation to this rigidly ethnocentric identification and demarcation, Y. J. Lee (2000, p. 100) has noted that within Korea, there is both conscious and unconscious avoidance of the use of a foreign language "which in turn inhibits not only oneself but others from practicing the language", and that there is

> cultural resistance to accepting English as a language for meaningful communication among the Korean public ... although there is a clear and compelling need to learn English, it is for use outside [with others/non-Koreans], not inside Korean circles [with self/Koreans].

This has led to citizens, and aspects such as national pride, blocking government plans to adopt (Standard American) English as a secondary official language within Korea (Ok, 2005), and has seen Korean EFL students "remain in a state of social ineptness as second language users ... being dependent learners and lacking a social identity as a second language user of English" (Y. J. Lee, 2000, p. 103). Further, as S. A. Kim (2000) points out, the goals of helping Korean EFL students understand the target (American) culture, broaden their horizons, gain a better understanding of Korean culture, improve their skills in (Standard American) English, and reduce ethnocentric attitudes toward the learners' own culture, "has almost been ignored by our language teachers" (p. 152).

It should also be mentioned that the 'collectivist' nature of Korean society illustrated by the Hofstede (1986) study, along with group-centeredness identified by Armitage (2001), would not by its very nature be at variance with a collaborative use of multimedia activities and computer mediated communication (CMC) if culturally attuned and adapted to the Korean EFL classroom (I. O. Kim, 2000). Yet, regardless of the group-oriented nature of Koreans, findings of research from this era shows that Korean students have difficulty gaining the full benefit from group activities (Armitage, 2001), and prefer structure and formality to group-based learning (C. C. Park, 2002). Armitage explained these findings in relation to the educational system where students mostly concentrated on memorization. How the impact of such traits affects learning with CALL initiatives, and use of collaborative CMC and network-based group tasks within the EFL classroom, was and has not been a focus of Korean-based EFL research. This is perhaps because, as I. O. Kim (2000, p. 39) has stated, "collaborative learning is predicated on a culture that values collectivism".

CALL and the Korean Cultural Learning Style

Following global trends, there has been much emphasis on the use in Korea of collaborative CMC and CALL activities that have focused on autonomous learning (S. Y. Kim, 2002a; Oh, 2003a). However, these activities may conflict with students' strong beliefs that the teacher is ultimately responsible for their learning. In addition, social customs, including respect for the teacher and the existence of senior-junior status levels amongst all members of Korean society, sees relationships and responsibilities formed between those of different status, gender, and age. Little research has been done on the way these customs might impact CMC and the use of technology-based activities, particularly in the L1 English speaker EFL classroom.

However, reduction of teacher-student talk, and an increase in student-student interaction, could see learners (in the terminology of Hofstede, 1986) engage in interaction with peers of relatively equal social power, as well as low social distance. In this regard, student-student interaction could be undertaken through collaborative-based CMC and network-based activities. Yet, perceived gender differentials stemming from a Confucian mindset may still impact upon this form of classroom interaction, as may the cultural traits of *noonchi* (reading another's mind, and using tact accordingly), *chemyon* (maintaining social face), and *uri* ('our', or rather the collectivist 'us' – and the importance of group identification) (see Breen, 1999; Cronin, 1995; and, Kosofsky, 1990). As such, any interaction between students and technology would need to be structured to reflect what is representative of Korean classroom expectations. These are believed to include: group dependence, allowing students to work towards consensus, and avoiding disagreements to obtain social harmony (Finch, 2000). Still, elements of intragroup interaction leading to differential performance among students may yet appear, resulting from the cultural bonds that guide relationships. As I. O. Kim (2000) asserts, most English as a foreign language students live in monolingual and/or monocultural environments and are culture-bound, as their entire world view is determined by values gained through a single cultural environment.

In this regard, the 'self-access approach' (Gardner & Miller, 1999) of computer-based activities appears to hold a place in the Korean EFL cultural learning environment. That is not to say that there is a need for complete reliance on such a system, but such activities, particularly if applied in a homework setting during the learning stage of language acquisition, could allow for the perception of the 'teacher as expert' paradigm to be transferred to computer-based applications (Spencer, 1999). This is one method of employing CALL while taking into account a Confucianist approach, and embodies elements of the Korean cultural learning style. The computer could then fulfill the role of a mentor-based system for students (Crook, 1994), affording them the direction and guidance they need when learning, and if associated activities are designed appropriately, could be extended to allow learners to negotiate meaning from activities, in sociocultural terms, from a zone of proximal development (see Vygotsky, 1978). In this manner, students could also become exposed to the nature of autonomous, independent, and interactive learning, and be led away from the more teacher dependent means of acquiring knowledge (Ahn, 2002; I. O. Kim, 2000).

Independent language learning with CAI can offer a 'self-contained learning environment' (Dickinson, 1987) in which students could become active rather than passive recipients of information (Klassen, Detaramani, Lui, Patri & Wu, 1998). This would assist in developing levels of learner independence and the functional English language skills that Lee and Pyo (2002) indicate that Korean students require when undertaking CALL activities focusing on autonomous learning. This is significant as we know from Ahn (2002) that it is the individual who must ultimately take the most important role in the development of their own language skills in such educational contexts. Further, use of self-access materials, activities, and applications would come to ensure delivery of the same content to students in mandatory study programs, such as the university English setting of Korea.

In addition, self-access approaches to technology-based activities, while rigorously providing for student needs and purposes (Conacher & Royall, 1998; Levy, 1997), can also allow for autonomous context-based learner-centered and learner-controlled study at a time and pace convenient for students. Such an approach could diminish the cultural bonds of perceived social status and the required interactions resulting from these bonds (see Min, 1998). One example of this includes the cultural factor of 'saving face', and in this regard, Song (cited in Min, 1998) refers to saving face as 'perfectionism'; that is, where perfectionism refers to the tendency to save face by not making mistakes in public, and avoiding situations which might lead to making such mistakes. It is further envisioned that the outward display of perfectionism by Koreans in public settings such as classrooms would also come into play within group interaction within class time, as well as one-to-one or collaborative CMC, seeing students working to lessen 'fear of failure' by not as actively engaging in learning – particularly "in a society in which saving face is vital to self-esteem" (Niederhauser, 1997, p. 9), and where "it might be said that most Korean students are what Krashen (1981, p. 15) calls *monitor over-users* who do not like to take any risk to protect their face" (J. T. Chang, 2003). However, with a sensitive and culturally attuned approach to the use of CALL, befitting the local cultural and educational context, it is suggested that such factors could be alleviated through the use of self-access multimedia-based applications in the homework learning phase, followed by, or combined with, appropriately applied classroom CMC in the practice phase, in addition to traditionally taught course methods and approaches. Such a context would not only lower affective filters (Krashen, 1985), but work completed individually in the multimedia environment would essentially become a private matter. Any errors made would potentially only be known by the learner (J. T. Chang, 2003). This would also provide students with a zone of comfort in which to make mistakes as they explore learning in an environment where fear of failure is minimized, and where errors could (in terms of a social constructivist paradigm) provide a scaffolding of knowledge that would allow students to autonomously and independently learn from their mistakes (see D. Chun, 1994; Erstad, 1996: Malhorta, 2002), and then, in turn, afford them the opportunity to actively apply this knowledge in practice.

D. ENGLISH LOANWORDS IN THE KOREAN CONTEXT

Background

Second Language Acquisition and the Native Language

In the field of teaching English as a foreign language (EFL), and from a teaching rather than a purely linguistic analysis perspective focusing on form, research on the applicability of loan terminology and the native language for assisting the foreign language acquisition process of students has been highlighted (refer to Canagarajah, 1999; Danhua, 1995; Nation, 1990, 2001, 2003; Weschler, 1997). Yet, only a small coterie of scholars have come to investigate the applicability of loanword terminology for vocabulary development in the Japanese and Korean EFL contexts (see Daulton, 1998, 1999a, 1999b, 2003; Kimura, 1989; Nation & Newton, 1997; Shaffer, 1999; Shepherd, 1996; Simon-Maeda, 1997; Yamaguchi, 2002). Such an approach views the first language loanword bank as a useful store of knowledge that can promote aspects of positive transfer, lighten the burden of learning throughout the process of foreign language acquisition, and provide scaffolding. The approach also establishes a building block for foreign language acquisition by using the native language as a resource and as a means of reference for adjusting to the target language (in this case, Standard American English). As Oka (2004) highlights, foreign language users are multi-competent language users rather than deficient native speakers: "language teaching can tap into a mind that already contains an L1 [first language]; that is to say, the new language is learned on the basis of the previous language" (Oka, 2004, p. 6).

Nation (1990, 2003) has recognized the value of using the student L1 in the foreign language classroom, both by the L1 speaker of English and L2 (second language) English speaking EFL instructor, citing studies by Lado, Baldwin, and Lobo; Mishima; Laufer and Shmueli that compare the effectiveness of vocabulary acquisition, showing that L1 translation is the most effective method and that focal points of learning emerge particularly when loanwords, and the base words from which they stem, differ significantly enough to confuse learners. Nation (2003) further states that arguments against L1 use can equally be applied to the use of demonstration, realia, and pictures, and that it is foolish to arbitrarily exclude the foreign language learners' proven means of communication. It may attest to be more difficult for L1 speakers of English to bring aspects of their students' L1 into the EFL classroom, compared to the L2 English speaking EFL instructor, but in either case, a balanced approach, as Wigglesworth (2002) agrees, is required to ensure that the L1 would not be overused.

The general pedagogical approach (see Yoon, 2004) assumes that Korean EFL students will need to relearn the context of loanwords when applying them in cross-linguistic discourse, relearning the 'English' that they already know in order to correctly understand and use those terms when undertaking discourse with L1 speakers of English. English language teaching texts, even today, predominantly leave this process up to the student, or to the teacher who has time to provide exercises in class where there is room for it in the syllabus.

Daulton (1998, 1999a, 1999b, 2003), Nation & Newton (1997), Shaffer (1999), and Yamaguchi (2002) have suggested that the bridge of commonality between English and the native language in the form of loanwords, as a pre-existing lexical resource, should not be ignored throughout the language learning process. This argument views loanwords as means from which to develop a 'common vocabulary core', which can be used as a base or a starting point for target language vocabulary development. If utilized effectively it is hypothesized that the English vocabulary acquisition progress of students could be advanced through the specific inclusion of loan terminology in EFL teaching materials tailored specifically for use in the Korean context, as it has in other settings (refer to Brown, 1995; Brown & Williams, 1985; Daulton, 1998; Kimura, 1989; and, Yoshida, 1978). Such materials not only take into account the local cultural context and learning environment, but allow for both incidental and intentionally directed vocabulary acquisition to occur. These materials could also be most easily incorporated within existing EFL syllabuses, particularly those of mandatory English language based courses at the university level, in the form of homework or self-access materials as part of the learning phase of language acquisition, while the classroom use of language remains focused upon establishing and providing learners with all forms of language practice through a range of approaches.

What is important to recognize initially is that the setting of foreign language acquisition is markedly different to that of initial language acquisition, as usually by the time a person desires to function in a foreign language, for university graduation requirements or other needs, the mind has adapted to a prescribed method of gathering and storing knowledge. The problem of foreign language acquisition is essentially worked upon by the mind's governing culturally adopted knowledge gathering process. "A person who knows a language has acquired a system of rules and principles – a 'generative grammar' in technical terms – that associates sound and meaning in some specific fashion" (Chomsky in Peck, 1992, p. 140). In this view, there are two things required to learn a language: principles (universal to all languages); and parameters (which are language specific). The learning of a first language sets these parameters in one fashion, while the learning of other languages becomes a process of appropriately adjusting the values of these parameters (Isobe, 2007). However, the dominant means of explaining the adaptation of loanwords in a number of languages, and in the analysis of English loanwords in Korean (Cho, 2001), is what Ito and Mester (1995b, 1999) have proposed to be the 'core-periphery model'. In this model, the native vocabulary exists as a lexical 'core', and satisfies all possible markedness constraints, while loanwords enter the L1 at the outer 'periphery' where fewer constraints are obeyed, and over time, gradually move inwards towards the core as they become nativized. This is in line with Chomsky (1986, p. 190): "The language that we then know is a system of principles with parameters fixed, along with a periphery of marked exceptions". This notion of 'periphery' contrasts 'prohibited segments', "segments that are systematically and immediately adapted or eliminated as soon as they are introduced in a language", with that of 'tolerated segments' – "segments which are sometimes adapted and sometimes not" (Paradis & Lebel, 1994, pp. 75-76). As such, "the periphery, like the core, results from parameter settings. In the periphery, however, parameters are set in such a way that they often yield constraint deactivation" (Paradis & Lebel, 1994, pp. 75-76), and as Chomsky (1986) notes, peripheral constructions relate to the core in systematic ways by relaxing certain core grammar conditions. Yet the periphery should not possess constraints that are not also present in the core.

> The core/periphery distinction suggests that we should not expect to find a language where a constraint holds in the foreign loanwords but not in the native vocabulary, or a situation where the stronger version of a constraint holds in the periphery and the weaker version in the core. What the core-periphery condition entails, then, is a notion of distance from the lexical core: As the distance increases, constraints are weakened and abolished, and the range of admissible structures increases (Ito & Mester, in Paradis & Lebel, 1994, p. 76).

Such aspects of loanword investigation lead to a primary concern with the phonological and syntactical nature of adopted terms. Shedding light on the means of how such transformations occur provides knowledge that can be applied to determine potential learner errors, or areas of interference, in EFL instruction (see Spolsky, 1989; Wardhaugh, 1970). This knowledge can also be used to determine what aspects of transfer can be identified as positive, and used as a base starting point for target language vocabulary development, by lightening the burden of learning through scaffolding, and by promoting incidental and directed vocabulary acquisition to enlarge receptive vocabulary recognition (see Daulton, 1998, 1999a, 1999b, 2003; Kimura, 1989; Nation, 1990, 2003; Nation & Newton, 1997; Nicholls, 2002; Shaffer, 1999; Shepherd, 1996; Simon-Maeda, 1997). In other words, by seeking to construct a 'common vocabulary core', determine what aspects of loanword terminology could prove useful in the target language acquisition process from within the Korean EFL context.

The parametric view, as illustrated by Koda (1997), provides plausible explanation for cross-linguistic variation in L1 acquisition that shows sentence comprehension and production as heavily constrained by the linguistic properties specific to each language. Also in the linguistic processing of different languages, qualitatively different mechanisms are involved, and "L1-based skills and strategies are transferred at various L2 [second language] processing levels" (Koda, 1997, p. 38). Further research also highlights that "orientation generated by L1 linguistic features not only influences L2 acquisition … but also constrains the cognitive procedures used in L2 processing" (p. 38). This sees aspects of both metalinguistic and linguistic knowledge, as well as the corresponding processing procedures, transfer from the L1 to foreign language production and comprehension in both written and oral forms.

Additionally, Nation (1990) asserts that L1 and foreign language vocabulary are stored together in a state that encourages both borrowing and (positive) interference. Also, that the more a teacher can draw similarities between first and foreign language vocabulary, the greater the opportunity for positive transfer. Alternatively, Ellis (1997) refers to interference as 'transfer', and as the influence that learners exert over the acquisition of a foreign language, and this is governed by perceptions about what is transferable depending upon the stage of foreign language development of the learner. Selinker (1971), Seliger (1998) and Ellis (1997) also comment upon interlanguage, where learners construct interim rules to guide their foreign language use based upon the native language when they perceive it will assist in the learning task, or when they have become sufficiently proficient in the target language for transfer to be possible. Ellis (1992, p. 48) also highlights, stemming from Vigil and Oller (1976), that fossilized "structures can be realized as errors or as correct target language forms". Ellis (1997) later raises an important distinction between learner 'errors' and 'mistakes' – mistakes reflect a lapse in performance while errors reflect knowledge gaps. This concept originated with Pit-Corder (1967), and prior to his work, interference was seen as inhibitory, but he did also point out that it can be facilitative and provide information about one's learning strategies.

Carroll (1964), Albert & Obler (1978), and Larson-Freeman and Long (1991) have concluded that foreign language learning is partly learned in terms of the kinds of meanings already learned in the first language. For example, connotations behind the word *fighting* in Korean and English differ, with the former used to encourage a person or cheer on a team and the latter referring to a dispute or argument, and this can affect foreign language acquisition. "In learning a second language, L1 responses are grafted onto L2 responses, and both are made to a common set of meaning responses", i.e. L2 expressions come to bear traces of the L1 (Bhela, 1999, p. 23).

Nicholls (2002) has emphasized that learners look for similarities between languages, and although interference can prove a hindrance, reliance on similarities between the native and target language exists, and through positive transfer, can assist the learner, and, as Kimura (1989) suggests, thus provide enhanced possibilities for EFL vocabulary acquisition. In one regard, as Daulton (1998) notes, recognition and recall of lexical items with loanword cognates is better than for those without. Nation (2001, p. 48) also mentions that "for some languages, the presence of loanwords makes learning much easier". For example, the learning burden of making form-meaning connections is light when the word is a cognate or a loanword shared between the native and target languages. That is, the strength of connections between form and meaning determine the ease for the learner in retrieval of meaning when seeing or hearing the word form or when retrieving the word form when wanting to express meaning.

However, as Selinker (1992) has pointed out, reliance on the first language may result in fossilization of an interlanguage. It can also be argued that without adequate knowledge of the use and misuse of loan terms and the development of a specific approach tailored to the local EFL learner, there is much danger of this 'fossilization' occurring naturally. This would be due to learners being unaware of their language misuse (Shaffer, 1999; Sheperd, 1996; Simon-Maeda, 1997) and teachers focusing on the syllabus that needs to be taught instead of adequately addressing the issue. There is evidence this may have already occurred in the Japanese and Korean contexts (see J. S. Kim, 2006). Further, in the case of local varieties of English, taking one example of institutionalized fossilization (Nickel, 1998), "undifferentiated tag questions by Indian English speakers is not [considered to be, like it once would have been,] a reflex of incomplete acquisition or fossilized interlanguage, but a manifestation of a steady-state cultural grammar of English in outer-circle contexts" (Bhatt, 2001, p. 537). So too, English loanwords used in Korean follow Korean morphosyntactic rules and have culture-specific meanings. It is these culture-specific meanings that are then brought into the target language classroom by Korean EFL learners.

The use and misuse of the loanword lexicon (see Shaffer, 1999; Sheperd, 1996; and, Simon-Maeda, 1997) among Korean EFL learners, when speaking in the target language (Standard American English), is a form of fossilization (see Quirk, 1990; and, Selinker, 1992), keeping in mind that fossilization results from stabilization, and that stabilization does not "imply a permanent cessation of learning" (Odlin, Alonso, & Alonso-Vasquez, 2006, p. 97). Nakuma (1998) states that

> fossilization is a performance-level phenomenon occasioned by the L2 learner's conclusion that a given L2 form need not be acquired because it is already available to the target L2 system from his or her pre-acquired language system(s) through transfer. Fossilization, then, is engendered necessarily by the interlingual identification of an L2 form with an L1 form by the L2 learner. Fossilization implies that the L2 learner has, at an early stage of the target L2 learning process, made the decision not to 'reacquire' the specific L2 form which will be perceived subsequently by others as fossilized. Furthermore, interlingually identified forms can be either positive (meaning that the pre-existing form perfectly overlaps the target L2 form with which it is identified, such that there is no perceptible deviation from the native L2 norm when the L1 form is performed out as a substitute), or negative (meaning that the two forms do not overlap perfectly and a deviation from the L2 native norm is perceptible when the L1 form is performed out as a substitute) (Nakuma, 1998, p. 252).

In this sense, fossilized forms are not the product of acquisition, but of avoidance and of no functional necessity for a particular aspect to develop further. It is these kinds of fossilized or 'stabilized' forms that continue to persist unless there is focused direction against the reasons behind the interlingual identification sustaining them. One tool, according to Tarone (2006), that was perceived to help in countering such forces of fossilization is language play, as either play with language form or play with semantic meaning, will stretch the learner system "beyond the limits of its current norm" (Tarone, 2006, pp. 162-164, 168). However, as Koda (1997) stressed, when learners mistakenly assume they know a word, particularly when reading, they tend to ignore various contextual clues highlighting the semantic incongruity resulting from the misidentification of the term. As such, this contributes to a failure to 'notice', and "learners must notice the difference between their own and new language forms in order to acquire the new form, then failure to notice means failure to acquire – and failure to acquire, over the long haul, means fossilization" (Schmidt, 1993, in Tarone, 2006, p. 160). Noticing is "a necessary and sufficient condition for converting input to intake" (Han, 2004, p. 130). So, "error detection depends not just on psycholinguistic factors, like availability of attention, but also on factors of social context such as the 'accuracy demand of the situation' and 'various listener-based discourse constraints'" (Kormos, 1999, in Tarone, 2006, p. 160). At a more global level, socio-psychological factors can also prevent foreign language learners from "identifying with certain interlocutors and adopting new linguistic norms used by those interlocutors. Learners in this situation may resist linguistic change, preferring their own stable IL [interlanguage] norms" (Tarone, 2006, p. 160).

Further, as Nicholls (2002) has stated, since the mother-tongue influences English learning, there will be as many varieties of 'Learner English' or 'World Englishes' as there are mother tongues. Tran (1997) and others (Crystal, 2003; Jenkins, 2003; Kachru, 2005; McArthur, 2003) have identified three key elements comprising a World Englishes perspective: (a) a 'repertoire' of English models exists; (b) localized innovations in English have a pragmatic base; and (c) English is viewed as belonging to all who use it. The constructs through which English is taught in the EFL environment, therefore, needs to improve learner understanding of both the language they are learning and the "key philosophical differences between the worldview in which they were socialized and the one in which they must now operate" when using the target language (P. Lee, 1997). Utilizing loanwords as a lexical base for teaching false-beginners semantic/conceptual differences between the native and target languages could then be provided through systemic attention (cf. contrastive analysis hypothesis). While Norrish (1997) not only highlights that a better language development setting derives from assigning an equal value to both the local and target language, but calls for English language teaching to take into account the manner that English forms a part of the local language. It is also recognized as important for learners, particularly those from Expanding Circle countries like Korea, to move their understanding and use of their local English 'variety' to one more appropriate when speaking 'standard' English or English as an international language (EIL). In this regard, Jenkins (2000) has drawn attention to 'mutual unintelligibility', while Tran (1997) has highlighted situations where Vietnamese workers were not able to understand Taiwanese or Korean bosses who were using their own varieties of English as standard in the international context. These issues, as they relate to EFL concerns, as Kachru and Nelson (in Tran, 1997) indicate, and as Bhatt (2001) has also highlighted, need to be undertaken through studies relating to variation, pragmatics of variation, varieties and cultures, and varieties and creativity. This view of English as a lingua franca (ELF), or English as an international language, as Brown (in Tran, 1997) sees it, then began to affect language education policy decisions in External Circle contexts, particularly regarding the choice of pedagogical models, standardized testing and examination standards, and development of material for listening and reading. These approaches ideally also need to include cross-cultural and cross-linguistic elements that could provide learners with bicultural and bilingual competence, since varieties of English were and still are used in diverse sociolinguistic contexts. Further, Bhatt (2001) has highlighted that pedagogical paradigms, including methods, models, and materials, have not revealed any sensitivity to local sociolinguistic contexts in regard to the use of local varieties of English. If developed, they would prove to be a step toward contextually sensitive pedagogy that is socially realistic as foreign language acquisition occurs in normative rather than native contexts.

Context

Loanwords in the Native Vernacular and Educational Applicability

Studies of loanword usage within the Korean language have been undertaken, but in the past, they have predominantly focused on the processes involved in adaption (Hirano, 1994; Kang, 1996; P. H. Lee; 1995; Lee, Lee, Park & Kang, 1999; Oh, 1996) and been mainly concerned with showing that Koreans transliterate loans (Yu, 1980). These loans normally come to conform to Korean phonological patterns (Colhoun & Kim, 1976), and when there is conflict between the syllable structure of English terms and Korean words, native Korean speakers intuitively reject the term or change it to conform with Korean syllable structure conditions (Nam & Southard, 1994). This serves to retain as much phonetic information from the source as possible while conforming to constraints of the recipient language. In this regard, Steraide (2001) has argued for the existence of a phonological module that would assist in determining the minimal modification required to fit foreign lexical items to the phonotactics of a native language. In addition, it has been shown that a move from reliance on Chinese character words to English loanwords has occurred in modern Korean vernacular (Shim, 1994), with Standard American English increasingly being the source (Kenstowicz, 2005).

In general, linguistic-based research on loanwords has come to focus upon the phonological process.; that is, input from the donor language (e.g. English) and output in the native language (e.g. Korean), centering first on rules and constraints and then later on perception. Optimality Theory (OT) (Prince & Smolensky, 1993), views auditory salience and similarity as the most critical factors in resolving the choice as to which aspects of the source term should be preserved or sacrificed (refer to

Kang, 2003). In OT, the grammar of a language is defined by 'a hierarchy of universal constraints' – Structural (Markedness) that reflects unmarked forms as defined by Universal Grammar (UG); and Faithfulness for preserving input properties (Shinohara, 2001). As such, the language acquisition process in OT consists of determining the ranking of universal constraints as well as inputs, and so OT has its heritage in the principles and parameters framework.

> In generative grammar, one task of the learner is to determine which of the possible grammars allowed by an innate Universal Grammar is compatible with the language she is learning. In a Principles and Parameters (P&P) framework, this task amounts to determining the correct settings of a number of usually binary innate *parameters*, while in an Optimality-Theoretic (OT) framework, the task amounts to determining the correct relative rankings of a number of innate *constraints* (Dekkers, van der Leeuw & van der Weijer, 2000, p. 25).

OT allows researchers to examine the extent of difference between adapted forms and how they not only differ from the native system but also conform to it. "Within the optimality perspective, it is reasonable to assume that the [pronunciation] difference between loanwords is due to the employment of different constraint sets and rankings between the source language and the borrowing language" (H. Yoo, 1996, p. 147). While Cloutier (2005) believes that in Korean, different constraint rankings "have a different rank order depending on the group to which the word belongs" (native terms, Sino-Korean terms, and terms borrowed from other languages), and as such, B. R. Lee (2001) argues that two levels of loanwords exist, those adapted and those nativized. However, once adaptation through specific loanword constraint ranking is complete, "outputs are stored in the Korean lexicon in the same pool as that for the native vocabulary", and when "used in Korean morphophonology in combination with other native words and the loanwords from different source languages, they will be evaluated by ... Korean phonotactic and phonological constraints with no discriminations as to their origin" (B. R. Lee, 2001, p. 102). This leads to a situation where the English word is spoken one way "when adopted as a loanword, but the same word may be mispronounced ... when considered as pure English" (B. R. Lee, 2001, p. 118). Kenstowicz (2005) also shows that Korean readily accepts the phonetic and grammatical faces of a lexical item where speakers have a robust intuition on the 'proper' means of adopting a word, and a number of researchers have uncovered generalizations that illustrate the complexity of this process (refer to Ahn, 1998; Y. J. Kang, 2003; and, Oh, 1996).

Perceived similarity (Kenstowicz, 2001; Steraide, 2001) seeks to determine if loanword adaptations are grammar-driven or if other factors such as perception also have a role to play in the process. However, it is recognized that a perception-only approach (Peperkamp & Dupoux, 2003) is too strong (Smith, 2006), and that the native language phonology also influences perception. "Diverse forces influence loanword phonology – including not only perceptual effects, but also orthographic information, and even interactions between loanword adaptation and other phonological constraints active in the L_b [borrowing language]" (Smith, 2006, p. 11). Nonetheless, and highlighting that linguists view loanword adaptations as part of native phonology and treat them as equals with other phonological factors within the borrowing language, Peperkamp and Dupoux (2003) argue that the perceptual process is more sensitive to the phonetic properties of language rather than the phonological. They argue that loanword adaptations take place during perception through a process of phonetic decoding, "which maps non-native sound patterns onto the phonetically closest ones" (p. 369) where *closest* is viewed as "either acoustic proximity or proximity in the sense of fine-grained articulatory gestures ... Phonetic decoding, then, acts as a filter, in that many fine-grained acoustic details of speech sounds are lost as these sounds are mapped onto phonetic changes" (p. 368). Peperkamp and Dupoux (2003) also suggest that our processing systems seem tuned to our native language, distorting the way we produce, memorize, and perceive foreign sounds – 'phonological deafness' – even in bilinguals. The role of perception can be "well summarized by the P[erceptual]-map hypothesis" (H. Y. Park, 2007, p. 2), where "a sound in the source language is adapted into the recipient language in a way that maximizes the similarity between the two sounds ... but without violating the phonotactics of the recipient language" (Shinohara, 2001, p. 2). Peperkamp (2004) also illustrates that for Korean, from a phonological analysis, there are rules and constraints that refer to loanwords only, but due to their nature, "a phonological account would require a special loanword module in order to accommodate the loanword adaptations" (Peperkamp, 2004, p. 5). As such, it is argued that

> If the borrowing process was purely phonological and the borrowers had complete access to the phonology of both languages, varied adaptions of a single sound would not be expected. Varied patterns in loanword adaptation such as those being shown in Korean loanwords from English are

difficult to explain without considering perceptual factors in the borrowing process (H. Y. Park, 2007, p. 3).

Silverman (1992) also suggests that the native system plays a central role in perception, in which a perceptual level filters out sounds that cannot be assimilated natively with an operational level, then adapting the resulting input based on structural constraints. Silverman considers the division of levels to be the same in both the bilingual and monolingual speaker, contradicting aspects of speech perception research (Flege, 1995). It has also been noted that when massive scale borrowing occurs, aspects of phonology from the donor language can be imparted onto the native system, resulting in mini-phonologies (Lees, 1961; McCawley, 1968). Although there is debate as to the extent to which this challenges the single grammar notion (Ito & Mester, 1995a), other research (Shinohara, 2001) has highlighted that it is rational to attribute loanword adaptations within the native language to the latent use of Universal Grammar.

Jacobs and Gussenhoven (2000) claim that a 'universal phonological grammar' exists, where humans can perceive all sounds from any language without mistake, and therefore perception plays no role in adaptation. This is in contrast to the view of Peperkamp and Dupoux (2003) as outlined above, and other research that shows infants lose their ability to discriminate speech sounds in foreign languages (Werker & Tees, 1984). Yet, it has been well recognized that loanword adaptation is carried out through a 'phonological grammar' (Smith, 2006; Yip, 2002). That is, for the speakers who first borrow a word through contact with a source language, the underlying representation of the loanword in the borrowing language closely resembles the source language form. The borrowing language's phonological grammar then maps the underlying representation to a surface representation, and as part of mapping, the loanword may be altered to satisfy the phonological requirements of the borrowing language. However, Smith (2006) notes that it is significant that languages such as Korean use feature change or deletion repairs in the native phonology, but loanword adaptation involves epenthesis (the insertion of an additional one or more sounds in a word). Kang (1996) also recognizes this, illustrating that Korean loanword phonology and Korean native vocabulary have separate constraint systems within OT. This implies that "nonloan phonology cannot be the only mechanism accountable for loanword adaptation – if it were, then the same repair strategy that is used for the nonloans would be chosen for loanwords as well" (Smith, 2006, p. 3-4). As a result, "researchers have proposed adding loanword-specific principles or constraints to the phonological system" (Smith, 2006, p. 4), as loanwords enter one language (with a set of constraints) from another language (with another set of constraints) (Yip, 1993).

"As UG or principles and parameters theory provides a framework for testing hypotheses about L2 acquisition" (Rodby & Winterowd, 2004, p. 5), OT provides a basis for understanding the entrenchment of loanwords in a matrix language. In interlanguage terms, this is a system that produces 'errors' as well as 'correct forms' (Rodby & Winterowd, 2004). It is these 'errors' or 'correct' forms that are perceived as L1 (negative) transfer or L1 (positive) transfer when Korean loanwords are used in the target language, and this extends from semantic use through to the phonological and phonetic forms (Jenkins, 2000). As Gass and Selinker (1994, in Han, 2004, p. 150) remind us, it is from the teacher (or researcher) perspective that a learner generates errors, and "for corrective feedback to be potentially useful, it is necessary that some sort of attention-getting mechanism be built in the feedback process to enable the learner to perceive it for what it is, and further, to recognize the gap between the feedback and his or her own output". Otherwise, "if the learner fails to discern the real difference between the information available in the correction and his or her error, fossilization is likely to result" (Han, 2004, p. 150). With this in mind, the study of foreign word adaptations can not only probe the final-state grammar of L2 but may also shed light on the initial state (Shinohara, 2001). The implication for acquisition is that the UG latent in L1 is accessible in a later stage in life, and so the rise of constraint-based frameworks such as OT have come to provide insight into native phonology by revealing relative ranking of faithfulness constraints that would otherwise remain 'hidden' (see Jacobs & Gussenhoven, 2003). Harely (1993) also makes claims that cross-lingual analysis can help undo fossilized (or stabilized) errors.

Predominantly, all of this research, focusing largely upon form, has highlighted a lack of research centering upon the practical applicability of loanwords in the EFL environment. As Rodby and Winterowd (2004) emphasize, much second language acquisition (SLA) research focuses on how the conditions for language are enacted rather than on the influence of social usage conditions, and the cognitive processes of the learner. In this regard, "scholarly work on input processing (VanPatten, 1996) and focus on form (Long & Robinson, 1998) suggests that acquisition benefits most when second language learners focus, not on linguistic form alone, or on communicative meaning alone, but on both form and meaning when they use the L2" (Tarone, 2006, p. 159). As such, it is essential to examine the usage aspect of loanwords, if seeking to utilize such terms in the foreign language acquisition process, in terms of both social usage and applicability for learning, for it is important to understand how the loanwords operate in the L1 and what influence they may in turn have upon foreign language communication. Particularly since learners who share the same L1 share the same conceptual framework, and "have highly homogeneous ways of conceptualizing and verbalizing their life experiences" (Han, 2004, p. 156). In addition,

> Borrowing is a very complicated process involving perceptual, non-perceptual, phonological, and morphological factors, as well as non-linguistic factors (e.g. historical reason, influence of orthography, frequency effect; thus it is difficult to give a unified explanation for all the loanwords even within one language (H. Y. Park, 2007, p. 25).

"Loanwords are words from one language which are incorporated into another, the borrowing language" (Haunz, 2003, p. 1). In this process, the borrowed terms are usually adapted to fit the governing sound system of the acquiring language. At times, these words are not only phonologically altered but the semantic meaning can be changed, and in this case, pseudo-loanwords can result. Such borrowings and adaptations in Korean have also resulted in adjustments to the grammatical structure, such as increased use of *deul*, an optional plural particle that is almost an equivalent of the plural inflection *s* and *es* in English, and the adoption in the 19th Century, not followed by Chinese and Japanese, of writing each Korean word unit separately (McArthur, 1992). The English loan and pseudo-loanwords that exist or were borrowed into Korean largely become propagated through the media and the use of technology (Doms, 2004). Newspapers have peppered these terms throughout news stories and titles, as have television advertisements and programming, along with internet sites and chat rooms coming to aid in the continuous spread, use, and entrenchment of these terms within the native vernacular ("Plagued by Mangled English, South Korea Struggles to Improve Skills," 2000).

English loanwords entering the Korean language can fit into one of six categories as presented in Table 1 (based on Miller, 2003). A summary of the assimilation of loanwords into Korean, based on Taylor and Taylor (1995), can be categorized as: (a) the majority of more modern loanwords appear to stem from the English language, and to a lesser degree other European languages; (b) shortening, limiting, combining, and extending English loanwords results in words that can be incomprehensible to an L1 speaker of English; (c) some loanwords tend only to be used as compound words; (d) loanwords tend to be nouns in the original language, but are incorporated into Korean for use in any word class; (e) loanwords are blended with other loans or the native language to coin new terms or pseudo-loanwords and false cognates; and (f) brand names take on semantic meaning.

Table 1
English Loanwords in Korean by Category

Category		Definition	Example Korean Term
Direct Loanwords		Loans with identical or phonetically modified pronunciation or meaning	*chyokoreiteu* (chocolate) *okeseuteura* (orchestra) *kopi* (coffee) *juseu* (juice)
Hybrid Terms		Loan terms incorporating words from both English and Korean	*binil-bongtu* (plastic bag, lit. vinyl envelope) *bang'ul-tomato* (cherry tomato, lit. bell tomato)
Substitution		Loanwords that have come to replace other loans or existing Korean terminology	*raiteo* (lighter, replacing *pul*, lit. fire) *paking* (parking, replacing the Sino-Korean *jucha*, lit. stop car)
Pseudo-Loanwords	Truncated Terminology	Loanwords formed from the shortening of English terms	*remocon* (*remo*te *con*trol) *remicon* (ready-*mi*xed *con*crete)
	False Cognates	Terms that are pronounced the same but hold different semantic meanings in English and Korean	*consent* (English: permission; Korean: power outlet) *steam* (English: water vapor; Korean: radiator heater)
	Fabricated Loans	Terms that sound like English but are not used by L1 speakers of English	*Dutch pay* (go Dutch) *hop* or *hof* (bar, *used interchangeably*) *wheel cap* (hub cap)

Considering their appropriateness for the EFL teaching context, English loanwords in Korean can fall into one of three categories: (a) forms that are not utilized in English, such as *remicon* meaning *rea*dy *mix*ed *con*crete, and for these terms, a background of sociocultural knowledge may be required of L1 speakers of English before they can guess the meaning of the word; (b) forms that can be expressed or understood, including words such as *omnibus* meaning *a collection of several items*, which can also consist of pseudo-loanwords that have their basis in the English language but may not be commonly heard in the 'English' speech community or are not used in the manner expressed in Korean, like *fighting* meaning *a struggle* in English but used to encourage a friend or cheer on a team in Korean; and (c) forms that are identical in English and Korean (e.g. *burger, chocolate, computer, lighter, orchestra*) which pose no or few problems for interpretation and can be used directly within contextual English language settings as no decoding on the part of the learner is required for the terms in this category and at the beginning phases of second language acquisition. Words of this type not only form a basis for using situational settings that are contextual with existing language knowledge, but also form a part of the target language, allowing for settings that provide for loanword use in the EFL context to be incorporated into lesson material, and in a manner reflective of 'real-life' contextual environments and topics that can come to promote realistic English language usage that is of relevance to student learning.

Loanword terms from each of these categories can also provide a means for students to identify and compare cross-cultural and cross-language use, granting them a more complete understanding of their own natural language use while developing English competence, allowing them to see how certain topics reflect and imply regularities between the seemingly alien native and target languages. Keeping in mind that "loanwords result, not from stupid straightforward copying: rather they result from phonological and semantic transformations that are complex and creative" (Tanaka, 1997, p. 2), and this is well established (see P. Y. H. Choi, 2001; Dimova, 2007; Peperkamp & Dupoux, 2003).

The problem for constructing an appropriate foreign language framework that utilizes loanwords from the L1 and testing the effectiveness of it is that the communicative competence provided by these loanwords must be used to promote aspects of positive transfer (Daulton, 1998; Kimura, 1989; Nicholls, 2002), lighten the burden of learning (Nation, 1990, 2003), and provide scaffolding (see Daulton, 1998, 1999a, 1999b, 2003; Kimura, 1989; Nation & Newton, 1997; Shaffer, 1999; Shepherd, 1996; Simon-Maeda, 1997) in order to develop communicative performance in the target language (Standard American

English). A further problem that must be considered is that the underlying phonological and grammatical competence possessed by knowledge of the loanword from the L1 may affect the learning of the underlying models and rules of performance in the target language (Standard American English). These issues were expected and dealt with during the development of an approach that has come to incorporate loanwords for use in the teaching of EFL in the Korean context, as well as in the construction of linguistic exercises relevant for imparting English language knowledge through the use of such terms, and this is detailed in Part Three of this book. Such a model of instruction, through use of loanwords, then comes to hold at its core utilization of aspects of linguistic competence already in possession of the students concerned (Daulton, 1998, 1999a, 1999b, 2003).

Pedagogy

Target Language Lexical Development through L1 Usage

Vocabulary acquisition is a gradual and complicated process – a process where there are three dimensions of knowledge that can be acquired to various degrees (see Henrickson, 1999).

The first dimension views word knowledge as a continuum rather than as either known or unknown, with learners possessing word knowledge that ranges from zero through to partial and on to precise. Korean EFL students' knowledge of English loanwords from their L1 lexicon sees many of these words, such as direct loanwords, fall on this continuum at a precise level. That is, students possess comprehensive understanding of the foreign language (Standard American English) term since it has been fully assimilated into Korean usage. However, some other loanword terminology (e.g. pseudo-loanwords and hybrid terms) may possess very different semantic and pragmatic meaning from the original language from which it was borrowed, and when used in the student L1, and in terms of English as a foreign language usage, would come to fall on the word knowledge continuum at a partial or even zero point level.

The second dimension refers to word knowledge types, and views depth of knowledge as requiring mastery of various lexical aspects, or as Qian (1999) indicates: how well learners know a word. In terms of loanwords in the native lexicon, Korean students possess many base words, and therefore the core meaning sense of much of the English vocabulary, but there is little relative depth to this knowledge. As a result, in the English as a foreign language acquisition process, the core meanings of these base words would need extending to cover the range of meanings usually possessed by the words when used in English, while different loanword types (pseudo-loanwords or false cognates, and hybrid terms) would require lexical meaning shifts to occur (see Daulton, 1999a, 1999b, 2003).

The third dimension of vocabulary acquisition involves both productive (use) and receptive (recognition) mastery of lexical items. In this regard, Melka (as cited in Schmitt, 2000) views receptive and productive mastery of vocabulary as poles of a continuum, and in relation to this, it is believed that much of the English loanword knowledge that students possess is active at the receptive level (on a point of the word knowledge continuum) but not active at the productive level. To this end, the students' receptive levels need reinforcement and their productive levels need activating with any approach that incorporates loanwords as viable lexical units from which to engage in the learning of EFL. Consequently, the mental lexicon cannot be seen as a module stored apart from other forms of knowledge in long-term memory (Hulstijn, 1997), but all words may be located within a single store with the subset of L1 words more strongly associated with each other than those of the foreign language as part of a dynamic system. This dynamic system allows words to be stored in unassociated fashions, which can then be linked by one formal or semantic feature and later by more features, with the strength of these associations for each word being different at various times with these individual associations increasing and decreasing over time.

Such an approach is designed to promote foreign language lexical development through structured use of the L1, and relies upon the production of communicative competence, much like the communicative language teaching (CLT) approach, to develop pragmatic competence. This technique is also akin to the lexical approach, in that development of learner proficiency occurs by focusing on lexis, or words and word combinations. An increase in competence and communicative power is achieved by extending the learners' repertoire of lexical phrases and collocational power, and increasing the mastery of pre-existing vocabulary familiar to the learner through their native language.

Lewis's (1993, 1997a, 1997b) lexical syllabus is based on word patterns, while Willis's (1990) lexical syllabus is word-based. The loanword approach for vocabulary building and teaching EFL to Korean students is akin to both of these. Since the lexical approach relies on word chunks (or groups of words as phrases) to develop the pragmatic competence of learners, and Korean students are not able to do this with L1 word forms that they use as part of the foreign language in loanword transfer, the loanword approach could be used as a step before the lexical approach. It can also extend the CLT approach by not just using English to teach

English but using the English inherent within the native vernacular to teach English. The lexical approach, like that of the loanword approach, does not require radical methodological changes either (Moudraia, 2001).

Several elements of how the loanword approach compares to the lexical, natural, and CLT approaches (based on Richards & Rogers, 2001; 2014) are detailed in Table 2.1, Table 2.2, and Table 2.3 respectively. The major characteristics of the loanword approach toward language and situated learning (see Tretiakov, Kinshuk & Tretiakov, 2003) are as follows:

1. The local cultural context and learning environment must be considered in the teaching of EFL (Critchley, 1998; Ellis, 1994; Oka, 2004; Weschler, 1997).

2. Specific and judicious use of the native language can provide support and scaffolding for learner target language development, with links and strengths of association between the native language use of loanwords and the use of these terms in English promoting the pragmatic and communicative competence of learners (Daulton, 1998, 1999a, 1999b, 2003; Kimura, 1989; Nation & Newton, 1997; Shaffer, 1999; Shepherd, 1996; Simon-Maeda, 1997).

3. For false-beginners, native language English loanword use can be particularly helpful for developing language/vocabulary acquisition in the target language learning phase (e.g. for homework, especially with large classes using set syllabuses such as in universities and high schools), with focus on production in the practice phase (e.g. in the classroom, particularly when set syllabuses are used and when learners are face-to-face with instructors) (Nation, 1990, 2001, 2003).

4. A loanword approach to EFL vocabulary teaching should be utilized or extended by the use of other approaches in contexts such as in Korea, where a large number of base words relating to loanwords can be found on such vocabulary lists as the general service list (GSL), the British national corpus (BNC) (Daulton, 1999b, 2003), the NGSL (New General Service List) and the COCA (Corpus of Contemporary American English).

Table 2.1

Comparing elements of the lexical approach to the loanword approach

Lexical Approach	Loanword Approach
Lexis plays a central role in language teaching and learning	Lexis that stems from English loanwords can play a central role in teaching and learning with students, viewing this lexis as a 'target language knowledge kernel'
Lexis should be the central organizing principle of any meaning-centered syllabus	Meaning-based activities need to be provided to learners, as lexis from the 'target language knowledge kernel' is used as the organizing principle
Importance of contrast in language awareness must be recognized	Importance of contrast and similarity between the L1 and foreign language in language awareness must be recognized

Table 2.2

Comparing elements of the natural approach to the loanword approach

Natural Approach	Loanword Approach
For beginners – designed to help them become intermediates	For false-beginners – designed to help them gain confidence, fluency, and develop pragmatic and communicative competence in the use of target language vocabulary
Emphasizes the primacy of meaning, with an importance on vocabulary	Emphasizes a primacy of meaning, with an importance on lexicon that is similar, or that allows for positive transfer between native and target languages to occur
Explicit attention placed on grammar is not required	Explicit attention placed on grammar is not required, rather explicit attention is placed on lexical use and misuse of loanwords (i.e. positive and negative transfer) and using this to develop learning gains

Table 2.3

Comparing elements of the communicative language teaching approach to the loanword approach

Communicative Language Teaching Approach	Loanword Approach
Uses English to learn English, although judicious use of the first language (including translation) is acceptable, with comprehensible pronunciation sought	Uses English and the English within the native vocabulary to learn English, with a view that limited and judicial translation is acceptable, with comprehensible pronunciation sought
Error correction generally occurs when it impacts meaning not accuracy, language being created by trial and error	Error correction (or perceived foreign language error correction) occurs when it affects meaning, this meaning can be linked associatively and then used to build appropriate use of vocabulary, hoping to minimize the trial and error process or misinterpretation of vocabulary use
Language items are contextualized in materials, centering on communicative functions	Language items, including loanwords, are contextualized within materials, centering around various functions including communicative needs
Language learning is learning to communicate and to communicate effectively, with communicative competence the aim	Language learning is learning to communicate and communicate effectively in both the national context (understanding the local 'variety' of English) and international context (understanding 'standard' English equivalents of locally used or misused English terms), where communicative competence is the aim
Motivation stems from interest in what is being communicated, with teachers helping learners in ways that motivate them to work with language, and sequencing is determined by any consideration of content, function, or meaning that maintains interest	Motivation stems from learners determining how it is that they use English, developing material to assist learners to work with the language, and sequencing is determined by any consideration of content, function, or meaning that maintains interest
Attempts to communicate are encouraged from the outset, with the struggle to communicate seen as the best process of acquiring the target language	Attempts to communicate are encouraged from the outset, with the struggle to communicate coupled with use of the L1 for scaffolding seen as the best process for acquiring higher levels of proficiency and fluency in the target language

Like the lexical approach and communicative language teaching approach, the loanword approach takes a view on the theory of language as communication with lexis as the basis of language. The goal of language teaching is to develop a 'communicative competence' (Hymes, 1972) that incorporates communication and culture. In other words, use of the loanword approach aims at allowing learners to be communicatively competent in the international as well as the national context, achieving proficiency in both the use of the local 'variety' of English as well as the English equivalents for this terminology, and therefore being proficient in two dialects of English. The loanword approach therefore subscribes to tenants of the theoretical base of both the lexical approach (Lewis, 1993, 1997a, 1997b), and the CLT approach (from Richards & Rogers, 2001; 2014). These are: (a) language is a system for the expression of meaning, and lexis is the basis of language; (b) interaction and communication is the primary function of language, meaning that successful language is a wider concept than accurate language; (c) structure reflects functional and communicative uses of language, with lexis being the guiding principle; and (d) grammatical and structural features are not the primary units of language, grammar is not the basis of language, and mastery of grammatical systems is not a prerequisite for effective communication.

Furthermore, "the language learner does not start with a *tabula rosa*" (Spolsky, 1989, p. 117). Contrastive analysis (CA) of two languages allows potential problems of interference to be predicted and addressed via carefully constructed instructional content. It also allows the linguist to use the best linguistic knowledge available to him or her in order to account for observed difficulties in foreign language learning (Spolsky, 1989; Wardhaugh, 1970). Selinker (1992) shows that there are "… at least three generally distinguishable sets of theoretical claims resulting from CA" (p. 21), and these claims could be extended to loanword usage as a basis for vocabulary acquisition in the Korean EFL context (see Table 3).

Ultimately this research, along with that of Nation (2003), emphasizes that "the L1 clearly has a very important role to play in the deliberate learning of vocabulary" (p. 4). Encouraging learners to notice borrowings and the use of loanwords to assist in the learning of English "is a very effective vocabulary expansion strategy" (Nation, 2003, p. 4), and one that involves the deliberate exploration of first and second language relationships. In terms of orthography, Schmitt (2000) has also mentioned that, when L1 and foreign language words are similar, due to either etymology or a loanword basis, they can facilitate learning. As recent research into teaching practices indicate, the L1 is being used as a learning resource, and "when the native language *is* used, practitioners, researchers, and learners consistently report positive results" (Auerbach, 1993, p. 18, original emphasis). Furthermore, Critchley (2002) has demonstrated that in communicative English language teaching, the L1 has a clear supportive role, and cites several researchers (e.g. Auerbach, Pellowe, and Burden) to support this claim.

Table 3
Contrastive analysis and loanword approach claims

Contrastive Analysis Claims	Loanword Approach Claims
The learner in an SLA situation 'expects to find' some 'equivalent' in the target language to native language structures: productively, receptively, or both	Use of direct loanwords shows learners that there is evidence of equivalence between the native and target language
Such a learner 'has to learn' to produce something different from his native language in his attempt at learning the target language	Elements, like truncated, hybrid, and shortened loans, must be produced differently in English
Such a learner has 'considerable trouble' (in some way) with a target language pattern which is different from the native language	There are terms that must be recontextualized, like pseudo loanwords and false cognates, before 'standard' English usage of the term can occur

Application

CALL System Foundations for Vocabulary Development

A number of CALL software systems, usually unable to deal with issues relating to cross-linguistic influence, have been developed that use aspects of transfer to assist learners with language acquisition (Bull, 1995). In part, these systems, by indicating similarities between target and other languages including the native language, may result in learning through positive comparison, as in many cases, the first language will be the dominant source of transfer. This conception of transfer is similar to what Lado (1952, p. 2) once described as individuals transferring "the forms and meaning, and the distribution of forms and meanings of their native language and culture to the foreign language and culture". In addition, Schachter (1996) argued that knowledge of a prior language would facilitate or inhibit foreign language acquisition in adults, depending on the similarity or dissimilarity between the languages. With these two perspectives in mind, what in the target language is exact or similar in the native language would be more easily absorbed by the learner as linguistic knowledge in an EFL situation. In regards to vocabulary acquisition, the understanding of meaning and usage for direct loanwords may be more easily acquired over that of pseudo-loanwords, and for the practical application of using pseudo-loanwords to assist in the vocabulary acquisition process, interlingual errors become a focus (see Richards, 1971). Furthermore, to solidify the usage or reconstruction of such native language material in the target language as a learner strategy for vocabulary acquisition, an intentional means of being able to do so must be pointed out and emphasized to students before positive transfer can occur. That is, explicit learning is consistently effective (see Beaton, Grunberg & Ellis, 1995; Laufer & Shmueli, 1997; Prince, 1996), as is direct versus an indirect means of vocabulary instruction (Folse, 2004; Johnson & Pearson, 1984; Zimmerman, 1997). Noticing can be enhanced and recycling opportunities provided through strategies of explicit lexical learning. It is these two factors, noticing and recycling, that effectively foster integration of vocabulary in long-term memory, provided that form and meaning are attended to appropriately (Prince, 1996). This explicit focus on similarity markedly contrasts with Lado's perception, whereby the role of language teaching appears to have been interpreted as essentially focusing upon the points of difference and then presenting these points of difference in a manner of massive practice. Kimura (1989) also provides support from the EFL context to challenge Lado's assertion that loanword knowledge limits the range of English meanings learners possess for a term, as loanword knowledge (from the L1) encourages learners to add meaning (acquired from the target language) to the pre-existing meanings they possess. This is particularly true in the case of pseudo-loanwords and hybrid terms, but also for direct loanwords that have undergone semantic narrowing when borrowed.

Technology application is conducive to vocabulary teaching according to Levy & Stockwell (2006), but for vocabulary acquisition to occur from a program of foreign language study, learners need to be exposed to a variety of contexts that include recycling of terms, "critical if they stand a chance of becoming readily accessible in long-term memory" (Koprowski, 2006, p. 1), and provide a complementary combination of both explicit teaching and implicit learning (Nation, 1990; 2001). A number of the key principles for explicit vocabulary teaching are highlighted by Sokmen (cited in Schmitt, 2000) and these are produced below. Each principle has been extended by taking into account research on learning with multimedia (Alessi & Trollip, 2001) and vocabulary acquisition (Nation,

1990, 2001), and to show how it relates to a loanword approach based CALL vocabulary teaching system:

- Build a large sight vocabulary, by utilizing modern processing and multimedia powers of modern systems along with their large storage capacity, and by using the lexical store of English terminology inherent within the native vocabulary as the lexical database.

- Integrate new words with old, through various exercises and activities in particular units or activities.

- Provide a number of encounters with a word, by incorporating terms throughout system activities and by allowing users to redo these activities as many times as they wish by providing links back to various points in the system.

- Promote a deep level of processing, achieved through the utilization of various techniques such as classification or sorting-based tasks, multiple-choice selection-based tasks, clue-type matching-based tasks, and so on.

- Facilitate imaging, by relating the terminology to both the L1 and foreign language setting through contextualization in activities, and in construction of the user interface.

- Make words 'real' by connecting them to the student world in some way through situated learning, by utilizing English loanwords from the native language and creating a culturally relevant interface focusing on the local setting.

- Use a variety of techniques, from activities to acquisition methods through to design elements.

- Encourage independent learning strategies, by utilizing aspects of the learning system to promote motivation and encourage students to focus on the vocabulary items and relate their foreign language usage to real life use and experience from the first language.

The lack of intelligence and interactivity of many multimedia-based software systems, as Warschauer (1996) has pointed out, can limit the ability of CALL to provide meaningful and authentic communication. However, Pusack and Otto (1997) have recognized that multimedia systems shift the emphasis of learning toward that of 'input and intake', and can facilitate authentic learning and an accurate portrayal of the target language as a result of housing vast quantities of virtual realia. Stoney and Oliver (1999) also indicate that multimedia develops and fosters cognitive engagement through its ability to hold and attract student focus and attention. Multimedia systems are also consistent (Hick, 1997) as they provide the same learning content to all learners. This is supported by Adams (in THINQ, n.d.) where it has been shown that a 59% variance occurs in instructor-delivered material as opposed to a 19% variance when learners participate in the use of multimedia-based modules. Computer-based instructional variance can perhaps be explained by the unique navigational selection of students (Schar, Schluep, & Schierz, 2000). The instructional consistency provided through multimedia can be viewed positively, particularly in the university English program setting of Korea where the reliability of delivering the same learning content and quality of service to a large number of students is important.

Non-linear navigation and the interactivity that can be built into multimedia environments offers advantages over other systems and distinguishes multimedia from other forms of CAI (Davies & Crowther, 1995). Software systems built on such platforms offer interactivity by providing students with the means to control aspects of the learning environment, and can integrate audio, graphics, text, and video within the learning environment. Further, Soper (1997) has also long shown that the individual use of multimedia systems allows students to review and apply knowledge for themselves as often as they like, receive rapid feedback, assessment, and answers, and put this knowledge to immediate use and learn from their mistakes. Soper (1997) also favors systems of single-user design, as they can develop within students the ability to complete work without supervision, and enable students to take more responsibility for their own independent learning. Whatever the system design, however, multi-user or single-user multimedia use requires students to be self-regulating.

For explicit language teaching, CALL software systems are ideally suited to provide such contexts through multimedia, and their re-use enables recycling to occur at the demand of the student, while assessment can be embedded within activities along with immediate and extensive feedback. Such abilities, including the patient, interactive, and reinforcing capabilities of CALL systems, have been widely documented (Ahmad, Corbett, Rogers, & Sussex, 1985; Alessi & Trollip, 2001; Ariew & Frommer, 1987; Levy, 1997). In fact, single-user courseware and applications allow for autonomous context-based learning at times that are convenient to students who are working at their own pace. They are learner-centered and learner-controlled, and can ensure the delivery of the same content to each individual participating in large-scale study programs like university English courses in Korea. It is such a system, in just such a context, that was designed, deployed, and empirically tested during the mid 2000s so that the effectiveness of using L1 vocabulary for lexical development in a practical Korean EFL setting during that time could be assessed. The design, development, and testing of this system is discussed at length throughout Part Three of this book.

Part Two Summary

Part Two of this book consists of four major segments, each focusing on research from the Korean context. The first and second segments place a focus on the Korean educational environment and aspects relating to EFL and ICT. The third section introduces the complex cultural environment of Korea, and advocates the necessity of taking the local cultural context into account when designing and implementing teaching materials. The final section then focuses on linguistic issues. A unique approach, one that comes to involve CALL and L1 usage, is then envisioned for the teaching of EFL in the local Korean educational environment.

Part Three will now begin by examining and detailing the methods by which the aforementioned approach was implemented and tested in the Korean context during the mid 2000s.

Part Three
DEVELOPMENT, IMPLEMENTATION,
INQUIRY, AND OUTCOMES

Part Three
DEVELOPMENT, IMPLEMENTATION, INQUIRY, AND OUTCOMES

Examining the Effectiveness of a Multimedia Curriculum

Overview

This part of the book highlights one means of developing and implementing a method for employing a loanword approach to the teaching of English as a foreign language (EFL) in the Korean context. Following this, the means used to trial the approach are explained, and the outcomes presented. Ultimately, this involved the development of several instruments (a survey, a pre- and post-test, and two multimedia-based computer assisted language learning modules), and their use in an experiment. The findings from this empirical investigation, along with the process of refinement and calibration of resulting data by the Rasch rating scale model, with results obtained from final administration of the instruments will then be detailed. Analyses applied to test the hypotheses also included a regression analysis and a one-way analysis of variance. These results will also be discussed, and in doing so, the association of computer assisted learning of English with the learning of pseudo-loanwords will be considered. The impact of instructional approaches on vocabulary acquisition will then be examined, and aspects of loanword utilization for foreign language development taken into account. Also considered are the consequences of the changing Korean cultural learning style, the influence of negative washback on the investigation, and the emergence of a 'stabilized interlanguage' in Korea. Finally, threats to the reliability and validity of the investigation will be discussed, along with several limitations to the investigation, before presenting answers to the lines of inquiry.

Introduction

Determining the effectiveness of applying a loanword approach to the teaching of English as a foreign language in the Korean context was not so straightforward. Ultimately, this involved distribution and group-administration of a survey, with participants of this survey then taking part in learning foreign language from one of two specifically developed multimedia-based computer assisted language learning (CALL) homework modules as part of an experiment. Data concerning the effectiveness of these modules was then collected from participants through the administration of a pre-treatment and a post-treatment test which is based on the learning material that participants were exposed to at treatment.

As such, the research method applied can be defined as a 'within methods' approach (Creswell, 1994), that is, quantitative data collection strategies employing both survey-method and experimental design. Such experimental research involves manipulation of one or more variables, and tests for the effect of this manipulation or treatment on one or more dependent variables. The one-group pre-test/post-test experimental design (pre-test, treatment, then post-test) that was applied is the same as that of the pre-test/post-test design, but there is no random assignment to multiple conditions, and is thereby considered quasi-experimental. The most common reason for employing a quasi-experimental design is the inability to randomly assign persons to conditions, as is the case during this investigation.

Further, the Rasch model was employed for data analysis, and there are two major reasons for this. First, to identify in the pre- and post-test the items that both top and bottom students got correct. Rasch analysis assists in determining items found not to be discriminating properly which serves to pinpoint data that is of no use, and therefore items that, after trialing, can be identified and improved upon before final instrument deployment. Second, item 'difficulties' can be calibrated to match the range of student 'abilities'. This means that both the test and survey instruments could be confirmed to be a good measure of the trait that each was designed to measure, with persons and items plotted along the same single measurement dimension. This is significant as Rasch analysis adheres to unidimensionality, measuring one attribute at a time, and therefore demands that a single construct underlies items making up the hierarchical continuum. After ensuring instrument reliability and validity, and refining the data in this manner, a process of multiple regression and the use of ANOVA was then employed to test the hypotheses.

A. DEVELOPMENT OF AN INVESTIGATIVE METHOD

Approach

The research method that was applied within this study can be defined as a 'within-methods' approach (Creswell, 1994), and it was selected as it allowed for multiple methods of investigation; that is, quantitative data collection strategies employing both the one-group pre-test/post-test experimental method, and also the survey method. Typically, the assumption behind the use of this approach is that any bias inherent in the study can be neutralized in conjunction with other data sources and collection procedures. As Borg and Gall (1989, p. 641) iterate, although powerful, "the experiment is not a perfect method"; even well designed experiments are refutable. Consequently, in addition to employment of the experimental method, the survey method allowed for data to be collected using variables not manipulated in the experiment but considered influential on the dependent variable.

Experimental research involves manipulation of one or more variables and tests for the effect of this manipulation or treatment on one or more dependent variables. It is a powerful method that can provide strong evidence for confirmation of hypothesized cause and effect relationships (Fraenkel & Wallen, 2003). The one-group pre-test/post-test experimental design (pre-test, treatment, then post-test) is the same as that of the pre-test/post-test design but there is no random assignment of multiple conditions, and it is thereby considered quasi-experimental. The most common reason for employing a quasi-experimental design is the inability to randomly assign persons to conditions, as was the case with this research. It is also such design types that are used "when experimental and control groups are such naturally assembled groups as intact classes, which may be similar" (Best & Kahn, 1993, p. 151).

The survey method provides systematic data collection relating to perceptions and attitudes of a given group (Fraenkel & Wallen, 2003), and, as Best and Kahn (1993) illustrate, surveys are useful assessment and evaluation tools. In the case of this study, attainment of the research objectives required collecting information from the subjects of the experiment about their disposition towards computer assisted learning of English to supplement the results from the experiment.

Inquiry

This research seeks to understand the interaction between multiple dimensions of computer assisted learning and English foreign language acquisition of Korean freshmen university students during the mid 2000s; in particular, to examine how the student's knowledge of English words adapted for use in the Korean vernacular – loanwords – was affected by their attitudes towards computerized instruction, their preference for certain methods of learning and teaching, and also by the attributes of computerized instructional packages.

The two core questions that emerged are:

1. Is student understanding of pseudo-loanwords associated with dispositions towards computer assisted learning of English as a foreign language?
2. Does the application of different computer assisted language learning instructional strategies affect student understanding of pseudo-loanwords?

Obtaining data to answer these lines of inquiry is contingent on the following objectives: (a) to develop a linear scale to measure Korean student dispositions towards computer assisted learning of English as a foreign language; (b) to develop a linear scale to measure Korean student understanding of loanwords for use as the pre-test and post-test in the experiment; and (c) to develop two computer assisted language instructional modules as the treatment in the experiment.

Research Design

The empirical design comprises of four stages. The first stage is development of an instrument to measure Korean student dispositions towards computer assisted learning of English as a foreign language (EFL), and also development of a test to measure Korean student understanding of loanwords. Second, the survey of student dispositions towards computer assisted learning of English as a foreign language was administered concurrently to the sample of students completing the pre-treatment test. Third, two computer assisted language instructional modules were administered as the experiment treatment to two different groups of students. Finally, the test of student understanding of loanwords was re-administered.

A multiple regression analysis (SPSS, 2003) was conducted to ascertain whether disposition towards computer assisted learning of English as a foreign language (the independent variable) is associated with student understanding of pseudo-loanwords (the dependent variable). The effect of the treatment on the dependent variable of student understanding of pseudo-loanwords was estimated by a one-way analysis of variance (ANOVA) (RUMM, 2002) between Rasch model calibrated pre- and post-treatment test scores.

Participant Population Target Sample

The target population is all the freshmen (first year students) in a mandatory university English program in a Korean university. To ensure that minimal linguistic differences between experimental groups exists, the sample was restricted to intermediate-level students from this program as determined by university placement tests. Participants therefore came from a cluster sample of almost 2,000 students, which were assigned to classes and instructors in blocks based on major, and this resulted in an available overall sample of approximately 150 students. Although such a small sample size, and restriction of the sample to one school, may limit the ability to generalize results, this has the advantage of affording the researcher greater experimental control (Fraenkel, Wallen, & Hyun, 2012).

Instrumentation

1. Survey of Student Attitudes towards Computer Assisted Learning in EFL (SSACAL)

Theoretical Framework
The survey is based on three postulated dimensions of student attitudes towards computer assisted learning in EFL: (a) disposition towards computer assisted instruction (CAI); (b) Korean learning style; and (c) English as a foreign language learning style.

Item Writing
Instrument items were developed by the researcher relying on existing questionnaires, including a survey examining changes in Korean cultural assumptions and attitudes toward English language learning (refer to Windle, 2003), along with a taxonomy framework of vocabulary strategies stemming from the Oxford Strategy Inventory for Language Learning (see Park, 2001). The survey (see Appendix One) comprised 114 items organized respectively into the following three major sections and subsections. For more detail on the content of the sections and subsections, refer to Appendix One.

The major sections and sub-sections of the instrument are:
Section One: Disposition towards computer assisted instruction.
   A). Computer competency;
   B). Preference for computer-based learning; and
   C). Preference for learning English through CAI.

Section Two: Korean learning style.
  A). In-class relations;
  B). Desired characteristics of instructors; and
  C). View of education.

Section Three: English as a Foreign Language learning style.
  A) Preference for cultural representation;
  B). Loanword use; and
  C). Vocabulary acquisition strategies.

2. Test of Student Understanding of Pseudo-Loanwords (SUPL)

To measure student understanding of pseudo-loanwords, a test (see Appendix Two) was constructed and administered pre- and post-treatment. The test was designed to determine the ability of students to identify the meaning of a Korean pseudo-loanword by selecting from one of four statements written in English.

The number of test items was limited to 50 so that the test could easily be completed within one lecture period, and they required recognition of the correct English meaning of pseudo-loanwords. These loanwords were selected at random from the vocabulary applied in the activities comprising the experimental treatment.

The test measures one aspect of EFL learning: student understanding of pseudo-loanwords expressed in English.

Item Writing

Multiple-choice is a common type of selected-response items used in classroom achievement tests. The format is easily understood, and students have had a high exposure to such test style formats (Mandernach, 2003). Multiple-choice items are also objective, and this supports speedy, reliable, and efficient scoring. In regards to the number of items tested, multiple-choice tests can be completed in a short period of time (Claycomb & Kysilko, 2000), and as Mandernach reminds us, their versatility sees them able to target a range of learning objectives such as analysis, comprehension, factual knowledge, and evaluation. The multiple-choice test constructed for this research sees each item contain a stem with four response options. The stem consists of a short statement, in which a single word, one that comes from the pseudo-loanword category, is underlined, and students must select its meaning from one of four response options. The response options immediately follow the stem, contain three distracters and, in the form of the English language definition, one correct answer.

3. CALL Modules

Conceptual Framework and Development of Modules

The two multimedia-based computer assisted language learning (CALL) modules, based on 'traditional-' and 'edutainment-based' learning, were built on an existing multimedia/hypermedia software system framework and share a common interface design. At the macro level, both modules employ three similar types of task, and thereby each module maintains the overall objectives that come to underpin each activity section (i.e. classification, multiple-choice, and identification). In the edutainment-based module, the exercises are in language puzzle form (see Backer, 1995), while those of the traditional-based module are similar to vocabulary exercises found in 'typical' language learning textbooks (refer to Chiquito, Meskill, & Renjilian-Burgy, 1997).

With this in mind, two instructional strategies needed to be chosen to differentiate the modules, and these are based on the phases of behavioristic CALL and communicative CALL (as presented by Warschauer & Healey, 1998), and involve taking on a restricted CALL and open CALL approach (see Bax, 2003). These approaches were selected since behaviorism and cognitivism are the two dominant theoretical positions in the field of learning with interactive courseware (Atkins, 1993; Hannafin, Hannafin, Hooper, Rieber, & Kini, 1996; Jonassen, 1991). In addition, the modules also take into account the more contemporary theories of interactive multimedia CALL, and hypermedia instructional design. It is important to note that software systems employing the communicative phase/open CALL approach can still include those of the drill-and-practice type akin to a behavioristic phase/restricted CALL approach. The difference between a behavioristic (restricted CALL) and communicative (open CALL) model in this case is the level of student choice provided, and levels of control and interaction. As "the dividing line between behavioristic and communicative CALL involves not only which software is used, but also how the software is put to use by the teacher and students" (Warschauer, 1996, p. 3). A more detailed explanation of the CALL modules is provided in Appendix Three.

Beta Testing of Modules

After the modules were fully developed, beta testing of the two software systems could begin. Several L1 English speaking EFL instructors trialed the software, which led to a number of minor bugs being corrected and the wording within several activities changed. Modules were then given to a small group of students, similar in composition to that of the sample population, for testing. This group of students was able to save activity data for submission, and reported no errors from engagement with the language activities that they were assigned to complete. After this testing period, the modules were produced for final distribution and readied for delivery by the instructor responsible for administering treatment.

Data Analysis

Data analysis of survey and test results was conducted using RUMM (Rasch Unidimensional Measurement Models) and SPSS (Statistical Package for the Social Sciences). The Rasch model was employed to refine and calibrate the data, while multiple regression and analysis of variance (ANOVA) were applied to test the hypotheses.

Procedure

Rasch Rating Scale Model Analysis

The Rasch model locates person ability and item difficulty on the same interval scale. To confirm that the survey and test instruments are measures, the residual and chi-square values of the data collected were estimated. A low residual ($< \pm 2.0$) means that an item's data fits the model well, with the actual response close to the expectation of the model, whereas a high residual indicates actual performance different to that expected. Chi-square probability for item-trait interaction indicates how well students agree on difficulties of items across the scale, and whether the analysis of a single trait, or assumption of unidimensionality, is reasonable (Cavanagh & Romanoski, 2004). A high chi-square probability ($p > 0.05$) represents a good match of the data to the model, while low chi-square probability ($p < 0.05$) shows a poor fit of the data to the model.

Multiple Regression Analysis

Data from the test of student understanding of pseudo-loanwords (SUPL) was used for regression analysis with pre-test data from the survey of student attitudes towards computer assisted learning in EFL (SSACAL). The survey dimension and the individual item were specified as the independent variables, and the test score logits as the dependent variable.

ANOVA

To examine the effect of the treatment, an item-by-item one-way analysis of variance between pre- and post-treatment test data was conducted. As there are two modules, or two forms of treatment (Modules One and Two), a separate ANOVA, which determined which questions were more successfully answered after the treatment, was required for each.

Survey Refinement

The distributed survey is based upon a developed and translated instrument, which had been used with focus groups and allowed for initial fine-tuning and refinement of questions in the native language for presentation to participants. Prior to distribution, for a final check on instrument appropriateness and validity, the survey was split into four mini-surveys, each of which being disseminated to one of four trial groups consisting of around 30 students each. Trial groups consisted of intermediate EFL level freshmen from a university English program at a tertiary institution different to that of the students who participated in the final empirical investigation. The data was then collected and examined, and taking the results of this analysis into consideration, the survey was then fine-tuned.

The survey fine-tuning process consists of examining two aspects of the data in SPSS: Cronbach alpha reliability, and the frequency of responses to each question item. These analyses were used to determine if the four-point Likert scale is working effectively, and if normal distribution of responses across the four categories exists.

For trial group one, the analyses found that items 1 to 41 of the survey shows consistent responses to the different items with an alpha reliability of 0.93, and that the middle two categories were most frequently selected with less in the *strongly disagree* and *disagree* categories. These items worked well, and no changes were made. Also no changes were required for items 94 to 121, distributed to trial group four, as category use was normally distributed for most items with an alpha reliability of 0.82.

Changes were required amongst items 42 to 59 distributed to trial group two, and to items 60 to 93 distributed to trial group three. Items 42 to 59 ($\alpha = 0.83$) were found to possess normal distribution for most of them, as were items 60 to 93. As items 54 to 59 formed part of a second construct or second section of the survey, these items were analyzed separately ($\alpha = 0.83$) and a number of changes considered. Items 54 and 57 were then removed, leaving four items under the 'in-class relations' construct ($\alpha = 0.54$). It also appears as though each student was responding differently to the different items 60 through 93 comprising the

'Korean learning style' construct. The solution was to use the existing data to identify items from this section, and across sub-sections, that elicited similar responses. A process of elimination identified 12 items (60, 61, 63, 64, 68 to 74, and 76) that elicited similar responses and maintained good internal reliability ($\alpha = 0.74$). It was then decided that the remaining items in the section would be deleted, while two items (68 and 69) were moved to a different sub-section. After these adjustments were made, a 95-item survey became ready for deployment.

Test Refinement

The test is based on an existing instrument developed by the author, and since it had been previously deployed, existing data was analyzed to determine the suitability of the instrument for this research. After determining test suitability and constructing an appropriate instrument, the test was trialed with a small group of around 50 students. Again, these students were intermediate EFL freshmen enrolled in a university English program at a tertiary institution different to that of the students who participated in the final empirical investigation, and are different students to those participating in the survey trials. Results were then collected and analyzed using RUMM so that individual item fit statistics could be examined. Any items showing disordered thresholds could then be identified and removed. Other items, such as those being too difficult or too easy, could also be identified and removed as necessary. The test instrument was then ready for distribution.

Hypothesis One

This research employed CALL as a learning treatment in the process of acquiring understanding of pseudo-loanwords. It is therefore important to determine if student disposition toward computer assisted learning of English as a foreign language is associated with student understanding of pseudo-loanwords. It was hypothesized that a relationship between these two variables exists and multiple regression analysis was performed to determine if this is the case.

Hypothesis Two

If utilized effectively, it was hypothesized that the English vocabulary acquisition progress of students can be advanced through the specific inclusion of loan terminology in EFL teaching materials tailored specifically for use in the Korean context. This would be evidenced by learning gains from all students involved in the experiment, and proved by comparison of pre- and post-test results. Further, it was expected that one instructional strategy or treatment would exhibit a greater effect, and this would be confirmed through ANOVA with the vast majority of test items for one treatment group showing a greater amount of statistically significant change than those of an alternate treatment group. Only after comparison of the significant changes in each of the treatment groups would this hypothesis be proved.

Reliability and Validity Mechanisms

Reliability is the expectation of an instrument to provide consistent and accurate results. Validity relates to the capacity of an instrument to measure what it is designed to measure. In Rasch analysis, reliability is estimated for both persons and items, with person separation reliability an estimate of how well persons can be differentiated on the measured variable, while validity stems from the ability of the instrument to measure a single trait or underlying construct. This means that person-item fit comes to confirm instrument reliability, and assists in determining validity by ensuring fit of an instrument to a unidimensional measurement scale, which in the case of this study is based on the individual trait(s) of the survey and test instruments. Factors concerning the internal validity of the instruments and treatment employed need considering, since "a well-designed experiment has to have high internal validity to be of value" (Ravid, 2000, p. 9).

To obtain reliable and valid data for hypothesis testing, the survey and test both underwent reliability and validity checks by trialing before final deployment, and Rasch analysis before use in hypothesis testing. The trialing and refinement process utilizing focus group interviews, piloting and trial groups, and undertaken with representative samples, was able to verify content validity of survey items and construct validity of test items, and to provide data to assist in fine-tuning the instruments. For the survey, internal consistency and response frequency were also examined to ensure scale effectiveness. These processes assisted in developing a valid and reliable instrument, and ensured the survey and test were appropriate for deployment and that the data obtained is appropriate for data analysis. This led to necessary refinement of the survey from a 121-item instrument to a 95-item well-measuring survey focused on specific constructs, and saw the pre- and post-test instrument reduced from 50 items to 40 in order to match the ability level of intermediate EFL students. Ultimately, Rasch analysis assisted in determining the reliability of the test in terms of person-item difficulty calibration as well as the survey in terms of person-item response calibration, and the validity of the test and survey by ensuring fit of the items to the model and thereby effective measure of a single trait. The trait for the survey is 'student attitude towards computer assisted instruction in EFL', and for the test, it is 'student understanding of the English meaning of pseudo-loanwords'.

To achieve consistency or reliability of answers and scores collected by instruments, or reliability, objective scoring methods were used along with a method for coding data for entry into a computer for analysis. In this regard, for each closed-ended question, the survey was designed to contain a 4-point Likert style response grade. This provided standardized data for analysis and coding by ensuring that all subjects responded to the same options. Also the pre- and post-test format is in the form of multiple-choice as this allows for the collection of data that is easily quantifiable and can be accurately and objectively assessed. Multiple-choice items were checked to ensure that there is only one correct response so that questions are not interdependent, and that the order of correct responses is randomized to reduce test wiseness. Further, students possessed a unique code so that neither data collector nor researcher could be aware of which student participated in what treatment when instruments were collected and when data was entered into the computer for analysis.

Due to the nature of treatment, identical data was presented to each participant: the same learning content, correction, and feedback. This is important since it is imperative that all participants received the same learning content. The CALL modules were designed to be homework-based so that they could be incorporated within an existing syllabus and therefore be less obtrusive on student work requirements and existing teacher in-class commitments. This also minimized instructor-bias, and it controlled attitudinal effect by incorporating treatment as part of normal taught-course homework-based procedure. Subject characteristic threats, however, may have been present as participants could have chosen to neglect the material or complete it in one sitting, and as such, incremental homework submission dates were established. Another danger is location threat, as the homework could have been done from anywhere (for example: dormitory, internet cafe, or home environment). The reliability and validity of the treatment was ensured through alpha testing of the software on several operating systems, and beta testing with instructors and target end users. The administrating instructor was also provided with training in how to utilize the modules so that assistance could be rendered to students as required.

Experiment participants were obtained from a sample of convenience, and to reduce maturation and mortality risks, appropriate treatment groups were formed through a process of stratified sampling while experiment runtime was limited to half a semester. While the short timeframe of two months for the treatment may be considered a limiting factor, experiments of this length are not unheard of in the literature (for example, Hegelheimer & Tower, 2004). The participating students were all of an intermediate level of English, and this assisted in limiting regression as lower or higher-level students may have performed better or worse throughout the experiment, which was refined to a single university for increased control. To expose each experimental group to identical data collector characteristics, a single instructor was responsible for collection and deployment of the survey as well as the pre-test, treatment, and post-test. This could have led to implementation threats but by using the same instructor, the same data collector bias was present for each experimental group. To alleviate data collector bias, specific instructions and coaching were provided regarding the deployment and collection of instruments. To reduce location threat, the instructor delivered both the survey instrument and pre- and post-tests in the same location and at the same time of the weekly class schedule. The survey was also translated to increase salience, with back-translation used as an error check, and a Korean assistant was on hand for support.

The specific impact of threats on the reliability and validity of this research, and the process as to how these were minimized, is discussed in depth in Section C of this Part of the book.

B. THE FINDINGS OF IMPLEMENTATION

Sample Characteristics

The subjects of the empirical investigation were 108 university freshmen (34 men and 74 women) enrolled in a university English program in Korea (see Table A4.1.1 in Appendix Four) who were grouped according to the following five majors: childhood education, electronics, elementary education, pharmacy, and occupational therapy (refer to Table A4.1.2 in Appendix Four). Each class met twice a week for an hour to engage in learning English conversation with the same L1 English speaking instructor as part of the university's general elective requirements. The instructor was a 35-year-old American female with eight years of EFL teaching experience in Korea, and she is the one who was responsible for survey, pre-test, treatment, and post-test distribution and collection. Participation was also voluntary, and signed consent was obtained from participants for use of the anonymously collected data.

Survey Refinement

The survey administered to the students was comprised of 114 items. Although the instrument had been carefully constructed, it was anticipated that when data from the instrument became available, data analysis would suggest that the instrument required modification. That is, some of the items were expected to elicit data that did not fit the requirements for objective measurement. The first stage in the survey refinement was a RUMM analysis of the 114-item data resulting in: summary test of fit statistics, ordering of thresholds, and individual item-fit statistics.

RUMM Analysis of the 114-Item Survey Data

Summary Test-of-Fit Statistics

Summary test-of-fit statistics were calculated for the 114 items and are presented in Table A4.2.1 in Appendix Four. When the data fits the model, the fit statistic has a mean near zero and a standard deviation near one. A negative fit statistic indicates that the data fitted the model closely whereas a positive fit statistic would indicate that some 'noise' is present. The means of 0.00 and 0.10 show the mean difficulty of the items was close to the mean of the student scores. The standard deviations of 0.71 and 0.42 shows a variance in student data that is lower than what would be observed in an ideal data-to-model fit. The power of the test-of-fit statistic, based on the separation index of 0.88, shows that the student logits (logarithmic units based on the logarithmic odds of answering positively) were well spread across a continuum. However the total chi-square probability value of 0.00 (<0.05) suggests the items were likely not eliciting data on a unidimensional attribute of the respondents.

Ordering of Thresholds

Ideally, the order of responses for an item should match the rank order of student ability to affirm the items. That is, students with a highly affirmative view should have consistently selected the 'strongly agree' category.

This is illustrated in Figure A4.1.1 and Figure A4.1.2, both found in Appendix Four, in which student locations (logits) are plotted on the horizontal axis. Students who found the item difficult to affirm are located on the left and students who found the item easy to affirm are on the right. The probability for a response category to be selected is plotted on the vertical axis. The four curves are labelled according to the respective response categories (0 for strongly disagree, 1 for disagree, 2 for agree, and 3 for strongly agree). The intercept on the horizontal axis corresponding to the intersection between two curves indicates the threshold (a logit value) between the two response categories.

Figure A4.1.1 shows disordered thresholds for item 66, 'the young should learn', where the intercept of Curves 0 and 1 has a higher logit value than for curves 1 and 2, and ideally, it should be lower.

Figure A4.1.2 shows the ordered thresholds for item 1, 'I use online learning', where it can be seen that curve intersection points and corresponding logit vales are ordered with increasingly higher values from negative to positive.

The ordering item thresholds for the 114-item survey are presented in Table A4.2.2, in Appendix Four, where seven items (31, 61, 66, 67, 85, 94, and 104) show disordered thresholds.

Individual Item-Fit Statistics

Individual item-fit statistics – locations, residuals and chi-square probability – were calculated for data from the 114-item survey (see Table A4.2.3 in Appendix Four), and the item locations show the relative difficulty that students demonstrated in responding affirmatively to the items. This was measured in logits – the log odds of responding affirmatively. The residual is the difference between the expected estimate and the actual values for each person-item summed over all items for each participant and summed over all participants for each item (see Styles & Andrich, 1993, p. 914 or Andrich & van Schoubroeck, 1989, p. 482 for the equations). When the data fits the measurement model, the fit statistics approximate a distribution with a mean near zero and a standard deviation near one. Negative values indicate a response pattern that fits the model too closely (probably because response dependencies are present; see Andrich, 1985), and positive values indicate a poor fit to the model, probably because other measures ('noise') are present. While residuals outside of ±0.75 are seen as unexpected (Bond & Fox, 2001), a limit of ±2.0 has been applied in previous learning environment instrument construction (see Waugh & Cavanagh, 2002). The chi-square test shows how well data from an item fits the model, and if the probability is less than 0.05, the divergence between the observed mean and the expected value is large relative to chance (RUMMLab, 2004).

Data from seven items (17, 43, 56, 57, 61, 78, and 79) was found to have high residual and/or low chi-square probability values. Eventually, after a 16 step iterative process of deleting data from various misfitting items and reestimating individual item-fit statistics, data from nineteen items was deleted.

RUMM Analysis of the 95-Item Survey Data

After 16 iterations of RUMM analyses and item deletion, the fit statistics from data for 95 items indicate that they are likely to be an objective measure of student attitudes comprising the trait that was under investigation.

Summary Test-of-Fit Statistics

Summary test-of-fit statistics were generated to determine the extent to which the 95-item data fits the Rasch model (see Table A4.3.1 in Appendix Four). The means of 0.00 and 0.09 are close to ideal, but the standard deviations of 0.68 and 0.44 illustrate that variance in student and item data is lower than what would be observed in an ideal data-to-model fit. For item-trait interaction, the total chi-square probability is 0.12. This result indicates that for the data, the scale is measuring a dominant and possibly unidimensional trait. The power of the test-of-fit statistic shows that the overall fit between the data and the model is excellent with a separation index of 0.87. Overall these results show a good data-to-model fit.

Ordering of Thresholds

Centralized item thresholds for the 95-item data were calculated and the results appear in Table A4.3.2 in Appendix Four. The data from all 95 items are shown to be exhibiting ordered thresholds.

Individual Item-Fit Statistics

For this data, item locations ranged from −1.91 to 1.80, all but two chi-square values are high ($p < 0.05$), and all residuals are lower than ± 2.0. This illustrates that the fit of the data from individual items to the model is good (see Table A4.3.3 in Appendix Four).

tem Map

To show the overall fit between persons and items, a RUMM item map (see Figure A4.2.1 in Appendix Four) was generated for the 95-item survey data. As can be seen, the distribution of person locations matches the distribution of item location very well, illustrating that the items 'targeted' the sample. All persons and items are located between the +2.0 and −2.0 logits.

Summary of the Survey Development and Refinement Process

The Rasch rating scale model was used to examine the data from the 114-item survey in order to refine the survey so that it was measuring a unidimensional trait of the respondents. In an iterative process, nineteen items (13, 17, 18, 31, 43, 45, 52, 56, 57, 61, 66, 67, 70, 78, 85, 94, 104, 110, and 114) that elicited data with disordered thresholds and/or poor fit to the model were discarded. The data from the remaining 95 items was considered interval and thus amenable to further analyses such as tests of correlation and multiple regression.

Test Refinement

RUMM Analysis of the 40-Item Test Data

Summary Test-of-Fit Statistics

To verify fit of the 40-item test data to the Rasch model, summary test-of-fit statistics were determined (see Table A4.4.1 in Appendix Four). Since the test was used before and after the intervention and needed to measure both pre- and post-intervention ability, data from both administrations were used for test refinement. The means of 0.00 and −1.21 show that many of the items were too hard for the students, and the standard deviations of 1.47 and 1.09 showed that the variance of item difficulty data was larger than in an ideal data-to-model fit. The total chi-square probability was 0.00, suggesting that the items were not eliciting data on a unidimensional trait of the students. The power of the test-of-fit statistic showed the overall fit between the data and the model was good with a separation index of 0.83. In summary, it is likely that the instrument could be improved.

Individual Item Fit Statistics

Individual item-fit statistics for the 40-item test data was calculated and are presented in Table A4.5.1 in Appendix Four, with the locations of these items ranging from −3.18 to 2.96. Seven of them (4, 20, 22, 34, 35, 36, and 38) had high residuals ($<\pm 2.0$) and/or low chi-square probability values ($p < 0.05$), and were therefore identified as eliciting misfitting data, and removed, leaving a 33-item refined test.

RUMM Analysis of the 33-Item Test Data

Summary Test-of-Fit Statistics

Summary test-of-fit statistics for the 33-item test data are presented in Table A4.6.1 in Appendix Four. The means of 0.00 and -1.55 show many of the items were too easy for the students, and the standard deviations of item difficulty and student ability of 1.35 and 1.20 show greater than ideal variance. The total chi-square probability was 0.00 suggesting the items were likely not eliciting data on a unidimensional trait of the students. The power of the test-of-fit was good with a separation index of 0.82. Interestingly, deletion of the seven items with poor individual data fit to the model did not improve the global fit statistics just presented. Similarly, deletion of more items failed to improve these statistics, so it was assumed that the 33-item instrument would be preferable to a smaller one.

Individual Item-Fit Statistics

Table A4.6.2 in Appendix Four shows the results of determining individual item fit statistics for the 33-item test. Item locations for the data ranged from –2.59 to 2.71, which shows that there is a wide range of difficulties within the items. Chi-square probability values were all above 0.05, and all residuals but one were between –2.0 and +2.0, which is low. These results show that the fit of the majority of the data to the model was good.

Item Map

A RUMM item map was created for the 33-item test so that the overall fit between person and item data could be established (see Figure A4.2.2 in Appendix Four). As can be seen, the person locations are lower than the item locations. Persons were located within a range of –6.0 to 1.0, and items within the range of –3.0 to 3.0. This highlights that the test was difficult for these students.

Summary of Test Refinement Process

The process applied to refine the test was similar to that used to refine the survey. The refined test comprised of 33 items where each elicited data with good fit to the model and the overall fit statistics were acceptable. While better fit statistics might have been desirable, this would have required writing new items and have caused a major delay in the progress of the research as well as presenting logistical problems associated with more data collection in Korea.

Associations between 95-Item Survey Data and Pre-treatment Test Data

To determine if test performance was dependent on the variables measured in the survey, a multiple regression analysis was undertaken. First, both pre-test student ability logits were correlated with survey dimensions which concerned dispositions towards computer assisted learning of English as a foreign language (see the correlation matrix in Table A4.7 in Appendix Four). Since the logits have both negative and positive values, all of them were converted into non-negative values by the addition to each of the absolute value of the lowest logit. In this way, the intervality of the scale was maintained but the lowest logit (the logit for the student with the lowest ability) is 0.00. The lack of moderate or strong statistically significant correlation coefficients suggests that the correlation analysis did not reveal associations between survey items and dispositions towards variables relating to computer assisted learning of English as a foreign language. Next, a regression analysis was performed with test logits treated as the dependent variable and the survey elements as independent variables (see Table A4.7.1 and Table A4.7.2 in Appendix Four).

Regression Analysis: Survey Variables (independent variables) and Pre-Test Logits (dependent variable)

The regression analysis model summary, presented in Table A4.7.1 in Appendix Four, shows that when 18 independent variables were entered into the prediction model, multiple R was 0.44 and R^2 was 0.19. This shows that 19% of the variance of the dependent variable (test logits) could be cumulatively predicted by the 18 independent variables.

In examining the coefficients, it can be seen in Table A4.7.2 in Appendix Four that only one independent variable (C1) accounted for a statistically significant variation ($t = 2.22$, $p = 0.03$) in the dependent variable (test logits). In this case, where there was a unit positive change in preference for cultural representation in EFL learning material, the student test performance increased 0.24. Since relations between the other 17 independent variables and the dependent variable were not confirmed by either the correlation analysis or the regression analysis, the results of these analyses do not support a positive response to the first line of inquiry.

Analysis of Variance Comparison of Pre-treatment and Post-treatment Test Data

An item-by-item one-way analysis of variance was conducted to compare student performance on the pre- and post-test calibrated scores for each of the 33 items. Since the treatment comprised either of two instructional modules, the analysis was conducted twice. The analyses were performed by RUMM which has provision for ANOVA as part of a test for differential item functioning. Table A4.8.1 in Appendix Four shows the F-ratio and probability value from the RUMM ANOVA output for each item for the first treatment group, and Table A4.8.2 in Appendix Four shows it for the second treatment group.

For the first treatment group (Module One users), the students performed at a statistically significant higher level in the post-treatment test than in the pre-treatment test for only one item (39). For the second treatment group (Module Two users) a statistically significant performance increase was shown for four items (6, 13, 26, and 29). Given that the total number of items was 33, the increase in student performance on the test after the treatments was small, although the increase was greater for the second treatment (Module Two). The ANOVA results did not provide strong support for a positive answer to the second line of inquiry concerning the effect of the application of computer assisted language learning strategies on student understanding of pseudo-loanwords.

C. EXPLORING THE LINES OF INQUIRY

Investigation

Line of Inquiry – Question One

Is student understanding of pseudo-loanwords associated with dispositions towards computer assisted learning of English as a foreign language? Answering this question involves determining if an association exists between the method of presenting learning content to students (computer assisted instruction) and the learning content itself (pseudo-loanwords).

Primary Investigation: Computer Assisted Instruction and Learning in EFL

Summary of the Results

Results indicate that no correlation was revealed between the trait measured by the survey and the understanding of pseudo-loanwords, as represented by test data. As such, the hypothesized relationship between survey variables and test performance is not proved.

Association of Computer Assisted Learning of English with the Learning of Pseudo-Loanwords

The trait 'student attitude towards computer assisted instruction in EFL' consisted of three postulated dimensions of student attitudes. First: disposition towards computer assisted instruction (focusing on computer competency), preference for computer-based learning, and preferences for learning English through computer assisted instruction (CAI) (see Alessi & Trollip, 2001; Chapelle, 2001). Second: Korean learning style, comprising of in-class relations, desired characteristics of instructors, and view of education (as per Cortazzi, 1990; Eastmond, 2000; Hofstede, 1986; Joo, 1997; Min, et al, 2000; Park & Oxford, 1988; Windle, 2003). Third: English as a foreign language (EFL) learning style, consisting of preference for cultural representation, loanword use, and vocabulary acquisition strategies (see Ahn, 2002; Finch & Hyun, 2000; Pak, 1999; Park, 2001).

The survey was refined so that the data is more closely aligned to the Rasch model. Even though the survey had to undergo some modification in order to more consistently measure the single trait desired, the items removed from the survey to achieve this are from all three constructs comprising the trait (i.e. seven items from disposition towards CAI, five from Korean learning style, and seven from EFL learning style). Hence, a consistent measure was developed – a unique and refined instrument for use in correlation.

Rasch model analysis results indicate that the survey measured the trait successfully. To determine if the data on test performance is linked to data on the variables measured by the survey, a process of multiple regression was undertaken. Test logits were used as the dependent variable, with survey dimensions and individual items as independent variables. The results suggest that there is minimal correlation between data on the trait being measured by the survey (student attitude towards computer assisted learning in EFL) and data on the understanding of the lexical content used in the treatment and test instruments (pseudo-loanwords). Consequently, the hypothesized relationship between the survey variables and test performance is not proved.

As such, variables that exist outside of the 'attitude of students towards computer assisted learning in EFL' impacted upon the results, and therefore computer use did not bias the results through the use of computer assisted language learning (CALL) in treatment. Since correlation predicts, rather than explains, the second line of inquiry can assist in defining aspects and elements of what extraneous variables exist, and determine why the treatment did not lead to learning gains as expected.

Line of Inquiry – Question Two

Does the application of different computer assisted language learning instructional strategies affect student understanding of pseudo-loanwords? This question involves examination of two factors that led to the primary investigation of the impact of CALL instructional approaches on second language (L2) vocabulary acquisition, and a secondary investigation that focuses on exploring the applicability of loanword utilization for foreign language development. Reflecting upon the results, each will be discussed in turn.

Primary Investigation: Impact of Instructional Approaches on Vocabulary Acquisition

Summary of the Results

Results indicate that behaviorist-based restricted CALL versus communicative-based open CALL instructional approaches provided largely the same learning gains to Korean university freshmen. This is supported by consistency in the level of performance, although the communicative-based open CALL approach does see marginally higher learning gains. Such results may have result from the pre-existing exposure that Korean students have had to both strategies in the EFL classroom, as evidenced by Jeong (2002, p. 251) who states, "there are two sharply different ways of learning English in Korea" – behaviorist and communicative. Traditionally, a behaviorist approach has been provided by Korean instructors in the grade school years, and a communicative approach provided by first language (L1) speakers of English at the tertiary level but now also at the school levels as a result of policy changes and revisions to the national English curriculum. Results would then appear to indicate that, as students become increasingly exposed to alternate strategies, the behaviorist focused Korean cultural learning style appears to change, as students are able to adopt and utilize communicative strategies effectively. This lends support to the belief that learning styles and strategies or approaches to learning can be taught, and it is the educational environment that molds students to patterns of classroom behavior and models of classroom expectations. This highlights a need for educators to reexamine the beliefs and stereotypes held about Korean learners, particularly when such learners are continually being grouped with Chinese and Japanese students as East Asian learners. In addition, research undertaken in one Asian nation is generalized as being true for the entire Asian context (see Finch, 2000; Liu & Littlewood, 1997; Rao, 2002).

Aside from this, students might have viewed the CALL systems as part of the university English program course, as desired, but this might have led to negative consequences. Students might have interpreted the material as 'homework to complete' rather than 'material to engage them in learning'. The impact of learner attitudes, and learner responses to homework use in the university English program might have then generated negative washback on the study. Although mechanisms were in place throughout the empirical investigation to prevent students from simply processing the material rather than practicing language with it, more controls might have been required. Such controls would need to take individual learner variables and aspects of Korean student self-efficacy, motivation, autonomy, and self-regulatory skills into account.

Consequences of the Changing Korean Cultural Learning Style

The local culture and learning context, constituting the Korean cultural learning style, was taken into account in the design of the two CALL modules employed in treatment. The first of these instructional systems focuses on behaviorist-based strategies via a restricted CALL approach. This approach was selected as a result of the academic literature showing that Korean students hold a Confucian consciousness, and that their classroom expectations align with the behaviorist learning mode, which has long been favored in the Korean classroom by Korean teachers, as Niederhauser (1997) has observed. The first CALL module was therefore based on the cultural and classroom expectations of the learner, as reported by academic literature and reported in practice (refer to Ahn, 2002; Cortazzi, 1990; Eastmond, 2000; Finch & Hyun, 2000; Hofstede, 1986; Joo, 1997; Min, Kim & Jung, 2000; Pak, 1999; Park, 2001; Schmitt, 1997; Windle, 2003). This instructional strategy is contrasted with a communicative-based open CALL approach, a common instructional strategy in contemporary systems, and one more akin to L1 English speaker learning content presentation, and the teaching style since advocated by the national English curriculum.

It was expected that both instructional approaches would lead to significant learning gains, but that the behaviorist-based restricted CALL approach would provide higher learning gains over the other – that is, if cultural expectations of the learner and the learner strategies presented in the academic literature, and incorporated within the CALL systems, are truly indicative of the contemporary Korean learner. In an attempt to ascertain this, a greater amount of statistically significant change amongst items in the first treatment would have had to appear over those of the alternate treatment. In fact, results show the effect of both treatments to be low, but that the second treatment group (i.e. communicative-based open CALL users) fared slightly better than the first treatment group (behaviorist-based restricted CALL users). One item of forty showed a significant improvement for the behaviorist, and four items showed a significant improvement for the communicative group. This illustrates that the Korean cultural learning style, presented within behaviorist-based restricted (Module One) and communicative-based open CALL (Module Two) vocabulary learning approaches, reveal no real statistically significant learning gains with either instructional method when L1 data was used as the source for foreign language learning material.

This indicates that although cultural expectations of students might be at play in the classroom context, vis-à-vis both Korean and L1 English speaking instructors, these expectations might not transfer to the CALL instructional method and the student/computer context in an autonomous self-directed learning mode. Although this is an area for further research, it does lend support to the view that learning styles and strategies can be taught, and what has been measured cannot be attributed to an overly generalized prescription for the 'way that Asian learners are' but more the 'way that Asian learners have been taught'. Educational contexts are more responsible for Asian learning styles than the learners themselves (Littlewood, 2000, p. 33), which is supported by Reid (1987, p. 100) who postulated that learning styles are "moderately strong habits rather than intractable biological attributes", even though Dunn and Griggs (1988, p. 3) state: "Learning style is the biologically and developmentally imposed set of characteristics that make the same teaching method wonderful for some and terrific for others".

Nonetheless, it is believed that teaching method policy changes made to the national English curriculums toward that of a communicative language teaching (CLT) focus will begin to see younger learners become more accustomed to the types of strategies central to communicative-based open CALL rather than being exposed to (what has previously been the case) a mix of approaches – behaviorist (in Korean teacher English language classrooms) and communicative (from the L1 speaker of English language classrooms). In fact, it is postulated that this past mix of exposure explains the similar levels obtained by the group of students looked at within this book, since they would have been accustomed to both types of teaching strategies from within the classroom context. This reinforces the belief that implementation of changes to the national curriculum will promote a change in the development of the Korean cultural learning style, and as this develops, and as results from this empirical investigation would appear to indicate, a need to reexamine exactly what this notion entails will be essential.

Taking the above into account, the results also imply that the Korean cultural learning style and classroom expectations, as evident in the literature (predominantly behaviorist), are changing (as hinted by Windle, 2003) to a more communicative orientation. Hence, culturally tailored CALL courseware systems based on current perspectives of Korean culture may not be as effective as they could be, as results presented within this book would seem to indicate. These results also support the argument put forth by Kubota (2001) that the perception of dichotomous differences between Asian and Western learners and teaching contexts is questionable. This also highlights the danger in arguing, as Rao (2002) does, that East Asian students possess the same learning style – a Confucian behaviorist transmission model with focus on accuracy through a process of analysis. Others such as Terry (2002) would assert that Asian students like to learn in a variety of ways. As such, by providing a wide range of classroom activities that cater to different learner needs and interests, teachers can help foreign language students develop their linguistic skills.

Instead of following what Rao (2001) has advocated – teachers adapting teaching methods to the way learners in particular communities learn – it is possible and may prove more beneficial to assist learners in developing a variety of strategies to approach learning, since this is a main factor in determining "how – and how well – our students learn a second or foreign language" (Oxford, 2003, p. 1).

Influence of Negative Washback

As a number of researchers indicate (see H. K. Choi, 2004; S. W. Lee, 2003; Schulz, 2001), learner perceptions and beliefs regarding a particular language learning activity can strongly influence the effectiveness of that activity in foreign language learning contexts. In response, it is important to consider what has in the past been referred to as learner representations (Holec, 1987), and take into account the 'subjective reality' of the learner (Riley, 1997). 'Subjective reality' can be considered an important stimulus for action since "what we believe we are doing, what we pay attention to, what we think is important, how we choose to behave, how we prefer to solve problems, form the basis for our personal decisions as to how to proceed" (McDonough, 1995, p. 9).

Although focusing on internet activity use in the EFL context with adult students enrolled in non-credit courses, as opposed to courseware systems, Oh (2003a, p. 157) discovered that when required as homework, "most students were reluctant to use them ... because they were 'lazy' or 'not ready to use the internet comfortably', or they didn't have 'strong will-power'". In a later follow up study with primary school students, Oh (2003b, p. 107) also found similar results, along with the opinion that computers were perceived primarily as an entertainment device.

> For them, 'computers are the place to be relaxed and to take a rest [and] not to be stressed'. So, when they were asked to do something on the computer in English as homework, they did the homework as quickly as possible not doing any extra works to learn English voluntarily.

This, as mentioned in Part Two of this book (and supported by C. H. Lee, 2000; Y. J. Lee, 2000; Lee & Kastner, 1999; Lee & Pyo, 2002; and, Y. S. Jung, 2000), indicates that autonomous learning is lacking in Korean EFL students. However, if greater autonomy can be promoted, then it appears that multimedia and internet use can lead learners to increased motivation, and provide them with not only a rich linguistic environment but also develop within them personal responsibility (C. J. Kwon, 2002). This also reiterates the concept of a need for students to be actively involved with learning from any CALL material they are required to use. Yet, as Lee and Pyo (2002, p. 78) indicate, this is problematic since

> first-year Korean university students are not ready nor prepared for this particular mode of learning. It is unfortunate to observe that most students show passive needs of teachers' direct guidance or control, feeling burdened for the responsibility given from autonomous learning.

Furthermore, Lee and Pyo indicate that Korean students exhibit a lack of learning responsibility if the system or teacher does not enforce it, and this emphasizes the need of having such checks in place to ensure that students complete only their homework, and do not copy it from others. They also go so far as to suggest that not only do Korean students need to possess minimal levels of functional English and high levels of motivation, but that they need to be purposely selected for participation in CALL, or more specifically, offline classes. "It is indispensable to choose a group of students who would maximize their learning opportunity through a screening process" (Lee & Pyo, 2002, p. 79), particularly when, as evidence suggests, Korean students with higher grades are more responsive to CAI while those with lower grades prefer traditional classroom lectures over CALL (W. K. Choi, 2002).

Even though low motivation and active involvement appear to be inherent problems for CALL–based learning initiatives in Korea, especially for compulsory courses such as freshman English in which the students participating in this empirical investigation were enrolled, the same attitudes may not be found within English language and literature students utilizing such courseware. Although no comparative study examining this concept is available, it is well recognized that individual learner variables ranging from motivation and attitude through to anxiety and beliefs can significantly impact upon language learning (Brown, 2000; S. W. Lee, 2005), and this extends to the use of CALL. S. W. Lee shows us that learner belief studies suggest that individuals' beliefs could affect motivation levels and behavior, as well as "reactions to certain instructional activities or methods" (S. W. Lee, 2005, p. 13). This is particularly true when

> the computer program simply produces relatively fixed feedback. Because the feedback has already been pre-programmed in conjunction with the specific situation, learners will not expect to receive feedback resulting in extra-positive learning effects. Such inflexibility may dampen the learner's motivation as the computer software repeatedly parrots the same pattern of comments or replies (H. Lee, 2005, p. 208).

In addition, Stoney and Oliver (1999) warn that the nature of multimedia products allowing for student control and self-paced completion of activities can see students unsuccessfully manage the completion of learning tasks, and in this sense then, program attributes allowing for the development of cognitive engagement can in fact prove an impediment to learning. So too, in the view of Laurillard, Stratfold, Luckin, Plowman & Taylor (2000, p. 2), because multimedia environments allow for learner control over navigational pathways, this can lead to the lack of a narrative line, as a narrative line is only established "from an interactive collaboration between the user and the program". User selections may thereby result in learners engaged with multimedia material as perceiving the software to be something very different to the expectations of the creator(s).

However, what multimedia environments inherently provide are multi-sensory experiences from the combination of various media types into a single medium, a heuristic environment that learners can control, and where there is flexibility in the distribution of learning content, with the same material delivered to students in either passive or active forms. Hick (1996) views this consistency as one of the benefits of employing multimedia with learners, and as such,

> teachers can therefore feel comfortable in using online resources as homework assignments, since (in addition to saving valuable class time) this allows students to acquire the required forms and functions at their own speed, and to perform the activities however many times it takes until successful cognition is achieved (Finch, 2004, p. 150).

Yet, the results from the empirical investigation conducted for this book come to indicate that perhaps higher learning gains could have been promoted by integrating the CALL modules and activities into the structure of the classroom, rather than "being an add-on part of the program. ... The active involvement of the teacher, such as modelling the activities, in-class feedback or follow-up quizzes, reinforces the effectiveness of CALL classes" (Lee & Yang, 2002, pp. 173–174). In such a manner, positive washback could have been promoted, and perhaps also, aspects of self-regulatory skills could have been taught as part of the course. Unfortunately, this would have been problematic in terms of the experiment coming to infringe upon the existing university English program curriculum. Nevertheless, the single-user design employed by the CALL modules did provide students with the ability to complete work without supervision, and would have to a certain extent, seen them become more responsible for independent and autonomous learning (Soper, 1997).

Ultimately though, Lynch (2003) recognizes that CALL can be detrimental when students lack self-regulatory skills, and that there needs to be a shift in research from hardware and software to 'humanware' by examining "which strategies for which learners using which technologies in which instructional contexts" (Lynch, 2003, p. 29). That being said, self-regulatory learners are proactive rather than reactive; they motivate themselves, possess self-efficacy, seek assistance when necessary, and modify their learning environment or move to a new one as required. Unfortunately, the self-regulation level of participants in the current study is unknown, but one advantage of the homework modules developed for the empirical investigation discussed in this book is that they could be applied in any location, and therefore allowed learners to be proactive in choosing where they would study, allowing them the ability to exercise "motivation and autonomy in ways conducive to personal learning choices" (Lynch, 2003, p. 37). Yet this could also be considered to be a threat to the experiment, and is discussed in more detail later in this section. Continuing, Lynch (2003, p. 33) draws our attention to Salomon who

> found that learners who express a preference for instruction using media tend to expect that it will be a less demanding way to learn. This expectation results in lower investment of effort and lower achievement levels when compared to instructional conditions that are perceived as more demanding (e.g. traditional instruction).

This belief can also be related to technological bias, the fallacy that technological use inherently grants increased human proficiency (Lynch, 2003). Although unmeasured, students using the CALL material could have believed that they were gaining some value from their activities "even while procrastinating because of the incorrect belief that work was being accomplished" (Lynch, 2003, p. 36). So too, students believing that the use of technology would allow them greater efficiency in learning may have completed the activities quickly and in a rushed manner, as Oh (2003b) indicates that young Korean learners are prone to do, particularly since students tend to believe that advanced technology is more effective pedagogically over other techniques (Bates, 1994).

Aside from the individual learner variables, and aspects ranging from low motivation, low self-efficacy, through to a lack of self-regulatory skills, the L1 learning content itself may have impacted upon the learning gains achieved through use of the CALL systems developed, seeing neither instructional strategy come to provide greatly beneficial learning over the other. This aspect of loanword utilization for L2 development is the focus of the secondary investigation of this line of inquiry, and will now be considered.

Secondary Investigation: Loanword Utilization for Target Language Development

Summary of the Results
Results of the empirical investigation indicate that the use of L1 vocabulary in the form of pseudo-loanwords to promote learning and understanding in the target language does work within the Korean CALL environment but with marginal and limited success. This is in contrast to reported successes in the use of loanwords in other contexts, such as non-CALL-based implementation of vocabulary acquisition with Japanese students of various ages in English as a second language (America) and English as a foreign language (Japan) contexts. Despite such hopeful reports of success for the use of direct loanwords elsewhere, in the

Korean case, learning and understanding may be inhibited due to aspects associated with the nature of pseudo-loanword vocabulary items themselves, as well as such factors that, for lack of more well-defined terminology in the academic literature (see Han, 2004), could be described as a 'stabilized interlanguage'.

Successful Application in Alternate Contexts Versus the Korean Context

Success in the application of loanwords for target language acquisition has been seen in contexts outside of Korea, most notably with Japanese learners in both English as a foreign language (EFL) and English as a second language (ESL) environments. Although researchers have postulated that loanwords provide negative interference with Japanese students of English (see Sheperd, 1996; Simon Maeda, 1995), positive transfer can be observed (refer to Brown, 1995; Brown & Williams, 1985; Daulton, 1998; Kimura, 1989; Yoshida, 1978;). The latter group of studies provides support for the loanword approach in various contexts, although none of these are CALL-based.

In the Yoshida (1978) study, it was found that English loanwords assisted a Japanese speaking child in the learning of Standard American English while living and attending nursery school in America. Loanwords were helpful in the learning of English due to their similarity as cognates, enlarging receptive vocabulary recognition, and in the comprehension of new English vocabulary items. Kimura (1989) examined both the EFL and ESL contexts and found that student scores were better for English base words than for non-base words. Brown and Williams (1985), stating that "students may do better when they make the English association on their own" (p. 141), also found that Japanese college level EFL students were better able to define words that were borrowed into Japanese from English over words that were not. Brown (1995) also came to indicate that loanwords in Japanese constitute a latent vocabulary base, showing that a 'borrowed word recognition phenomenon' allows Japanese students to more easily identify and apply loanword terms over non-loanwords. So too, Daulton (1998) further confirms that Japanese college level EFL students were better able to recognize and recall base words over non-base words. This implies that loanwords, as a pre-existing lexical resource, can provide scaffolding, enhance vocabulary acquisition, and lighten the learning burden (Nation, 1990).

In comparison to the investigation outlined in this book, the aforementioned research predominantly focuses upon loanword cognates or direct loanwords. However, this book presents as the first line of inquiry an examination of the pedagogical applicability of pseudo-loanword vocabulary items for foreign language acquisition. This research is also the first to examine the use of such items from a CALL-based context, and the first to do so in the Korean (EFL) environment. Preliminary results suggest that students were unable to consistently build new form-meaning connections between pseudo-loanwords in Korean and the meaning of Standard American English equivalents. Although CALL-based contexts may require different vocabulary learning strategies over that of the classroom, these are not considered to be the primary factors leading to this result.

The fact is that pseudo-loanwords maintain the need for learners to engage in radical semantic shift from the L1, versus direct loanwords, when using the foreign language. Where such 'subtle distinctions' are required, the learning of meanings can potentially be very difficult (Oller & Ziaohosseiny in Brown, 2000, p. 212).

> Examples of subtle distinctions at the lexical level may be seen in false cognates like the French word *parent*, which in the singular means 'relative' or 'kin', while only the plural (*parents*) means 'parents'. ... In recent years, research on CLI [Cross Linguistic Influence] has uncovered a number of instances of subtle differences causing great difficulty (Sjoholm, 1995)" (Brown, 2000, p. 213).

In this regard, foreign language acquisition research shows that aspects of language exhibiting greater difference between what is familiar and what is to be learned, can be acquired more easily over that which exhibits 'subtle distinctions' or 'minimal learning distance'. Such a principle may be in effect within the empirical investigation presented within this book, where one cognate has already been acquired in the form of a pseudo-loanword, producing an L1 form-meaning association. In the process of English language acquisition, the Korean learner is often required to keep the pseudo-loanword form constant – the form is always identical in the case of false cognates – while replacing the meaning, as opposed to other vocabulary items where form is essentially replaced and meaning is kept constant in the development of new form-meaning associations. This also implies that unlike previous loanword use studies, applying associative tasks in the learning process, pseudo-loanwords may specifically require recontextualisation tasks before learning can occur and a new meaning schema solidifies.

This relates to the information processing model, as presented by Brown (2000, 2014), which depicts learners as engaging in linguistic processing from either an L2/EFL oriented or a meta-language (L1) oriented perspective. This sees learners, when presented with loanwords, initially engaging in linguistic processing from an L1 (metalinguistic) orientation, and this is particularly evident when the provided input is beyond L2 (second/foreign language) capability, or where background information sought for linguistic retrieval was initially encoded in the first language. This would support Selinker's (1992) claim that

> L2 learners often conduct a cognitive inter-lingual comparison, or some sort of CA [comparative analysis] between the linguistic form they have noticed in the input, and knowledge of their native language. Therefore, instruction which provides CMI [contrastive metalinguistic input] may assist the learner in conducting an L1-L2 comparison, and arriving at the correct L2 generalization (Kupferberg, 1999, p. 3).

That is, where CMI is "defined as teacher-induced salience which foregrounds differences between the learner's L1 and L2 which have been established as areas of difficulty in studies independent of CA" (Kupferberg & Olshtain, in Kupferberg, 1999, p. 3). An L1-L2 comparison is defined "within a model of attention and memory in L2 acquisition as a conceptually-driven activity conducted in short-term memory between the specific input to which the learners are exposed and the knowledge (including L1 knowledge) stored in their long-term memory" (Kupferberg, 1999, p. 4).

The above indicates that pseudo-loanwords, compared to other vocabulary items, exhibit 'minimal learning distance', involve interlingual comparison from a metalinguistic orientation, and are consequently more problematic for learners in the foreign language acquisition process. In other words, the original L1 form-meaning association causes greater interference in the learning process for pseudo-loanwords compared to other loan terms and lexical items. The use of pseudo-loanwords over direct loanwords could have proven inherently more problematic for learners, and this may have impacted on participants of the empirical investigation undertaken in this book, and therefore come to affect the results obtained by this investigation compared to that of other loanword studies. This now leads us into a discussion concerning the stabilization of lexical use by learners involved in the experiment.

Vocabulary Acquisition and Interlanguage Stabilization

Han (2004) notes that there are a multitude of definitions for fossilization, but in general it refers to the "phenomenon of the non-progression of learning despite continuous exposure to input, adequate motivation to learn, and sufficient opportunity for practice" (Han, 2004, p. 213). The lack of uniformity in understanding the term has seen it applied in various contexts from "stabilized errors (e.g. Schumann, 1978), a learning plateau (e.g. Flynn & O'Neil, 1988), ingrained errors (e.g. Valette, 1991), systemic use of erroneous forms (e.g. Allwright & Bailey, 1991), errors made by advanced learners (e.g. Selinker & Mascia, 1999)" right through to "errors that are impervious to negative evidence (e.g. Lin & Hedgcock, 1996)" and "persistent difficulty (e.g. Hawkins, 2000)" (Han, pp. 218-219). In the case of Nakuma (1998), fossilization, as a performance level phenomenon, is based on the learner's conclusion that a given foreign language form need not be acquired because it is already available to the foreign language from the L1 (through transfer). As such, there is perceived to be no need to acquire a new form-meaning association; that is, since interlingually identified forms of vocabulary can be viewed as either positive (perfectly overlapping in the L1 and the other language) or negative (non-overlapping), seeing either imperceptible or perceptible deviation from foreign language native norms. In a process akin to what Nakuma describes as learners continually relying on fallback to L1 form-meaning associations, Selinker (1992) has conceived of interlingual fossilization as the consequence of learner reliance on the first language.

Results of the current study suggest that perhaps a naturally occurring interlingual fossilization, probably more suitably termed 'lexical stabilization' since the term 'fossilization' holds connotations of permanence, is indeed evident within Korea. Support for the cause of such a phenomenon has been linked to the Englishization of Korean (Baik & Shim 1998; J. J. Lee, 2004; Shim, 1994). Specifically, native Korean words and Sino-Korean words are being replaced by English ones, and use of new phonemes (from English) and phonological rules amongst the younger generation of Koreans are starting to appear. So too, many L1 speakers of English residing in Korea are using the pseudo-loanwords of their students when communicating, not only with them in social contexts, but also with other L1 speakers of English residing in-country ("English Teachers Risk Losing Skills", 2006). This serves to illustrate how pervasive, and accepted, the use of such terms have become in Korea. So too, Shim (1999) illustrates the appearance of Korean English forms in English language learning textbooks used in schools, contrary to expectations or opinions of the wider Korean populace. This also highlights that Korean learners, perhaps inadvertently, are beginning to 'make the language their own' (Kachru, 1998, 2005). It also provides an understanding as to why Korean students at all levels (from beginner to advanced), persist in the use of pseudo-loanwords in English communication, and are often unaware of their misuse (Shaffer, 1999) in terms of the target language (i.e. standard American English).

Although fossilization has been recognized as idiosyncratic (see Nakuma, 1998; Selinker, 1972; Selinker & Lamendella, 1978), as Larson-Freeman (1997) indicates, the specific L1 of learners also produces a distinctive interlanguage. This dictates a specific interlanguage for Korean learners, at the global fossilization level, but at the individual or local fossilization level, individuals might be able to employ specific lexical items in particular contexts – as perhaps evidenced by the results showing marginal improvement. This can assist in understanding why "by the time they enter college, Korean students usually have completed six years of English classes, yet most are unable to carry on simple conversations with native speakers or write sentences free of basic grammatical errors" (Niederhauser, 1997, p. 9). It also assists in explaining why participants in this study, although possessing the specific knowledge of terms such as pseudo-loanwords, were not able to gain control over the meanings and usage of such words in Standard American English as a stabilized use of interlanguage was being employed.

This lexical stabilization phenomenon can be related to the aforementioned theories of Henrickson (1999), Qian, (1999), and Melka (in Schmitt, 2000), as presented in Part Two, where vocabulary acquisition is viewed as a continuum of knowing, rather than lexical items which are either known or unknown. To move pseudo-loanwords along the continuum first relies on achieving depth of lexical knowledge through a process of semantic shift. In addition, a shift from productive L1 form-meaning association and receptive foreign language form-meaning association to that of productive and receptive foreign language form-meaning association needs to occur. It is asserted that through the continued use of the L1 (Korean) form-meaning association by L1 English speaking and Korean English speakers and instructors in-country, the process of semantic shift to the foreign language (Standard American English) form meaning association is being slowed, or even inhibited, within Korea.

The affective cognitive model of Vigal and Oller (1976), while relating predominantly to structural fossilization, can serve to illustrate the aforementioned notion. This model distinguishes between affective feedback (i.e. approval or disapproval encoded in kinesic mechanisms such as gestures, facial expressions, and so on), and cognitive feedback (i.e. understanding or lack of understanding provided by sounds, phrases, structures, discourse, and the like). Although the former was identified as not necessary for language learning, negative cognitive feedback is important, as Vigil and Oller indicate, and Schachter (1983, p. 183) noted, "unless learners receive appropriate negative input, fossilization will occur".

Fossilization is the result of a learner's utterances that gain positive affective feedback ("Keep talking") as well as positive cognitive feedback ("I understand"), the latter serving to reinforce an incorrect form of language. It is interesting that this internalization of *in*correct forms takes place by means of the same processes as the internalization of correct forms (Brown, 2014, p. 265).

A traffic signal metaphor sees that

The 'green light' of the affective feedback mode allows the sender to continue attempting to get the message across; a 'red light' causes the sender to abort such attempts. ... A green light here symbolizes noncorrective feedback that says 'I understand your message'. A red light symbolizes corrective feedback that takes on a myriad of possible forms ... and causes the learner to make some kind of alteration in production (Brown, 2000, pp. 235-236).

Pushing the metaphor further, a

yellow light could represent those various shades of color that are interpreted by the learner as falling somewhere in between a complete green light and a red light, causing the learner to adjust, to alter, to recycle, to try again in some way. Note that fossilization may be the result of too many green lights when there should have been some yellow or red lights. The most useful implication of Vigil and Oller's model for a theory of error treatment is that cognitive feedback must be optimal in order to be effective ... ignoring erroneous behavior has the effect of a positive reinforcer (Brown, 2000, p. 236).

Relating the aforementioned model to the instructional emphasis on communication, as opposed to accuracy, presented in the CLT approach, EFL instructors would allow, or green light, the use of understandable pseudo-loanwords in the Korean communicative classroom. This is in opposition to red lighting or yellow lighting the terms, and providing association or recontextualisation with English equivalent terminology and seeing, in the words of Han (2004), instruction promoting fossilization. However, such language use on the part of learners could also be "due to lack of willingness to take risks. It is 'safe' to stay within patterns that accomplish the desired function even though there may be some errors in those patterns" (Brown, 2000, p. 150). However, it is more likely that 'communicative borrowing' occurs, a strategy where learners fall back to the L1 in order to get their message across. The danger here is that successful communication does not depend entirely on formal correction, as persistent errors can lead to fossilization where a learner, uncorrected, is "still able to successfully get their message understood, has no sociofunctional *need* to alter their IL [interlanguage] and so it fossilizes in that state" (Powell, 1998, p. 8). It is therefore not inconceivable that use of the communicative language teaching (CLT) approach, as employed by L1 English speaking and Korean instructors alike, has led to a 'stabilized interlanguage' for Korean EFL students. As noted,

> The most intuitive account for fossilization focuses on the notion of entrenchment. When we practice a given skill thousands of times, we soon find that it has become automated or entrenched. The more we continue to practice that skill, the deeper the entrenchment and the more difficult it becomes to block the use of the skill (MacWhinney, 2005, p. 18).

The emergence of a stabilized interlanguage in Korean learners could even support why unlearning could occur due to student hypothesis testing for language use, although the type of words and the small number of the sample participating in this books empirical investigation cannot provide definitive proof for this theory, or why the use of L1 pseudo-loanwords for foreign language acquisition led to minimal learning gains. For that, a lengthy longitudinal study conducted over many years would be required, ranging from five to perhaps even twenty years (as indicated by Han, 2004). Further, as James (1998) reminds us, aside from lists of 'common mistakes' or false cognates, it is not easy to find systematic methods to assist learners in gaining advantage from research into fields such as error analysis. Further, as in the Brown (1995) and Brown and Williams (1985) loanword studies, the word level of the borrowed terms as used in the L1 is not known, and it is also recognized that this is a potential weakness of the empirical investigation herein. In regards to this, threats to internal validity and reliability will now be considered.

Impact of Threats on Internal Reliability and Validity

According to Bailey (1998), there will always be some tension between reliability and validity, and gains in one have to be balanced against losses in the other. Reliability, or achieving consistency of scores and answers provided by instruments used throughout the investigation, was obtained by utilizing objective scoring methods and coding data for entry into computer for analysis. In addition, due to the nature of treatment, the CALL modules were able to present identical data to each participant, providing the same learning content, correction, and feedback to all.

Rasch analysis was also employed to measure person-item fit, thereby determining the level of instrument reliability and assisting with validity by ensuring fit of the instruments to unidimensional measurement scales.

However, since the empirical investigation was quasi-experimental, it did not utilize random assignment and therefore relied on alternate techniques to control and reduce any threats to internal validity (Fraenkel, Wallen, & Hyun, 2012). Overall threats that may have impacted upon the one-group pre-test/post-test experimental design include: subject characteristics, mortality, data collector characteristics, data collector bias, history, maturation, regression, and implementation. The specific threats range from location, instrumentation, and instrument decay for the survey, through to instrument decay, testing, and attitudinal threats for the pre- and post-tests, and maturation, location, and subject characteristic threats for the treatment. Each of these threats will now be discussed, although it was perceived that attitudinal and treatment location threats would have been the most influential.

The One-group Pre-test/Post-test Experimental Design

Participants were obtained from a sample of convenience, which is often necessary in the case of educational research (see Borg & Gall, in Best & Kahn, 1993), and the treatment was distributed through a process of stratified sampling based on class roll sheet order. All students were of an intermediate English level as ranked by university placement tests, and so they are believed to be on relatively the same level in terms of linguistic knowledge of English. This therefore promoted a reduction in the risk of regression, as beginner or advanced level students may have performed better or worse due to their pre-existing English levels.

Through use of an appropriate and well selected treatment group, along with confining experiment runtime to the period of half a semester, maturation is limited and mortality risk is reduced. University policy dictating eight class hours absent as an automatic failure for the course required attendance, and thus also assisted in alleviating mortality risks. In fact, only a loss of five students occurred. This left a sample of 108 and a mortality rate of 4.4%, which is small and is likely to provide only very marginal impact on the results. Further, only participants who completed the survey, the pre- and post-tests, and the treatment are included in data analysis. Students who did not complete one of the instruments, or failed to submit homework on time, are excluded from the research. The five students who were dropped from the study were absent due to illness, or their need to attend to personal or other school matters, rather than due to failing the course or dropping out of university. The majors of the lost students were: one from electronics (no post-test), one from pharmacy (no pre- or post-test), and three from occupational therapy (no post-tests), while no subjects from the early childhood education and elementary education classes were lost.

Although participant backgrounds in terms of their majors were different, it is believed that this did not hold a detrimental impact on the use of treatment. This is due to the majority of students having had similar prior computer exposure at secondary school level, and they were not engaged in any other online learning activities at the tertiary level during the semester in which the experiment was conducted. In addition, even though participants consisted of 31% males and 69% females, gender is not perceived to be influential on the results of the study, although it was thought that attitudes towards the study, and use of the material in homework mode would have proved the highest threat regarding effective material use, learning, and appropriate data collection. Further, the characteristics of students attending low ranked universities, such as the one where the experiment was conducted, may have impinged upon the study as opposed to having run the experiment at a 'SKY' university (Seoul National University, Korea University, and Yonsei University, which are regarded as being the top three ranking schools in the country). Unfortunately, limited research is available that examines the learner characteristics of freshmen attending these elite level universities to that of freshmen attending very low ranked universities in Korea. Nonetheless, it is believed that such characteristics as pertaining to attitude toward learning, at least in the initial years of university, may include such aspects as those already discussed as impinging factors: low self-efficacy, low self-esteem, and low motivation.

Additionally, as the sample size was rather small, this naturally imposes limitations on the ability to generalize results, and further compounding this is the refinement of the experiment to a single school, although both factors do ensure greater experimental control (Fraenkel, Wallen, & Hyun, 2012). The short time frame of two months for the study may also be considered a limiting factor. However, for new and experimental techniques to be considered effective and viable tools for continued use in educational environments, it can be argued that gains in learning need to occur in such a short timeframe. In fact, the experiment ran for more than half of the in-class teaching time allotted during the sixteen-week semester after events such as festivals, sports days, and midterm and final exams were deducted from the schedule. Further, experiments of this length are not unheard of in the academic literature (e.g. Hegelheimer & Tower, 2004).

To ensure that each experimental group was exposed to identical data collector characteristics, a 35-year-old American female instructor with eight years of EFL teaching experience in Korea (seven at the workplace where the experiment was conducted) was responsible for the collection and deployment of the survey, pre-test, treatment, and post-test. Although the use of only a single instructor could have led to implementation threats, the same bias toward the study, intentional or unintentional and positive or negative, would have been equally provided to each participant. Subsequently, to alleviate data collector bias, specific instructions were provided regarding the deployment and collection of instruments. These included: specifying the weeks of semester when the tests would be delivered, the homework distributed and associated data collected, as well as the length of time permitted for the proctoring of each test. Instruments were provided just prior to required distribution, and returned for analysis immediately upon student submission. Additionally, students were provided with a unique code so that both the data collector and researcher were not aware of which specific students had participated in which treatment when instruments were being collected, and when the scores were being entered into the statistical package for data analysis.

Any unanticipated or unplanned events were controlled by providing instruments to each class during the same week of semester, while taking such factors as university events and public holidays into account. However, much like treatment location threats, it is unclear what history threats may have impacted upon individual students during their use of treatment throughout the homework process. Also, since all students had the option to redo activities if required, then students reattempting certain sections of the homework, if they felt any external influences may have made an impact, could alleviate such a threat.

Survey of Student Attitude Towards
Computer Assisted Learning in EFL

A translation of the survey was administered to participants in the same location, as all had the same classroom, and in the first lecture period of each class during week four of semester. This minimized location threat on the study. Further, as already mentioned, the same instructor was responsible for distribution and collection of the instrument for each class. Administration of the survey was also handled by a Korean assistant, who remained on-hand in case students experienced difficulties. As for instrumentation, translation was necessary since salience assists in obtaining accurate information and higher response rates (Borg & Gall, 1989). Back-translation was also employed as a means of checking translation accuracy. Translation and piloting of the instrument with representative samples, as part of a focus group, also served to verify the content validity of translation before distribution to trial groups. Further, to establish internal consistency of the instrument, alpha coefficients were calculated on trial group data to confirm reliability, and response frequency was examined to ensure scale effectiveness. Any necessary modifications were then made to the survey before final deployment. This initial screening assisted in verifying that extraneous material had been omitted, and that the survey is a representative or reliable measure of the trait under examination.

Direct administration of the survey within class time offered several advantages, the main ones being the high response rates as well as the ability of an administrator to take and answer questions prior to survey completion (Fraenkel, Wallen, & Hyun, 2012). As the survey was designed to be completed within a twenty- to thirty-minute timeframe, instrument decay was alleviated, as students could take the entire fifty-minute lecture period to complete the survey if necessary. The survey also contains a four-point Likert-style response grade for each closed-ended question. The advantage of this is that all subjects responded to the same options, providing standardized data for analysis and coding (Fraenkel, Wallen, & Hyun, 2012). Examination of the frequency of responses then assisted in determining if missing data exists, and in such cases, the Rasch model can compensate (Bond & Fox, 2001). Rasch analysis also highlights items with low indices of reliability and validity, which were then discarded. The essential criterion is compatibility of items with the model, or item fit to the measurement scale: disposition toward computer assisted learning of English as a foreign language. Consequently, the survey came to provide interval data for correlation analysis in the multiple regression phase of data analysis. In addition, the trait being measured was specifically based on data from the academic literature (such as Ahn, 2002; Cortazzi, 1990; Eastmond, 2000; Finch & Hyun, 2000; Hofstede, 1986; Joo, 1997; Min, et al, 2000; Pak, 1999; Park, 2001; Schmitt, 1997; Windle, 2003), and was consistent in terms of gathering data on the three constructs under examination.

Test of Student Understanding of Pseudo-loanwords

Discrete-point tests, such as the multiple-choice test developed and employed as the pre- and post-tests for the empirical investigation undertaken for this book, are advantageous as they allow for the collection of data that is easily quantifiable, and can be accurately and objectively marked. Item difficulty was varied by choice of pseudo-loanwords and the choice of English words used in test item statements, with particular care not to mix the level of difficulty within single items. By varying the closeness of meaning between distracters and the key, it was easy to modify items to varying degrees of difficulty (Nagy, Herman, & Anderson, 1985). When writing test activities, items were checked to ensure that they had only one viable correct response and were not interdependent. The order of correct responses was also randomized, so that test wiseness could be further reduced. In addition, distracters were developed that would be both plausible and equally appealing to students who did not know the correct answer.

Location threat was diminished as both the pre- and post-tests were delivered in the same location, by the same instructor, and at the same time of the weekly class schedule. That is, the first lecture period of week six of semester for the pre-test, and the last lecture period of week fourteen for the post-test. It was also important during the testing phase to consider the effect of student exposure to the pre-test when delivering the post-test. If the second test was administered too soon, students would have recall of the items from the first test, and an alternate one would need developing. If the test was administered too late, then no reliable measure would have been obtained (Fraenkel, Wallen, & Hyun, 2012). Since the period of delivery between each test was eight weeks, it was not perceived necessary to develop a second test instrument for the post-test.

It is important to note that when multiple-choice tests are created, the test banks often do not provide balanced keys. Although this seems to violate the conventional wisdom of multiple-choice answer creation, previous studies in fact note that balanced keys are not a significant factor in testing, as no more errors are made in any case where one series of particular options is correct over another (Kujawski Taylor, 2005). In addition, since Korean students are used to taking tests similar to the style of the TOEFL and TOEIC, the multiple-choice test developed for this study came to mirror the TOEFL structure section and presented students with a cloze-type statement along with four answer choices. Although new versions of the TOEFL and TOEIC have since been introduced, due to student familiarity with such tests at the time, three distracters and one key were consciously selected for use. This decision was made even though research indicates that three choices (two distracters and the key) are optimal for multiple-choice type tests (see Rodriguez, 2005), with four being the most common probably due to face validity while still allowing for an acceptably valid and reliable test, albeit more difficult (Taylor, 2005).

As with the survey, the test underwent reliability and validity checks by trialing before final deployment, and Rasch analysis before use in hypothesis testing. Trialing assisted in accurately developing a reliable and valid instrument by ensuring that the test was appropriate for deployment. Rasch analysis also assisted in determining the reliability of the test in terms of person-item difficulty calibration, and the validity by ensuring fit of the items to the model and therefore effective measurement of a single trait: student understanding of the English meanings of pseudo-loanwords used in Korean. In this manner, the measures ar used for hypothesis testing.

CALL Modules

The CALL modules used in the treatment are homework-based so that they would not impinge upon the existing syllabus schedule, thereby being less obtrusive and more easily implemented within the existing university English program curriculum. This also came to assist in minimizing instructor-bias as treatment involved measuring performance of student linguistic understanding and development resulting from completion of material outside the classroom. However, this could have led to subject characteristic threats, where participants neglected homework completion or completed materials in one sitting, rather than throughout the semester, and this was reduced by implementing standard-practice controls (i.e. incremental homework submission due dates: four submissions in total, one for every two weeks of treatment).

Since all of the classes taught by the instructor were using one of the CALL treatments, it is perceived that no novelty effect was in place. Although it is novel to be using CALL of this type in the tertiary sector with EFL students, even today, this is not believed to have provided an overtly positive or negative impact on data collected for the experiment. This is primarily due to the exposure that students have to computers in other areas of their lives as digital natives (Prensky, 2001) such as in the home environment and from the ubiquitous penetration of devices. Further, control of attitudinal effect stemmed from incorporating learning content into the classroom as part of normal taught-course homework procedure. However, as already discussed, student interpretation of the CALL modules as part of the university English program may have introduced a negative washback effect that could have come to impact upon the results obtained.

The only threat that was not directly controlled is treatment location: the places where students elected to engage in the use of the CALL homework modules. While it is expected that most students would take the homework seriously, allocate an appropriate time to complete the language learning activities, and do so in an appropriate and suitable place, the modules could have been completed in various locales ranging from dorm rooms (with four students per room possibly distracting the user), internet cafes (with many customers providing a 24-hour noisy gaming environment), school computer labs (with limited space and time availability), private bedrooms (away from campus in the students' hometowns), or on the go (on public transport). At the particular university where the experiment was conducted, most freshmen live in dormitories and travel home for the weekend, so it is presumed that the latter two venues would be the most likely. Although being a considerable threat to the results obtained, any form of computer-based homework provided to students would be subject to the same circumstances, and would need to prove effective under similar conditions. To alleviate such a threat, the researcher could have required the distributing instructor to book computer lab time on campus, or to have students bring their own devices to class, so that they could be assured of a place and time to complete the homework. Such a condition would, however, impinge upon the notion of promoting learner autonomy and self-regulatory behavior, and would prevent students from completing the homework in locations and at times more convenient to them.

No technical glitches were reported by the administering instructor concerning the provision and use of the modules for homework, most likely due to the contingency measures of providing the instructor with training in how to use the CALL materials so as to provide assistance to students on an as-needed basis. Still, it has been recognized that those students who need the most assistance are generally also the most reluctant to ask for it (Newman, 1994). Ultimately, the language exercises were checked for appropriateness by L1 English speaking EFL instructors while they trialed the software, and before the modules were piloted with a representative student group. After these testing periods, small modifications were made to the two systems before they were made available for final distribution, and as a result, it is believed that no student experienced major technical difficulties in the completion or submission of their CALL-based homework. Through all of the above-mentioned actions, it is believed that a course of reliable and valid treatment was provided to students throughout the empirical investigation undertaken.

D. SIGNIFYING INVESTIGATIVE OUTCOMES

The ultimate aim of this book is to examine the educational effectiveness of using the English inherent within the native language of Korean EFL students for the development of linguistic competence and the enhancement of attitudes towards learning in a mandatory university English language program, and to strategically investigate utilizing specifically developed computer assisted language learning (CALL) homework modules for such a purpose. Therefore, the investigation conducted seeks to understand the interaction between multiple dimensions of computer assisted learning and English foreign language acquisition of Korean freshmen university students; in particular, to examine how the students' knowledge of English words adapted for use in the Korean vernacular – loanwords – was affected by their attitudes towards computerized instruction, their preference for certain methods of learning and teaching, and also by the attributes of computerized instructional packages. At the end of this section, Tables 4.1 and Table 4.2 provide a summary of the contributions arising from the book where these are listed by the primary focus of each aspect, and identifiable from the resulting major outcome.

Conclusions Concerning the Line of Inquiry

The first line of inquiry question and objective seeks to determine if there is any association between the method of presenting learning content to students (in the form of computer assisted instruction), and the learning content itself (in the form of pseudo-loanword vocabulary), and how any association may impact upon results obtained during the course of treatment. The investigative question is: Is student understanding of pseudo-loanwords associated with dispositions towards computer assisted learning of English as a foreign language?

The study did not find a correlation between student disposition towards computer assisted learning of English as a foreign language (the trait measured by the survey) and the understanding of pseudo-loanwords (as represented by test data).

The second line of inquiry question and objective focuses on examining the impact of CALL instructional approaches upon vocabulary acquisition, and investigating the applicability of loanword utilization for foreign language development. The investigative question is: Does the application of different computer assisted language learning instructional strategies affect student understanding of pseudo-loanwords?

Table 4.1

Summary of book sections by aspect, primary focus and associated outcomes

Aspect	Primary Focus	Major Outcome
Korean cultural learning style	Affirm the traditional view held by the literature	The Korean cultural learning style appears to be changing, and accepted 'stereotypes' presented by the literature need to be reexamined
L1 use in the EFL context	Extend upon the success of direct loanwords applied in other (non-CALL-based) EFL and ESL contexts	Students were consistently unable to build new form-meaning connections between Korean pseudo-loanwords and English equivalents, implying 'lexical stabilization'
CALL module development	Develop two CALL modules to be used in an experiment utilizing the L1 as the source for foreign language learning	Introduces a means of examining the use of Korean pseudo-loanwords in EFL through the use of a computer-based multimedia learning solution
Survey instrument	Develop a unique and refined instrument with constructs consisting of disposition towards CAI, Korean learning style, and English as foreign language learning style	Measured the association between the method of presenting learning content to students (CAI), and the learning content itself (pseudo-loanwords)
Analysis	Utilize Rasch analysis techniques with the data	Expands the literature base of studies applying Rasch analysis in Korean CALL
Review of academic literature: Education, technology, culture, and language	Comprehensively investigates areas pertaining to EFL and the application of computer technology in the Korean education system, as well as the cultural influences on computer assisted learning of English as a foreign language, and on loanword use in the Korean context	Identifies a significant number of gaps in the academic literature, all of which highlight potential areas of future research

Table 4.2

Summary of book objectives and outcomes

Objectives	Primary Focus	Major Outcomes
Objective 1	Determine the impact of using CAI with Korean students	Computer use in the Korean EFL context would not bias any results obtained through use of computer assisted instruction (particularly during the treatment phase)
Objective 2(a)	Examine the educational effectiveness of using English inherent within the native vernacular (pseudo-loanwords) for development of English language linguistic competence and enhancement of attitudes towards learning	Pseudo-loanwords can be applied in Korean EFL teaching, and provide somewhat positive learning results, albeit that these are marginal and limited
Objective 2(b)	Investigate the utility of using researcher developed CALL homework modules	Both the behaviorist-based restricted and communicative-based open CALL approaches provide similar learning gains when applying L1 data as the source for foreign language learning material in the context of Korean freshmen university English classes

This question was explored through construction of a linear scale to measure Korean student understanding of loanwords, used as the pre-test and post-test in the experimental phase of investigation, and the development of two computer assisted language learning instructional modules as treatment. Evidence is found to indicate that the use of L1 vocabulary, in the form of pseudo-loanwords, can work to promote learning and understanding in the Korean CALL context, but with only marginal success. Although the communicative-based open CALL approach did produce marginally higher effects, consistency in the level of results obtained also shows that both behaviorist-based restricted CALL and communicative-based open CALL instructional approaches provide similar learning gains for Korean university freshman enrolled in general English language courses teaching Standard American English.

Limitations

As with many endeavors, the empirical investigation presented herein has several limitations. In particular, the experiment consisted of only a small number of participants, and as such, this comes to limit the ability to generalize the results obtained. This is certainly not a factor unique to this investigation, with a large number of peer-reviewed journal articles focusing on Korean students having the same limitation. The use of a limited number of subjects in empirical studies is a worrying trend. Regardless, most educational research studies, including the present study, rely on samples of convenience, and the advantage of restricting the sample to one school and to a smaller sample size is that it can afford greater experimental control to the researcher (Fraenkel, Wallen, & Hyun, 2003).

Treatment materials were provided to students as homework modules, and it may be argued that this is a limitation, as incorporating the empirical materials within the existing curriculum during class time may have been more fruitful. This concern must await another later study. In addition, time allotted for use of the CALL modules is short, and more positive outcomes might have been produced with more time on task. However, longer use of the software would have gone against the notion of using courseware material over a single semester, and needing it to be effective during that time period. These restrictions as well as the single-semester homework-based use were specifically imposed upon the investigation so that any English conversation instructor employing the material with their classes would not be overburdened, nor the English curriculum interrupted.

A final limitation is that the empirical investigation was conducted at a low-ranking university. In this case, the students themselves (in terms of low self-efficacy, low self-esteem, and low motivation), along with other learner variables such as those involving socio-economic background, social capital, or home environment, could have held sway more than what is visible from the data. In any case, multimedia education systems need to work with these types of students too (and not just those attending higher ranked schools where such learner variables may not prove to be as significant).

Part Three Summary

Part Three of this book came to specify the methods and analysis that was applied to implementing the loanword approach in the Korean context. In the first section, the experiment that is designed to test the effectiveness of this approach, along with the conceptual framework behind it, is outlined along with two core questions or lines of inquiry. The target population and sample, the instrumentation, and the data analysis techniques are also introduced, as are aspects of instrument and treatment reliability and validity. In section B, the findings of the empirical investigation are then presented in terms of the results of statistical tests, used for instrument refinement, as well as for analysis pertinent to the lines of inquiry. Emergent implications arising from the data are then discussed in section C. For the first hypothesis, this involves the examination of the association of computer assisted learning of English with the learning of pseudo-loanwords. It has been determined that computer use did not bias the results obtained through use of computer assisted language learning (CALL) in treatment, and as such, other extraneous variables must have held an impact on the results obtained. This then leads into a discussion of issues centering on hypothesis two, which involves the impact of instructional approaches on L2 vocabulary acquisition, and revolves around discussing the consequences of the changing Korean cultural learning style, and the potential influence of negative washback on the results presented. Following this, there is a discussion on loanword utilization for foreign language development, which examines the issue of successful application of loanwords in alternate contexts versus the Korean context, as well as the notion of vocabulary acquisition and interlanguage stabilization in Korea. Aspects of reliability and validity are also considered, with treatment location and attitudinal effect arising as the largest concerns. Before coming to a close, with section D and a discussion delving into the potential limitations of the empirical investigation, the potential contributions the work presents to the field are highlighted as are the ultimate outcomes of the experiment undertaken, and conclusions regarding the lines of inquiry.

Part Four
IMPLICATIONS

Part Four
IMPLICATIONS

Implications of the Study

There are a number of implications arising from the findings presented in this book, and the most significant relate to (a) the usability of computer-based English as a foreign language (EFL) instruction in the Korean tertiary education sector, (b) a need for reinterpretation of the Korean cultural learning style as it relates to EFL, and (c) the existence of a stabilized interlanguage on the Korean peninsula.

Significance and Recommendations

One of the most noteworthy insights gleaned from the results of the empirical investigation presented from within this book is the need to reexamine the stereotypes about Korean learners as presented in the EFL literature. There appears to be a movement away from traditional views of language learning and teaching by Korean students and instructors (see Finch, 2004; Windle, 2003); for example, Koreans no longer regard the teacher (university instructor) as an authoritative figure who should go unquestioned (Finch, 2004; Windle, 2003). Korean students do not want to passively sit in class receiving knowledge (Finch, 2004). As Reid (1987) indicates, from a group of nine language backgrounds, Koreans were the most visually oriented but favor kinesthetic and tactile learning experiences. Further, Korean concern for harmony within a group, as presented by Armitage (2001), is by its very nature not at variance with a collaborative use of multimedia activities and computer mediated communication (CMC) if attuned and adapted to the context of the Korean EFL classroom. This is important to recognize since to date, the "received truth" relating to the educational traditions of the East Asian learning context (see Pierson, 1996, p. 52) perceives these learners as individuals who are "conditioned by a pattern of cultural forces that are not harmonious to learner autonomy, independence or self-direction" (Liu, 1998, p. 5). From a field level perspective, the changing traits and classroom expectations of Korean learners will come to impact the EFL sector in Korea. It is therefore important to further examine the changing aspects of Korean students and the educational context in which they operate, and develop materials for these students that enables education to be provided in a manner in which teaching and learning is the most effective.

Also at the practitioner level, it is important to keep in mind the influence that the Korean cultural learning style holds over students. Consequently, it is believed that any application of computer assisted language learning (CALL), particularly in EFL environments, will need to take into account the local cultural and learning context. This means that beliefs and preferences are controlling factors in language learning, and need to be taken into account when generating an up-to-date profile of EFL students in Korea. This then holds implications for materials development and for teacher training programs as well (Finch, 2004), especially when we recognize the "need to match the different aspects of autonomy with the characteristics and needs of learners in specific contexts" (Littlewood, 1999, p. 71). This is important, since learner autonomy is a central issue for the success of most computer-based initiatives. Indeed, empowering students as learners is the essence of 'autonomy' according to Holec (in Benson and Voller, 1997, p. 1), who views it as "the ability to take charge of one's learning". Yet, as Briguglio (2000, p. 1) recognizes, the aim of education is to produce confident, independent, self-directed learners, but students like those from Korea require a more structured and gradual approach to transition them "to become confident and independent learners". Research shows that the most successful students are those that possess the ability to monitor their own learning progress (Schapiro & Livingston, 2000), and self-discipline and motivation have been found to be predictors of online course success (Waschull, 2005). Students who can monitor their own learning perform significantly better in computer-based instructional environments, as independent learner strategies are critical to achieving academic success from such instruction (Williams & Hellman, 2004). In this regard, it is essential that teachers applying CALL with their students focus upon structuring learning content appropriately, and seek to develop motivation and foster aspects such as self-efficacy in their language students.

Results of the investigation undertaken in this book also indicate that there is a significant lack of understanding of the English equivalents of pseudo-loanwords among Korean EFL students, and that it is difficult for them to establish additional semantic properties for these lexical items. This lack of understanding of English equivalents for pseudo-loanwords is the result of students having no socio-functional need to alter their use of this interlanguage, which in turn promotes 'lexical stabilization'. The challenge that arises here for teachers and material developers alike is to make students more aware of their language use and misuse, and to provide material that focuses on assisting students in understanding and using the English equivalents for these terms. To this end, alternate tasks, like recontextualisation, may prove more appropriate than the associative tasks used by the empirical investigation herein, and used in previous research on the effectiveness of employing direct loanwords in an EFL context for learning. As this occurs, further research will be needed to ascertain which aspects of the first language (L1) are most beneficial for use with Korean students engaged in learning English as a foreign language, so that support material for language practice and study can be developed.

Finally, it is increasingly essential for university administrators and the departments providing university English programs in Korea to implement CALL, especially the development of culturally adapted software systems for language learning. This need has emerged as a result of current graduation requirements, which require not only English skills but functional information communication technology (ICT) skills. More fundamentally, learners will eventually demand alignment of the university sector with government initiatives put in place at the grade school level concerning e-learning. Although the integration of computer-based learning and information communication technology use within the large majority of mandatory university English programs in Korea is something that has yet to occur, inevitably students will begin to demand a multimedia supported learning environment and associated teaching methods at the tertiary level. Administrators will also need to ensure that certain conditions are met when developing and using CALL in the university English programs of Korea. Teachers should not be assigned to a lab or computer classroom, say once a week, then be left to their own devices (K. W. Lee, 2000); they need classroom support and adequate training in computer applications and the means to integrate these into their instructional practice. Further, students need to be made aware of their responsibilities in terms of using computers and other devices for learning, such as when and how to complete assigned work using the applications and tools made available to them (Hubbard, 2004). The technology itself is also important, and administrators must ensure that adequate and functional devices, computers, and software are provided and adequately maintained for teachers. Otherwise, a computer could sit dormant in the classroom for months on end due to a problem as simple as a dirty mouse preventing interaction with software (Cuban, 2001). Most importantly, the usability and effectiveness of multimedia device-based EFL instruction in the Korean tertiary education sector must be built upon effective content and sound instructional design principles.

Areas of Future Research

As there have been no previous pseudo-loanword CALL studies undertaken in Korea, the data presented within this book has been able to identify a number of areas where research is lacking, as well as a number of areas for future research, and these will now be discussed.

There are several areas of interest for further investigation, including the impact of culture on media use in the Korean EFL context, and the need to focus on development of learner responsibility in Korean students using CALL for language study. There is a need for the design and delivery of multimedia device-based university English program materials that are built on the basis of effective pilot programs and research. Future research needs to be conducted utilizing Rasch analysis techniques, and the application and reexamination of the loanword approach in different contexts and from different approaches needs to be undertaken.

To date, there has been limited examination by scholars of the influence of the Korean cultural learning style on the application of CALL initiatives within Korea. Also, there is limited literature detailing specifically how Korean culture impacts practical learning in the Korean EFL classroom and in turn comes to affect the use of media and computer systems for language learning. Much more research is required in regard to how Korean culture impacts CALL initiatives, and how it can be advantageous for transitioning students to more active participation in their own second language (L2) learning.

There has been limited research on the impact of software and courseware use with Korean EFL learners, and what exists largely focuses on the collaborative use of materials or tools. So too, like teacher studies, research examining learner responses as well as their degree of satisfaction with CALL material is available, but it remains largely limited in scope to CMC or web based instruction (see H. K. Choi, 2004; Hwang, 2002; C. J. Kwon, 2004; O, 2005; Oh, 2003a, 2003b). Further studies are needed to examine the Korean student use of CALL-based instruction, particularly multimedia systems designed for individual private study, and to determine how such materials can foster the development of learner responsibility in Korean students, increase their motivation for language learning, and promote active involvement in the language learning process. This is important since it is well recognized that it is ultimately the individual who is responsible for his or her own progress, and the development of his or her own language skills (Ahn, 2002).

Despite the "focus on the need to promote and develop multimedia assisted teaching methods in university education" (C. J. Kwon, 2005, p. 169), there is a contrast between grade school level reforms concerning e-learning with that of educational practice at the tertiary level. Although numerous individual educators are adopting aspects of CALL instruction and applying it within their tertiary level EFL classes, there have only been a small number of CALL systems applied in regular university English programs (Lee & Yang, 2002). Even so, these "systems are not being used properly in an integrated and standardized form within the regular university curriculum" (Hoh, 2005, p. 341). In this regard, software systems and multimedia tools could be integrated properly alongside the university English program curriculum so that research-based pilot programs can determine the most effective means for learning content development and deployment for these students. In addition, by investigating other aspects such as student perceptions and attitudes, and how they undertake language learning activities, useful information about these learners in the Korean educational environment could be obtained. For example, their beliefs, motivations, likes and dislikes, and their preferences and choices, and this would ultimately allow for the development of knowledge that can be effectively applied when designing e-learning systems for these learners.

Some of the above issues may be addressed with the implementation of various social strategies and government led reforms, in particular, those coming to place emphasis on promoting e-learning in order to strengthen national competitiveness. This would lead to changes for the native English speaking instructor working in Korea and the use of CALL in the tertiary level EFL classroom, and these changes would provide a wide range of future research possibilities.

In addition, the empirical investigation undertaken by this book is among the first Korean CALL-based research endeavors to employ Rasch analysis, and many empirical studies that have been conducted in Korea might have yielded vastly different results if analysis techniques such as Rasch were applied. Particularly since

> ANOVA is extensively utilized in studies in which an independent variable is routinely examined for interactions with another independent variable. The discovery of spurious interaction effects produced under ANOVA of raw scores (Embretson, 1993, 1996), when Rasch transformations of the raw scores could easily have been employed, calls this use into question. Embretson found that when untransformed raw scores are subjected to multi-factor ANOVA, spurious interaction effects between

the independent variables regularly occur. Since the interaction effect in many cases reflects the major research hypothesis, this finding should be of concern to researchers and statisticians alike (Romanoski & Douglas, 2002, p. 234).

Hence, there is a need for Korean researchers to adopt such techniques and apply them locally, and when this happens, it will be informative to review the data analyzed by applying Rasch analysis, and in turn to evaluate the claims concerning Korean EFL students and CALL that begin to emerge.

Further, examination of the effectiveness of using such terminology as loan words, particularly pseudo-loanwords, in a practical Korean EFL setting has not been assessed and, unfortunately, the predominance of research that does exist largely focuses on form (e.g. Colhoun & Kim, 1976; Kang, 2003; McArthur, 1992; Nam & Southard, 1994; Shim, 1994; Yu, 1980;). Although the empirical investigation herein examines the viability of implementing a loanword approach in the Korean EFL context, only one aspect of the approach was tested: pseudo-loanword use from CALL-based instruction. To more accurately determine the limits and transferability of such an approach, further testing in different contexts will be necessary. Modifications may include using recontextualisation tasks as opposed to the associative tasks employed by this and other studies using direct loanwords as a basis: changing the core linguistic base from pseudo-loanwords to direct loanwords; or, operating the experiment while maintaining emphasis on in-class work over the deployment of homework modules.

In many ways this book has touched on all of the above areas, providing further insight into each. All are potential research agendas and worthy of further study. It is now hoped that the contributions presented will allow future scholars to build upon the concepts and practicalities herein explored.

REFERENCES

Ahmad, K., Corbett, G., Rogers, M., & Sussex, R. (1985). *Computers, language learning and language teaching.* Cambridge: Cambridge University Press.

Ahn, B. (1995). Issues in the application of multimedia to English education in Korea. *Multimedia and the information highway in language education* (pp. 145-158). Chonnam National University Language Research Center International Workshop Proceedings.

Ahn, B. (2002). An instructional model for college English incorporating the World Wide Web. *Journal of the Applied Linguistics Association of Korea, 18*(1), 195-218.

Ahn, S. C. (1998). *An introduction to Korean phonology.* Seoul: Hanshin Publishing.

Albert, M., & Obler, L. (1978). *The bilingual brain: Neuropsychological and neurolinguistic aspects of bilingualism.* New York: Academic Press.

Alessi, S. M., & Shih, Y. F. (1989). *Discrimination errors and learning time in computer drills.* 31st ADCIS Conference Proceedings. Bellingham, WA: Association for the Development of Computer Based Instructional Systems.

Alessi, S., & Trollip, S. (2001). *Multimedia for learning: Methods and development* (3rd ed.). Needham Heights, Massachusetts: Allyn & Bacon.

Andrich, D. (1985). A latent trait model for items with response dependencies: Implications for test construction and analysis. In S. E. Emreston (Ed.), *Test design: Developments in psychology and psychometrics* (pp. 245-275). Orlando, FL: Academic Press.

Andrich, D., & van Schoubroeck, L. (1989). The general health questionnaire: A psychometric analysis using latent trait theory. *Psychological Medicine, 19*, 469-485.

Ariew, R., & Frommer, J.G. (1987). Interaction in the computer age. In M. Rivers, (Ed.), *Interactive Language Teaching* (pp. 177-193). Cambridge: Cambridge University Press.

Armitage, L. (2001). *Factors affecting the adjustment of Koreans studying in Australia.* Sydney, NSW: Australia-Korea Foundation.

Atkins, M. J. (1993). Theories of learning and multimedia applications: An overview. *Research Papers in Education, 8*(2), 251-271.

Atkinson, D. (1999). TESOL and culture. *TESOL Quarterly, 33*, 625-654.

Auerbach, E. (1993). Reexamining English only in the ESL classroom. *TESOL Quarterly, 27*(1), 9-32.

Backer, J. (1995). *Teaching grammar with CALL: Survey of theoretical literature.* Retrieved from http:// ietn.snunit.k12.il/gramcall.htm.

Bae, J., & Rowley, C. (2001). The impact of globalization on HRM: The case of South Korea. *Journal of World Business, 36*(4), 402-428.

Baik, M. J., & Shim, R. J. Y. (1998). Martin Jonghak Baik and Rosa Jinyoung Shim: reply. *World Englishes, 17*(2), 273-279.

Bailey, K. (1998) *Learning about language assessment: Dilemmas, decisions, and directions.* Boston, MA: Heinle and Heinle.

Beaton, A., Grunberg, M., & Ellis, N. C. (1995). Retention of foreign vocabulary using the keyword method: A ten-year follow-up. *Second Language Research, 11*(2), 112-120.

Benson, P., & Voller, P. (1997). *Autonomy and independence in language learning.* London: Longman.

Bernstein, N. (1967). *The coordination and regulation of movements.* New York: Pergamon Press.

Best, J. W., & Kahn, J. V. (1993). *Research in education* (7th ed.). Boston, Massachusetts: Allyn and Bacon.

Bhatt, R. (2001). World Englishes. *Annual Review of Anthropology,* 527-550.

Bhela, B. (1999). Native language interference in learning a second language: exploratory case studies of native language interference with target language usage. *International Education Journal, 1*(1), 22-31.

Boling, E. (1995, June). *Issues in multimedia for learning.* Paper presented at the Multimedia and the Information Highway in Language Education Conference, Gwangju, Korea.

Bolinger, D. (1965). Pitch accent and sentence rhythm. In I. Abi & T. Kanekiyo (Eds.), *Forms of English: Accent, morpheme, order* (pp. 139-180). Cambridge, MA: Harvard University Press.

Bond, T. G., & Fox, C. M. (2001). *Applying the Rasch model: Fundamental measurement in the human sciences*. New Jersey: Lawrence Erlbaum Associates.

Borg, W. R., & Gall, M. D. (1989). *Educational research an introduction* (5th ed.). New York: Longman.

Breen, M. (1999). *The Koreans*. London: Orion Business.

Briguglio, C. (2000). Self directed learning is fine - if you know the destination! In A. Herrmann and M.M. Kulski (Eds.), *Flexible Futures in Tertiary Teaching: Proceedings of the 9th Annual Teaching Learning Forum*. Perth, WA: Curtin University of Technology.

Brown, H. D. (2000). *Principles of language teaching*. New York: Addison Wesley Longman.

Brown, H. D. (2014). *Principles of language learning and teaching: A course in second language acquisition*, (6th ed.). New York: Pearson.

Brown, J. B. (1995). Is Gairaigo English?. *The Internet TESOL Journal. 5*(1).

Brown, J. B., & Williams, C. J. (1985). Gairaigo: A latent English vocabulary base? *Eibungaku, 76*, 129-146.

Brown, P. C. (2002). A model of SLA and its andragogical implications in teaching EFL to young adult Japanese learners. *The Language Teacher Online, 3*. Retrieved February 26, 2006, from http://.jalt-publications.org/tlt/articles/2002/03/brown.

Bond, T., & Fox, C. (2001). *Applying the Rasch model: Fundamental measurement in the human sciences*. New Jersey: Lawrence Erlbaum Associates.

Bull, S. (1995). Handling native and non-native language transfer in CALL: Theory and practice. In E. Wakely, A. Barker, D. Frier, P. Graves & Y. Suleiman (Eds.), *Language teaching and learning in higher education: Issues and perspectives* (pp. 97-108). London: Centre for Information on Language Teaching and Research.

Canagarajah, A. S. (1999). Interrogating the 'Native-Speaker Fallacy': Non linguistic roots, non pedagogical results. In G. Braine (Ed.), *Non native educators in English language teaching* (pp. 77-92). Mahwah, NJ: Lawrence Erlbaum.

Card, J. (2005, November 30). Life and death exams in South Korea. *Asia Times*.

Carey, S. (2002). Constructionism and motivational use of technology for EFL teachers. *English Teaching, 57*(1), 45-57.

Carrol, J. (1964). *Language and thought.* Englewood, NJ: Prentice-Hall.

Cavanagh, R F., Kent, D. B., & Romanoski, J. T. (2005, December). *An illustrative example of the benefits of using a Rasch analysis in an experimental design investigation.* Paper presented at the Annual Conference of the Australian Association for Research in Education, Sydney, Australia.

Cavanagh, R. F., & Romanoski, J. T. (2004, January). *Application of the Rasch model to develop a measure of classroom information and communication technology learning culture.* Paper presented at the Second International Rasch Conference, Perth, Western Australia.

Chapelle, C. (2001). *Computer applications in second language acquisition: Foundations for teaching, testing, and research.* Cambridge: Cambridge University Press.

Chiquito, A., Meskill, C., and Renjilian-Burgy, J. (1997). Multiple, mixed, malleable media. In M. Bush, & R. Terry (Eds.), *Technology-enhanced language learning* (pp. 47-76). Lincolnwood, Illinois: National Textbook Company.

Cho. Y. Y. (1999). Language change and the phonological lexicon of Korean. In L. J. Brinton (Ed.), *Historical linguistics 1999: Selected papers from the 14th international conference on historical linguistics* (pp. 89-104). Amsterdam: John Benjamins.

Choi, H. K. (2004). EFL students' perceptions on synchronous English text chatting: Implications for its implementation. *Multimedia Assisted Language Learning, 7*(2), 35-63.

Choi, P. Y. H. (2001. Borrowings as a semantic fact. *Marges Linguistiques, 1.*

Choi, S. H. (2005, May 9). In South Korea, students push back. *International Herald Tribune.* Retrieved from http://www.iht.com/articles/2005/05/08/news/korea.php.

Choi, S. Y., & Shin, H. Y. (2002). A study of the effective use of CD-ROM developed for English teachers in Korean elementary schools. *Multimedia Assisted Language Learning, 5*(2), 156-181.

Choi, S. Y., Kim, K. S., Lee, C. K., & Sol, Y. H. (1999). Effective use of multimedia computer courseware in English language teaching and learning. *Multimedia Assisted Language Learning, 2*(1), 179-256.

Choi, W. K. (2002). Web-based application in a university reading class: A case study. *A new paradigm for innovative multimedia language education in the 21ˢᵗ century* (pp. 228-237). Seoul: Korean Association of Multimedia Assisted Language Learning.

Chang, J. T. (2003). The mask mechanism: Anxiety, motivation and oral proficiency in CMC. *A new perspective on the use of CMC (Computer-Mediated Communication) in foreign language education* (pp. 119-133). Daejon, Korea: Korean Association of Multimedia Assisted Language Learning.

Chomsky, N. (1986). *Knowledge of language: Its nature, origin, and use.* New York, USA: Preager.

Chujo, K., & Nishigaki, C. (2004). Creating e-learning material to teach essential vocabulary for young EFL learners. *IWLeL 2004: An interactive workshop on language e-learning* (pp. 35-44).

Chun, D. (1994). Using computer networking to facilitate the acquisition of interactive competence. *System, 2*(1), 17-31.

Chun, D. M., & Plass, J. L. (2000). Networked multimedia environments for second language acquisition. In M. Warschauer, and R. Kern, (Eds.). *Network-based language learning* (pp. 151-170). Cambridge: Cambridge University Press.

Chun, H. H. (2002). The CD-ROM review and evaluation guidelines for listening and speaking in the high school English textbook of Korean 7ᵗʰ curriculum. *A New Paradigm for Innovative Multimedia Language Education in the 21ˢᵗ Century* (pp. 353-363). Seoul, Korea; Korean Association of Multimedia Assisted Language Learning.

Clarke, R. E. (1994). Media will never influence learning. *Educational Technology Research and Development, 42*(2), 21-29.

Claycomb, C., & Kysilko, D. (2000). The purposes and elements of effective assessment systems. *The Policy Framework: the State Education Standard, Spring,* 7-11.

Cloutier, R. (2005). An optimality theoretic approach to consonant clusters of foreign loanwords in Korean. *Issues in EFL, 3*(1), 97-111.

Colhoun, E. R., & Kim, T. W. (1976). English loanwords in Korean. *Applied Linguistics, 8*(2), 237-220.

Conacher, J. E., & Royall, F. (1998). An evaluation of the use of the Internet for the purposes of foreign language learning. *Language Learning Journal, 18*, 37-41.

Cook, V. (1993). *Linguistics and second language acquisition.* London: The Macmillan Press.

Cortazzi, M. (1990). Cultural and educational expectations in the language classroom. In B. Harrison (Ed.), *Culture and the Language Classroom* (pp. 54-65). London: Macmillan Press.

Creswell, J. W. (1994). *Research Design.* California: Sage Publications.

Critchley, M. (1998). *Design and Implementation of a Communicative Approach for Entry-Level University Students.* Kiyou: Josai International University.

Critchley, M. (2002, November). *The role of Japanese in communicative ELT.* Paper presented at the JALT 2002 National Conference, Shizuoka, Japan.

Cronin, M. (1995). Considering the cultural context in teaching and learning for Korean tertiary students by western teachers. In L. Summers (Ed.), *A focus on learning* (pp. 53-56). Perth, WA: Edith Cowan University.

Crook, C. (1994). *Computers and the collaborative experience of learning.* London: Routledge.

Crowder Han, S. (1995). *Notes on things Korean.* Seoul: Hollym.

Crystal, D. (2003). *English as a global language.* USA: Cambridge University Press.

Cuban, L. (2001). *Oversold and underused: Computers in the classroom.* Cambridge: Harvard University Press.

Cunningham, K. (2000). Integrating CALL into the writing curriculum. *The Internet TESOL Journal, 6*(5).

Danhua, W. (1995). Medium of instruction in the L2 classroom. *Teanga: The Irish Yearbook of Applied Linguistics, 15*, 21-29.

Daulton, F. E. (1998). Japanese loanword cognates and the acquisition of English vocabulary. *The Language Teacher Online, 22*(1).

Daulton, F. E. (1999a). English loanwords in Japanese – the built in lexicon. *The Internet TESOL Journal. 5*(1).

Daulton, F. E. (1999b). List of high-frequency base word vocabulary for Japanese students. *The Internet TESOL Journal, 5*(7).

Daulton, F. E. (2003). List of high-frequency base word vocabulary for Japanese students #2. *The Internet TESOL Journal, 9*(3).

Davies, J. (1997). *The world wide web: A technology to enhance teaching and learning?* Retrieved from http://www.ualberta.ca/~jedavies/owston/index.htm.

Davies, M., & Crowther, D. (1995). The benefits of using multimedia in higher education: Myths and realities. *Active Learning, 3*.

de Jong, K. (1994). Initial tones and prominence in Seoul Korean. *Osu working papers in linguistics, 43*, 1-14.

Dekkers, J., van der Leeuw, F., & van der Weijer, J. (Eds.). (2000). *Optimality theory: Phonology, syntax, and acquisition.* New York: Oxford University Press.

Deubel, P. (2003). An investigation of behaviorist and cognitive approaches to instructional multimedia design. *Journal of Educational Multimedia and Hypermedia, 12*(1), 63-90.

Dickinson, L. (1987). *Self-instruction in language learning.* Cambridge: Cambridge University Press.

Dimova, S. (2007). English, the internet and computer terminology in Macedonia. *World Englishes, 26*(3), 373-387.

Doms, D. E. (2004). *English and Korean speakers' categorization of spatial actions: A test of the Whorf hypothesis.* Unpublished master's thesis, University of Birmingham, Edgbaston, Birmingham, United Kingdom.

Duffy, T. M., & Cunningham, D. J. (1996). Constructivism: Implications for the design and delivery of instruction. In D. H. Jonassen (Ed.), *Handbook of research for educational communications and technology* (pp. 170-198). New York: Simon and Schuster Macmillan.

Dunn, R., & Griggs, S. (1988). *Learning styles: Quiet revolution in American schools.* Reston, VA: National Association of Secondary School Principals.

Eastmond, D. (2000). Realizing the promise of distance education in low technology countries. *Educational Technology, Research, and Development, 48*(2), 100-125.

Elgort, I., Marshall, S., & Mitchell, G. (2003, July). *NESB student perceptions and attitudes to a new online learning environment.* Presentation at the Higher Education Research and Development Society of Australasia Conference, Christchurch, New Zealand.

Ellis, G. (1994). Contributions of cross-cultural research in the transfer of western teaching styles to Vietnam. *Asia-Pacific Exchange Journal, 1*(1), 199-212.

Ellis, R. (1992). *Understanding second language acquisition.* Oxford: Oxford University Press.

Ellis, R. (1997). *Second language acquisition.* Oxford: Oxford University Press.

English Teachers Risk Losing Skills (2006, April 20). *ELT News.* Retrieved from http://www.eltnews.com/news/archives/2006_04.shtml.

Erstad, O. (1996). Multimedia in educational settings: Prospects for learning. *Manuscript Series on Communication: Technology and Culture.* Retrieved from http://www.intermedia.uio.no/ktk/notater/pdf/notat4.pdf.

Eum, S. W. (2015, July 6). Number of foreign residents in S. Korea triples over ten years. *The Hankyoreh.* Retrieved from http://english.hani.co.kr/arti/english_edition/e_international/699034.html

Finch, A. E. (2000). *A formative evaluation of a task-based EFL programme for Korean university students.* Unpublished Ph.D. Thesis. The University of Manchester, Manchester, United Kingdom.

Finch, A. E. (2004). Web-based peer-assessment of student multi-media projects. *Multimedia and language testing* (pp. 149-156). Seoul: Korean Association of Multimedia Assisted Language Learning.

Finch, A. E. (2004, October). *An attitudinal profile of tertiary EFL learning in Korea.* Paper presented at the 2nd Asia International TEFL Conference, Seoul, South Korea.

Finch, A. E., & Hyun, T. D. (2000). *Tell me more!* Seoul: Hakmun Publishing.

Flattery, B. (2007). *Language, culture, and pedagogy: An overview of English in South Korea.* Retrieved from http://www.chass.utoronto.ca/~cpercy/courses/eng6365-flattery.htm.

Flege, J. (1995). Second language speech learning: theory, findings and problems. In W. Strange (Ed.), *Speech Perception and Linguistic Experience: Theoretical and Methodological Issues* (pp. 233-277). Baltimore, MD: York Press.

Folse, K. S. (2004). *Vocabulary myths.* Ann Arbor, MI: The University of Michigan Press.

Fraenkel, J., Wallen, N., Hyun, H. H. (2012). *How to design and evaluate research in education* (8th ed.). New York: McGraw-Hill.

Fujita, M., & Sano, T. (1988). Children in American and Japanese day-care centres: Ethnography and reflective cross-cultural interviewing. In H. T. Trueba & C. Delgado-Gaitan (Eds.), *School and Society: Learning through culture* (pp. 125-163). New York: McGraw-Hill.

Gardner, D., & Miller, L. (1999). *Establishing self-access: From theory to practice.* Cambridge: Cambridge University Press.

Gray, R. (1998). Confucian conundrums: Higher education and ESL teaching in Korea and Japan. *Advancing our profession: Perspectives on teacher development and education.* Seoul: Korea TESOL. Retrieved from http://www.kotesol.org/pubs/proceedings/1998/gray.pdf.

Graziadei, W. (1995). *Putting multimedia into the teaching-learning scholarship environment.* Retrieved from http://surryfact.buffalo.edu/cit95/papers/CIT95-PA.GRAZIA-1.

Guimaraes, N., Chambel, T., & Bidarra, J. (2000). From cognitive maps to hypervideo: Supporting flexible and rich learner-centered environments. *Interactive Multimedia Electronic Journal of Computer-Enhanced Learning, 2*(3). Retrieved from http://imej.wfu.edu/articles/2000/2/03/index.asp.

Hachigian, N. (2002). The internet and power in one-party East Asian states. *The Washington Quarterly, 25*(3), 41-58.

Han, Z. H. (2004). Fossilization: Five central issues. *International Journal of Applied Linguistics, 14*(2), 212-242.

Han, Z. H. (2004). *Fossilization in adult second language acquisition.* UK: Multilingual Matters Ltd.

Hannafin, M., Hannafin, K., Hooper, S., Rieber, L., & Kini, A. (1996). Research and research with emerging technologies. In D. H. Jonassen (Ed.), *Handbook for research for educational communications and technology* (pp. 378-402). New York: Simon & Schuster Macmillan.

Harely, B. (1993). Instructional strategies and SLA in early French immersion. *Studies in Second Language Acquisition, 15*, 245-259.

Haunz, C. (2003, May). Grammatical and non-grammatical factors in loanword adaptation. *Theoretical and Applied Linguistics University of Edinburgh Postgraduate Conference.* Retrieved from http://www.ling.ed.ac.uk/~pgc/archive/2003/proc03/Christine_Haunz03.pdf.

Healy, D. (1999). Classroom Practice: Communicative skill-building tasks in CALL environments. In J. Egbert & E. Hanson-Smith (Eds.). *CALL environments: Research, practice and critical issues* (pp. 116-136). Alexandria, VA: TESOL.

Hegelheimer, V., & Tower, D. (2004). Using CALL in the classroom: Analyzing student interactions in an authentic classroom. *System, 32*, 185–205.

Henrickson, B. (1999). Three dimensions on vocabulary development. *Studies in Second Language Acquisition, 21*(2), 303-317.

Hick, S. (1997). *Benefits of interactive multimedia courseware.* Retrieved from http://www.carleton.ca/~shick/mypage/benefit.html.

Higgins, J. (1986). The computer and grammar teaching. In G. Leech, & C. Candlin (Eds), *Computers in English language teaching and research* (pp. 31-45). New York: Longman.

Higgins, J. (1988). *Language, learners, and computers.* New York: Longman.

Hirano, H. (1994). A constraint based approach to Korean loanwords. *Language Research, 30*(4), 707-739.

Hofstede, G. (1986). Cultural differences in teaching and learning. *International Journal of Intercultural Relations, 10*, 301-320.

Hoh, H. J. (2005). Integrating an on-line education program into the university system. *E-learning and language education* (pp. 341-345). Chungbuk, Korea: Korean Association of Multimedia Assisted Language Learning.

Holec, H. (1987). The learner as manager: Managing learning or managing to learn? In A. Enden, & J. Rubin (Eds.), *Learner strategies in language learning* (pp. 145-156). London: Prentice Hall.

Holliday, A. (1999). Small cultures. *Applied Linguistics, 20*, 237-264.

Hong, S. G. (2002). Editing and using of sound files. *A new paradigm for innovative multimedia language education in the 21ˢᵗ century* (pp. 307-308). Seoul: Korean Association of Multimedia Assisted Language Learning.

Hope, G., Taylor, H., & Pusack, J. (1984). *Using computers for teaching foreign languages.* Orlando: Harcourt Brace Jovanovich.

Hubbard, P. (1987). Language teaching approaches, the evaluation of CALL software, and design implications. In W. Smith (Ed.), *Modern media in foreign language education: Theory and implementation* (pp. 227-254). Illinois: National Textbook Company.

Hubbard, P. (2004). Learner training for effect use of CALL. In S. Fotos, & C. M. Browne (Eds.), *New perspectives on CALL for second language classrooms* (pp. 45-68). New Jersey: Lawrence Erlbaum Associates.

Hulstijn, J. (1997). Mnemonic methods in foreign language vocabulary learning. In J. Coady, and T. Huckin (Eds.), *Second language vocabulary acquisition: A rationale for pedagogy* (pp. 203-224). Cambridge: Cambridge University Press.

Hwang, J. B. (2002). The state of web-based instruction in Korean elementary and secondary schools. *A new paradigm for innovative multimedia language education in the 21ˢᵗ century* (pp. 213-226). Seoul: Korean Association of Multimedia Assisted Language Learning.

Hymes, D. (1972). On communicative competence. In J. B. Pride and J. Holmes (Eds.), *Sociolinguistics* (pp. 269-293). Harmondsworth: Penguin.

Hyun, K. (2001). Sociocultural change and traditional values: Confucian values among Koreans and Korean Americans. *International Journal of Intercultural Relations, 25*, 203-229.

Im, I. S. (2002). The application of interactive game using pictures, sounds dictionary and java. The mechanism of changes to adapt ICT in education in Korea. *A new paradigm for innovative multimedia language education in the 21ˢᵗ century* (pp. 301-303). Seoul: Korean Association of Multimedia Assisted Language Learning.

Isobe, Miwa. (2007).The acquisition of nominal compounding in Japanese: A parametric approach. In Alyona Belikova, Luisa Meroni, and Mari Umeda, (Ed.), *The 2ⁿᵈ conference of generative approaches to language acquisition* (pp. 171-179). Somerville, MA: Cascadilla Proceedings Project.

Ito, J., & Mester, A. (1995a). Core-periphery structure of the lexicon and constraints on reranking. *University of Massachusetts Occasional Papers in Linguistics, 18*, 181-209.

Ito, J., & Mester, A. (1995b). Japanese phonology. In J. A. Goldsmith (Ed.), *The handbook of phonology theory*. Oxford: Blackwell Publishers.

Ito, J., & Mester, A. (1999). The phonological lexicon. ROA-256, *Rutgers Optimality Archive.*

Jacobs, H., & Gussenhoven, C. (2000). Loan phonology: perception, salience, the lexicon and OT. In J. Dekkers, F. van der Leeuw, & J. van de Weijer (Ed.), *Optimality theory: Phonology, syntax and acquisition* (pp. 193-210). Oxford: Oxford University Press.

James, C. (1998). *Errors in language learning and use*. Harlow: Addison Wesley Longman.

Jenkins, J. (2000). *The phonology of English as an international language*. New York: Oxford University Press.

Jenkins, J. (2003). *World Englishes: A resource book for students*. USA: Routledge.

Jeon, J., & Kim, E. (2001). Teacher training through self-observation. *Journal of the Applied Linguistics Association of Korea, 17*(2), 157-177.

Jeon, I. J., & Hahn, J. W. (2006). Exploring EFL teachers perceptions of task-based language teaching: A case study of South Korean secondary school classroom practice. *Asian EFL Journal, 8*(1), 1-27.

Jeong, K. C. (2002). Web-based language learning: A case study. *A New Paradigm for Innovative Multimedia Language Education in the 21ˢᵗ Century* (pp. 254-263). Seoul: Korean Association of Multimedia Assisted Language Learning.

Johnson, D D., & Pearson, P. D. (1984). *Teaching reading vocabulary.* (2nd ed.). New York: Holt, Rhinehart & Winston.

Jonassen, D.H. (1991). Objectivism versus constructivism: Do we need a new philosophical paradigm? *Educational Technology Research and Development, 39*(3), 5-14.

Joo, Y. (1997). Teaching the grammar of narratives to Korean EFL students, in "Modules to Teach Grammar from Discourse". *Journal of English Grammar on the Web, 1*. Georgia State University.

Joyce, B., & Weil, M. (1986). *Models of Teaching* (3rd Ed.). Sydney: Allyn and Bacon.

Jun, S. A. (1996). *The phonetics and phonology of Korean prosody: Intonational phonology and prosodic structure.* New York: Garland Publications.

Jung, I. (2000). Korea's experiments with virtual education. *Education and Technology Notes Series, 5*(2). World Bank Human Development Network.

Jung, Y. S. (2000). Effects of a cooperative learning approach to MALL (Multimedia Assisted Language Learning). *Multimedia Assisted Language Learning, 3*(1) 9-46.

Jung, Y. S. (2001). Toward an effective EFL teacher development program focusing on multimedia and the internet. *English Teaching, 56*(4), 141-162.

Kachru, B. (1998). English as an Asian language. *Links & Letters,* 5, 89-108.

Kachru, B. (2005). *Asian Englishes: Beyond the canon.* Hong Kong: Hong Kong University Press.

Kang, H. S. (1996). English loanwords in Korean. *Studies in Phonetics, Phonology and Morphology, 2,* 21-48.

Kang, H. S. (2000). A study of the effectiveness of internet English reading class. *Multimedia Assisted Language Learning, 2*(2), 88-103.

Kang, J. (2002). Reorganization of CD-ROM titles for the 3rd and 4th grades of elementary school using multimedia tools. *A new paradigm for innovative multimedia language education in the 21st century* (pp. 295-298). Seoul: Korean Association of Multimedia Assisted Language Learning.

Kang, Y. J. (2003). Perceptual similarity in loanword adaptation: English postvocalic word-final stops in Korean. *Phonology, 20*(2), 219-273.

Keem, S. U. (2000). A field study: Multimedia assisted English instruction to cultivate communicative competence. *Multimedia Assisted Language Learning, 3*(1), 139-166.

Kenstowicz, M. (2001). The role of perception in loanword phonology. A review of Les emprunts linguistiques d'origine europenne en Fon by Flavien Gbeto, Koln: Rudiger Koppe Verlage. *Linguistique Africaine, XX.*

Kenstowicz, M. (2005, February). *The phonetics and phonology of Korean loanword adaptation.* Paper presented at the First European Conference on Korean Linguistics, Leiden, Netherlands.

Kent, D. B. (1996). *Kent Konglish Dictionary,* [Software Download]. Kent Interactive Labs. Retrieved from http://www.geocities.com/Tokyo/Towers/5067/kkd.html

Kent, D. B. (1997). The practice of TESOL and the effect of individual variables upon TESOL students. *The Internet TESOL Journal, 4*(4).

Kent, D. B. (2000). Speaking in tongues: Chinglish, Japlish, and Konglish. *Teaching English: Asian contexts and cultures,* (pp. 197-209). Seoul: Korea TESOL.

Kent, D. B. (2001, October). *Teaching Konglish: Selected resources for students and teachers.* Paper presented at the 2001 Korea TESOL International Conference, Seoul, Korea.

Kent, D. B. (2004). CALL initiatives and the Korean cultural learning context. In J. B. Son (Ed.), *Computer-Assisted Language Learning: Concepts, Contexts, and Practices* (pp. 59-82). New York: iUniverse.

KERIS (2001). *Adapting education to the information age: A white paper.* Korea: Korean Education and Research Information Service.

Kim, D., Kim, K., Park, Y., Zhang, L., Lu, K., & Li, D. (2000). Children's experience of violence in China and Korea: A transcultural study. *Child Abuse and Neglect, 24*(9), 1163-1173.

Kim, I. O. (2000). Accommodating language learners' different learning styles with multimedia technology. *Multimedia Assisted Language Learning, 3(2),* 36-52.

Kim, J. R. (1999). A study of developing elementary English course design incorporating multimedia technology. *Multimedia Assisted Language Learning,* 2(1), 74-99.

Kim, J. S. (2006 August, 24). Konglish as a second language? *The Korea Herald.*

Kim, S. A. (2000). Enhancing cultural understanding: An instructional model. *English Teaching, 55*(4), 141-166.

Kim, S. Y. (2002a). Korean college students reflections of English language learning via CMC and FFC. *Multimedia Assisted Language Learning, 5*(2), 9-28.

Kim, S. Y. (2002b). Teachers' perceptions about teaching English through English. *English Teaching, 57*(1), 131-148.

Kimura, M. (1989). *The effect of Japanese loanwords on the acquisition of the correct range of meanings of English words.* Unpublished master's thesis, Bringham Young University, Provo, Utah, USA.

Klassen, J., Detaramani, C., Lui, E., Patri, M., & Wu, J. (1998). Does self-access learning at the tertiary level really work? *Asian Journal of English Language Teaching, 8*, 55-80.

Koda, K. (1997). Orthographic knowledge in L2 lexical processing: A crosslinguistic perspective. In J. Coady, & T. Huckin (Eds.), *Second language vocabulary acquisition: a rationale for pedagogy* (pp. 35-52). Cambridge: Cambridge University Press.

Koehler, R. (2006 July, 10). Koreas growing internationalization. *Seoul Today.*

Koh, B. I. (1996). Confucianism in contemporary Korea. In W. Tu (Ed.), *Confucian traditions in East Asian modernity* (pp. 190-201). USA: Harvard University Press.

Kolarik, K. (2004). *Loosening the grip on the communicative ideal – A cultural perspective.* Paper presented at the17th Educational Conference, Adelaide, Australia.

Koprowski, M. (2006). Ten good games for recycling vocabulary. *Internet TESL Journal, 7*(7).

Kosofsky, D. (1986). *Common problems in Korean English.* Seoul: Waygook eh yeonsusa.

Kosofosky, D. (1990). Exploring Korean culture through Korean English. *Korea Journal, 30*(11), 69-83.

Kozma, R. B. (1994). The influence of media on learning: The debate continues. *School Library Media Research 22*(4).

Krashen, S. D. (1985). *The input hypothesis: Issues and implications.* London: Longman.

KRNIC. (2000). *Internet statistics information system.* Korea Network Information Center.

Kubota, R. (2001). Discursive construction of the images of U.S. classrooms. *Tesol Quarterly, 35*(1), 9-38.

Kupferberg, I. (1999). The cognitive turn of contrastive analysis: Empirical evidence. *Language Awareness, 8*(3), 210-222.

Kwon, C. J. (2002). A study on the attitude and perception of university students words using computers and the internet for learning English. *Foreign Languages Education, 9*(3), 185-210.

Kwon, C. J. (2004). University students perceptions of multimedia-assisted language learning. *Multimedia Assisted Language Learning, 7*(1), 55-81.

Kwon, C. J. (2005). Developing effective multimedia-assisted teaching in university education. *Multimedia Assisted Language Learning, 8*(1), 169-196.

Kwon, O. Y. (2000). Korea's English education policy changes in the 1990s: Innovations to gear the nation for the 21st century. *English Teaching, 55*(1), 47-91.

Lado, R. (1952). *Linguistics across cultures*. Michigan: University of Michigan Press.

Larson-Freeman, D. (1997). Chaos, complexity science, and second language acquisition. *Applied linguistics, 18*(2), 141-65.

Larson-Freeman, D., & Long, M. (1991). *An introduction to second language acquisition research*. New York: Longman.

Laufer, B., & Shmueli, K. (1997). Memorizing new words: Does teaching have anything to do with it? *RELC Journal, 28*, 89-108.

Laurillard, D., Stratfold, M., Luckin, R., Plowman, L., & Taylor, J. (2000). Affordances for learning in a non-linear narrative medium. *Journal of Interactive Media in Education, 2*.

Lee, B., Lee S. H., Park, C. B., & Kang, S. K. (1999). Korean speakers' perception and production of English word-final voiceless stop release. *Malsori, 38*, 41-70.

Lee, B. R. (2001). The liquid lexicalization and nativization in Sino-Korean and English loans. *Studies in Phonetics, Phonology and Morphology, 7*(1), 101-124.

Lee, C. H. (2000). Communicative activities applicable to CALL: Based on computer simulations. *Multimedia Assisted Language Learning, 3*(2), 70-99.

Lee, C. H., & Pyo, K. H. (2002). The development and implementation of the online/offline English language education program (OELEP). *A new paradigm for innovative multimedia language education in the 21st century* (pp. 69-80). Seoul: Korean Association of Multimedia Assisted Language Learning.

Lee, C. I., & Yang, E. M. (2002). Integrating CALL into classroom practices: Its theory and application. *A new paradigm for innovative multimedia language education in the 21st century* (pp. 169-183). Seoul: Korean Association of Multimedia Assisted Language Learning.

Lee, C. I. (2000). The effectiveness diagnosis of 'TOWUMI'. *Multimedia Assisted Language Learning, 3*(1), 247-263.

Lee, H. (2005). Psychological human-computer interface model in individual and collaborative CALL under classroom situations. *Multimedia Assisted Language Learning, 8*(1), 197-219.

Lee, H. J. (2001). *The role of native-English-speaking teachers in the Korean EFL education system.* Retrieved from http://www.mantoman.co.kr/issues/m032/m3201.htm.

Lee, I. S. (2002). Gender differences in self-regulated on-line learning strategies within Korea's university context. *Educational Technology, Research, and Design, 50*(1), 101-121.

Lee, J. J. (2004). The impact of English on the Post-1945South Korean Vernacular. *Karen's Linguistic Issues, March 2004.*

Lee, K. W. (2000). English Teachers' barriers to the use of computer-assisted language learning. *The Internet TESL Journal, 6*(12).

Lee, M. (2001). *A critical analysis of mandatory computer education for elementary school children in Korea: In the aspect of intellectual development.* Paper presented at the Enhancement of Quality Learning through Information and Communication Technology International Conference in Education, New Zealand.

Lee, P. (1997). Language in thinking and learning: pedagogy and the new Whorfian framework. *Harvard Educational Review, 67*(3), 430-472.

Lee, P. H. (1995). Korean loanword phonology: An optimality perspective. *Korean Journal of Linguistics, 20*(2), 121-151.

Lee, S. W. (2003). Korean ESL Learners' experiences in computer assisted classroom discussions. *English Teaching, 58*(4), 371-394.

Lee, S. W. (2005). ESL Students' beliefs about the utility of synchronous online discussion (SOD) in language learning and their participation in the SOD. *Multimedia Assisted Language Learning, 8*(2), 9-31.

Lee, Y. J. (2000). Integrating multimedia with communicative EFL methodology. *Multimedia Assisted Language Learning, 3*(1), 94-118.

Lee, Y. J., & Kastner, M. (1999). Multimedia in performance-based EFL classes. *Multimedia Assisted Language Learning, 2*(1), 21-34.

Lees, R. (1961). *The phonology of modern standard Turkish*. Bloomington: Indiana University Press.

Legenhausen, L., & Wolff, D. (1987). CALL at the crossroads? In L. Legenhausen, & D. Wolff (Eds.), *Computer assisted language learning and innovative EFL methodology* (pp. 3-10). Augsburg: Thomas Finkenstaedt und Konrad Schroder.

Levy, M. (1997). *Computer–assisted language learning: Context and conceptualization*. Oxford: Clarendon.

Levy, M., & Stockwell, G. (2006). *CALL dimensions: Options and issues in computer-assisted language learning*. New Jersey: Lawrence Erlbaum Associates.

Lewis, M. (1993). *The lexical approach: The state of ELT and the way forward*. Hove, England: Language Teaching Publications.

Lewis, M. (1997a). *Implementing the lexical approach: Putting theory into practice*. Hove, England: Language Teaching Publications.

Lewis, M. (1997b). Pedagogical implications of the lexical approach. In J. Coady & T. Huckin (Eds.), *Second language vocabulary acquisition: A rationale for pedagogy* (pp. 255-270). Cambridge: Cambridge University Press.

Li, D. (1998). It's always more difficult than you plan and imagine: Teachers' perceived difficulties in introducing the communicative approach in South Korea. *TESOL Quarterly, 32*(4), 677-703.

Lim, B. J. (2001). The role of syllable weight and position on prominence in Korean. *Japanese/Korean Linguistics, 9*, 420-433.

Lim, H. Y., & Griffith, W. I. (2003). Successful classroom discussions with adult Korean ESL/EFL learners. *The Internet TESL Journal, 9*(5).

Littlewood, W. (1999). Defining and developing autonomy in East Asian contexts. *Applied Linguistics, 20*(1), 71-94.

Littlewood, W. (2000). Do Asian students really want to listen and obey? *ELT Journal, 54*(1), 31-35.

Liu, D. (1998). Ethnocentrism in TESOL: Teacher education and the neglected needs of international TESOL students. *ELT Journal, 52*(1), 3-10.

Liu, N. F. & Littlewood, W. (1997). Why do many students appear reluctant to participate in classroom learning discourse? *System, 25*(3), 371-384.

Lynch, R. (2003). Media technology and language learning: Maximizing the potential – the need for a learner-centered teaching and research agenda. *Media technology and its impact on foreign language education: Past, present, and future* (pp. 29-44). Seoul: Korean Association of Multimedia Assisted Language Learning.

MacWhinney, B. (2005). Emergent fossilization. In Z. Han, & T. Odlin *Perspectives on fossilization*. UK: Multilingual Matters.

Malhotra, B. (2002). *Shut the classroom doors! The computers must stay! Or reintegrating reading and writing skills through computer-mediated-communication.* Paper presented at the Second National ELT Conference, Muscat, Oman.

Mandernach, J. (2003). *Multiple-choice*. Retrieved from http://captain.park.edu/facultydevelopment/multiple-choice.htm.

Mayer, R. (2001). *Multimedia learning*. United Kingdom: Cambridge University Press.

McArthur, T. (1992). *The Oxford companion to the English language*. New York: Oxford University Press.

McArthur, T. (2003). *The Oxford guide to world Englishes*. USA: Oxford University Press.

McCawley, J. (1968) The phonological component of a grammar of modern Japanese. The Hague: Mouton.

McDonough, S. H. (1995). *Strategy and skill in learning a foreign language*. New York: E. Arnold.

MEHRD. (2002). *Education in Korea 2001-2002*. Korea: Ministry of Education and Human Resources Development.

Miller, J. (2003). *A word by any other meaning: Konglish*. Retrieved December from http://www.macmillandictionary.com/MED-Magazine/March2003/05-Korean-English.htm#1.

Min, B. (1998). A study of the attitudes of Korean adults toward technology-assisted language learning. *Multimedia-Assisted Language Learning, 1*(1), 63-78.

Min, S. J., Kim, H. K., & Jung, K. T. (2000). A paradigm shift in English education in Korea: Integration of the textbook to a web-based curriculum. *Multimedia Assisted Language Learning, 3*(1), 119-138.

MOGIT. (n.d.). *Information technology landscape in Korea.* USA: American University, Management of Global Information Technology.

MOJ. (2015). *The Sojourn Guide for Foreigners.* Korea Immigration Service.

Moudraia, O. (2001). Lexical approach to second language teaching. *CAL Digest.*

Nagy, W. E., Herman, P., & Anderson, R. C. (1985). Learning words from context. *Reading Research Quarterly, 20*, 233-253.

Nakuma, C. (1998). A new theoretical account of 'fossilization': implications for L2 attrition research. *International Review of Applied Linguistics in Language Teaching, 36*(3), 247-257.

Nam, J. Y., & Southard, B. (1994). Orthographic representation and resyllabification of English loanwords in Korean. *Language and speech, 37*(3), 259-281.

Nation, P. (1990). *Teaching and learning vocabulary.* Boston: Heinle and Heinle Publishing.

Nation, P. (2001). *Learning vocabulary in another language.* Cambridge: Cambridge University Press.

Nation, P. (2003). The role of the first language in foreign language learning. *Asian EFL Journal, 5*(2), 1-8.

Nation, P., & Newton, J. (1997). Teaching vocabulary. In J. Coady, & T. Huckin (Eds.), *Second vocabulary acquisition: a rational for pedagogy* (pp. 238-254). Cambridge: Cambridge University Press.

National Computerization Agency. (2006). *Informatization white paper 2006.* Retrieved from http://www.ipc.go.kr/ipceng/public/public_view.jsp?num=2360&fn=&req=&pgno=1.

NCiC. (2015). National Curriculum of Korea Source Inventory. Retrieved from http://ncic.kice.re.kr/english.kri.org.inventoryList.do.

Newman, R. S. (1994). Academic help seeking: A strategy of self-regulated learning. In D. H. Schunk, & B. J. Zimmerman (Eds.), *Self-regulation of learning and performance: Issues and educational applications* (pp. 283-301). Hillsdale, NJ: Lawrence Erlbaum Associates.

Nicholls, D. (2002). What is learner English? *MED Magazine, 1*(10).

Nickel, G. (1998). The role of interlanguage in foreign language teaching. *International Review of Applied Linguistics in Language Teaching, 36*(1), 1-10.

Niederhauser, J. S. (1997). Motivating learners at South Korean universities. *Forum, 35*(1), 8-16.

NIIED. (2002). *Korea's education system.* Korea: National Institute for International Education Development.

Norrish, J. (1997). english or English? Attitudes, local varieties and English language teaching. *TESL-EJ, 3*(1), 1.

O, K. M. (2005). University students' reactions to taking a web-based English reading achievement test. *Multimedia Assisted Language Learning, 8*(1), 250-280.

O'Donnell, T. J. (2006). Learning English as a foreign language in Korea: Does CALL have a place? *Asian EFL Journal, 10*, 1-27.

O'Hagan, C. (1999). Embedding ubiquitous educational technology: Is it possible, do we want it, and, if so, how do we achieve it? *Educational Technology and Society, 2*(4), 19-22.

Odlin, T., Alonso, R., & Alonso-Vazquez, C. (2006). Fossilization in L2 and L3. In Z. H. Han, & T. Odlin (Eds.), *Studies of fossilization in second language acquisition* (pp. 83-99). UK: Multilingual Matters.

Office for Government Policy Coordination. (2006). *Selected Public Policies of Korea.* Retrieved from http://www.korea.net/kois/eng_il_read.asp?book_no=54.

Oh, M. (1996). Linguistic input to phonology. *Studies in Phonetics, Phonology and Morphology, 2*, 117-126.

Oh, M. (2003a). Beginning-level adult English learners' initial beliefs about MALL. *A new perspective on the use of CMC (Computer-Mediated Communication) in foreign language education* (pp. 155-159). Daejeon, Korea: Korean Association of Multimedia Assisted Language Learning.

Oh, M. (2003b). A group of primary school children's initial beliefs about MALL. *Media technology and its impact on foreign language education: Past, present, and future* (pp. 105-108). Seoul: Korean Association of Multimedia Assisted Language Learning.

Ok, K. Y. (2005). Discourses of English as an official language in a monolingual society: The case of South Korea. *Second Language Studies, 23*(2), 1-44.

Oka, H. (2004). A non-native approach to ELT: Universal or Asian? *Asian EFL Journal, 6*(1), 1-8.

Oxford, R. L. (2003). Language learning styles and strategies: An overview. *GALA 2003*. Retrieved from http://www.education.umd.edu/EDCI/SecondLangEd/TESOL/People/Faculty/Dr. Oxford/StylesStrategies.doc

Oxford, R., Rivera-Costillo, Y., Feyten, C., & Nutta, J. (1998). *Computers and more: Creative uses of technology for learning a second or foreign language*. Retrieved from http://www.insa-lyon.fr/Departments/CDRL/computers.html.

Pak, Y. (1999). College English textbooks: An analysis of their cultural content. *English Teaching, 54*(1), 43-66.

Palloff, R. M., & Pratt, K. (2001). *Lessons from the cyberspace classroom: The realities of online teaching*. San Francisco: Jossey-Bass.

Pang, M. S. J. (2002). The mechanism of changes to adapt ICT in education in Korea. *A New Paradigm for Innovative Multimedia Language Education in the 21st Century* (pp. 281-288), Seoul: Korean Association of Multimedia Assisted Language Learning.

Pankuch, B. (1998). *Multimedia in lectures and on the world wide web*. Retrieved from http://www.eclipse.net/~pankuch/Newsletter/Pages_News/Archive/MM-Prin-FINAL2.pdf.

Paradis, Lebel, (1984). Contrasts from segmental parameter settings in loanwords: Core and periphery in Quebec French. In Carrie Dick (dir.). *Proceedings of the MOT Conference in Phonology*, 75-95. University of Toronto: Department of Linguistics.

Park, C. C. (2002). Crosscultural differences in learning styles of secondary English learners. *Bilingual Research Journal, 26*(2), 443-459.

Park, H. Y. (2007). Varied adaption patterns of English stops and fricatives in Korean loanwords: The influence of the P-map. *IULC Working Papers Online, 7*, 1-25.

Park, J. E. (2001). Korean EFL learners' vocabulary learning strategies. *English Teaching, 56*, 4, 3-30.

Park, S. O. (1998). Globalization in Korea: Dream and reality. *GeoJournal, 45*(1), 123-128.

Park, Y., & Oxford, R. (1998). Changing roles for teachers in the English village course in Korea. *System, 26*, 107-113.

Paul, P. V., Stallman, A. C., & O'Rourke, J. P. (1990). *Using three test formats to assess good and poor readers' word knowledge* (Technical report no. 509) University of Illinois at Urbana-Champaign: Center for the Study of Reading.

Peck, J. (1992). *The Chomsky reader.* New York: Pantheon Books.

Pennington, M. & Vance Stevens (Eds.) (1992). *Computers in applied linguistics: An international perspective.* Clevedon: Multilingual Matters.

Pennycook, A. (1994). *The cultural politics of English as an international language.* New York: Longman.

Pennycook, A. (1996). Borrowing others' words: Text, ownership, memory, and plagiarism. *TESOL Quarterly, 30*, 201-230.

Peperkamp, S. (2004, February). *A psycholinguistic theory of loanword adaptations.* Paper presented at the 30th Annual Meeting of the Berkeley Linguistics Society.

Peperkamp, S., & Dupoux, E. (2003, August). *Reinterpreting loanword adaptations: the role of perception.* Paper presented at the 15th International Congress of Phonetic Sciences.

Pierson, H. D. (1996). Learner culture and learner autonomy in the Hong Kong Chinese context. In R. Pemberton, E. S. L., Li, W. W. F., Or & H. D. Pierson (Eds.), *Taking Control: Autonomy in Language Learning* (pp. 49–58). Hong Kong: Hong Kong University Press.

Pit Corder, S. (1967). The significance of learners' errors. *International Review of Applied Linguistics, 5*, 161-169.

Plagued by mangled English, South Korea struggles to improve skills (2000, June 2). *The Korea Herald.*

Postman, N. (1993) *Technopoly: The surrender of culture to technology*. New York: Vintage Books.

Powell, G. (1998). *What is the role of interlanguage in fossilization?* Working papers. Lancaster University: Centre for Research in Education.

Prensky, M. (2001). Digital natives, digital immigrants. *On the Horizon, 8*(5).

Prince, P. (1996). Second language vocabulary learning: The role of context versus translations as a function of proficiency. *The Modern Language Journal, 80*, 478-493.

Prince, A., & Smolensky, P. (1993). *Optimality theory: Constraint interaction in generative grammar*. USA: Blackwell publishing.

Pusack, J., & Otto, S. (1997). Taking control of multimedia. In M. Bush, & R. Terry (Eds.), *Technology-Enhanced Language Learning* (pp. 1-46). Illinois: National Textbook Company.

Qian, D. (1999). Assessing the roles of depth and breadth of vocabulary knowledge in reading comprehension. *The Canadian Modern Language Review, 56*(2).

Quirk,R. (1990). Language varieties and standard language. *English Today, 21*, 3-10.

Raschio, R. (1986). Communicative uses of the computer: Ideas and directions. *Foreign Language Annals, 19*(6), 507-513.

Rao, Z. H. (2001). Matching teaching styles with learning styles in East Asia. *The Internet TESOL Journal, 7*(7).

Rao, Z. (2002). Bridging the gap between teaching and learning styles in East Asian contexts. *TESOL Journal, 11*(2), 5-11.

Ravid, R. (2000). *Practical statistics for educators* (2nd Ed). Maryland: University Press of America.

Reid, J. M. (1987). The learning style preferences of ESL students. *TESOL Quarterly, 21*(1), 81-111.

Richards, J. C. (1971). A non-contrastive approach to error analysis. *English Language Teaching, 25*(3), 204-219.

Richards, J. C., & Rogers, T. S. (2001). *Approaches and methods in language teaching: A description and analysis* (2nd Ed.). Cambridge: Cambridge University Press.

Richards, J. C., & Rogers, T. S. (2014). *Approaches and methods in language teaching: A description and analysis* (3rd Ed.). Cambridge: Cambridge University Press.

Riley, P. (1997). The guru and the conjurer: Aspects of counselling for self-access. In P. Benson, & P. Voller (Eds.), *Autonomy and independence in language learning* (pp. 114-131). New York: Longman.

Robertson, P. (2002a). Asian EFL research protocols. *Asian EFL Journal, 4*(1).

Robertson, P. (2002b). The pervading influence of neo-Confucianism on the Korean education system. *Asian EFL Journal, 4*(2).

Robertson, P. (2003). Teaching English pronunciation skills to the Asian learner: A cultural complexity or subsumed piece of cake? *Asian EFL Journal, 5*(2), 1-26.

Rodby, J., & Winterowd, W. R. (2004). Grammar and language diversity. Additional chapter from companion website. In J. Rodby & R. W. Winterowd, *The uses of Grammar* (pp. 1-49).

Rodriguez, M. C. (2005). Three options are optimal for multiple-choice items: A meta-analysis of 80 years of research. *Educational Measurement, Issues and Practice, 24*(2), 3-7.

Romanoski, J., & Douglas, G. (2002). Test scores, measurement, and the use of analysis of variance: An historical overview. *Journal of Applied Measurement, 3*(3), 232-242.

RUMMLab. (2004). *Interpreting RUMM 2020*. Perth, Western Australia: RUMMLab.

Schachter, J. (1983). Nutritional needs of language learners. In M. A. Clark, & J. Handscombe. (Eds.). *On TESOL '82: Pacific Perspectives on Language Learning and Teaching* (pp. 175-189). Washington, DC: TESOL.

Schachter, J. (1996). Maturation and the issue of Universal Grammar in second language acquisition. In W. Ritchie, & T. Bhatia (Eds.), *Handbook of second language acquisition* (pp. 159-194). San Diego: Academic Press.

Schapiro, S. R., & Livingston, J. A. (2000). Dynamic self-regulation: The driving force behind academic achievement. *Innovative Higher Education, 25*(1), 23-35.

Schar, S., Schluep, S., Schierz, C., & Krueger, H. (2000). Interaction for computer-aided learning. *Interactive Multimedia Electronic Journal of Computer-Enhanced Learning, 1*(3).

Schmitt, N. (1997). Vocabulary learning strategies. In N. Schmitt, & M. McCarthy (Eds.), *Vocabulary: Description, Acquisition, and Pedagogy* (pp. 199-227). Cambridge: Cambridge University Press.

Schmitt, N. (2000). *Vocabulary in language teaching.* Cambridge: Cambridge University Press.

Schulz, R. A. (2001). Cultural differences in student and teacher perceptions concerning the role of grammar instruction and corrective feedback. *The Modern Language Journal, 85*(2), 244-258.

Seliger, H. (1998). Psycholinguistic issues in second language acquisition. In L. Beebe (Ed.), *Issues in second language acquisition: Multiple perspectives.* New York: Longman.

Selinker, L. (1971). The psychologically relevant data of second language learning. In P. Pimsleur, & T. Quinne (Ed.) *The psychology of second language learning.* London: Cambridge University Press.

Selinker, L. (1972). Interlanguage. *IRAL, 10*(2), 209-31.

Selinker, L. (1992). *Rediscovering interlanguage.* London: Longman.

Selinker. L, & Lamendella, J. (1978). Two perspectives on fossilization in interlanguage learning. *Interlanguage Studies Bulletin, 3*(2), 143-91.

Seth, M. J. (2002). *Education fever.* USA: University of Hawaii Press.

Shaffer, D. (1999, October). *Picture that! – Drawing techniques for teaching false cognates.* Paper presented at the Second Pan-Asian International Conference, Seoul, Korea.

Shaffer, D. (2001). A new approach for a new language. *The Internet TEFL Journal, 35.*

Sheperd, J. W. (1996). Loanwords a pitfall for all students. *The Internet TESOL Journal 2*(2), 1-8.

Shim, J. Y. (1994). Englishized Korean: Structure, status and attitudes. *World Englishes, 13*(2), 225-244.

Shim, Rosa Jinyoung. (1999). Codified Korean English: Process, characteristics, and consequence. *World Englishes, 18*(2), 247-258.

Shin, Gi-Wook. (2003). *The paradox of Korean globalization* (Working paper). Stanford University: Asia/Pacific Research Center (APARC).

Shinohara, S. (2001). Emergence of universal grammar in foreign word adaptation. In R. Kager, J. Pater, & W. Zonneveld (Eds.), *Fixing priorities: constraints in phonological acquisition.* Cambridge: Cambridge University Press.

Silverman, D. (1992). Multiple scansions in loanword phonology: Evidence from Cantonese. *Phonology, 9*, 289-328.

Simon-Maeda, A. (1997) Language awareness: Use/misuse of loan-words in the English language in Japan. *The Internet TESOL Journal, 1*(2).

Smith, J. (2006). Loan phonology is not all perception: Evidence from Japanese loan doublets. *Japanese/Korean Linguistics, 14*, 63-74. Prepublication version.

Son, B. (Ed.). (2004). *Computer-assisted language learning: Concepts, contexts, and practices.* New York: iUniverse.

Soper, J. (1997). Integrating interactive media in courses: The WinEcon software with workbook approach. *Journal of Interactive Media in Education, 97*(2), 1-39.

Spencer, K. A. (1999). Educational Technology – An unstoppable force: A selective review of research into the effectiveness of educational media. *Educational Technology & Society, 2*(4), 23-34.

Spolsky, B. (1989). *Conditions for second language learning: Introduction to a general theory.* USA: Oxford University Press.

Stepp-Greany, J. (2002). Student perception on language learning in a technological environment: Implications for the new millennium. *Language Learning & Technology, 6*(1), 165-180.

Steraide, D. (2001). Directional asymmetries in place assimilation: A perceptual account. In E. Hume, & K. Johnson (Ed.), *The role of speech perception in phonology* (pp. 219-50). San Diego: Academic Press.

Stoney, S., & Oliver, R. (1999). Can higher order thinking and cognitive engagement be enhanced with multimedia? *Interactive Multimedia Electronic Journal of Computer-Enhanced Learning, 2*(7).

Styles, I., & Andrich, D. (1993). Linking the standard and advanced forms of the Raven's Progressive Matrices in both the pencil-and-paper and computer-adaptive testing formats. *Educational and Psychological Measurement, 53*(4), 905-925.

Tanaka, T. (1997). *Gairaigo origins – Japanese loanwords with interesting origins.* Retrieved from http://www.cs.indiana.edu/hyplan/tanaka/other_tanaka/gairaigo.txt.

Tarone, E. (2006) Fossilization, social context and language play. In Z. H. Han, & T. Odlin (Eds.), *Studies of fossilization in second language acquisition* (pp. 157-172). UK: Multilingual Matters.

Taylor, A. K. (2005). Violating conventional wisdom in multiple choice test construction. *College Student Journal, 39*(1), 141-148.

Taylor, M. B., & Perez, L. M. (1989). *Something to Do on Monday.* La Jolla: Athelstan Publishers.

Taylor, I. S., & Taylor, M. M. (1995). *Writing and literacy in Chinese, Korean and Japanese.* Philadelphia: John Benjamins.

Taylor, R. (Ed.). (1980). *The computer in the school: Tutor, tool, tutee.* New York: Teachers College Press.

Terry, M. (2001). Translating learning style theory into university teaching practices: An article based on Kolb's experimental learning model. *Journal of College Reading and Learning, 32*(1), 68-65.

THINQ. (n.d.). *How e-learning can increase ROI for training.* Retrieved from http://www.thinq.com/pages/new_wp_IncreaseTheROI.htm.

Tran, T. (1997, December). *Why a world Englishes perspective should be infused into English language education programs?* Paper presented at the Australian association for research in education conference, Brisbane, Australia.

Tretiakov, A., Kinshuk, A., & Tretiakov, T. (2003, July). *Designing multimedia support for situated learning.* Paper presented at the 3rd IEEE international conference on advanced learning technologies. Athens, Greece.

Trofimovich, P., & Baker, W. (2006). Effect of L2 experience on prosody and fluency characteristics of L2 speech. *SSLA, 28*, 1-30.

Troudi, S. (2005). Critical content and cultural knowledge for teachers of English to speakers of other languages. *Teacher Development, 9*(1), 115-129.

Underwood, B. J., Runquist, W. N., & Schulz, R. W. (1959). Response learning in paired-associate lists as a function of intralist similarity. *Journal of Experimental Psychology, 58*(1), 70-78.

Underwood, J. (1984). *Linguistics, computers, and the language teacher: A communicative approach.* Rowley, MA: Newbury house.

UNESCO (2002). *ICT for Education in Asia-Pacific.* United Nations Educational, Scientific and Cultural Organization.

Vercoe, T. (2007, June). *'Playing with myself again' - L1 interference in the L2 and Konglish.* Paper presented at the 2007 KNU-KOTESOL International Conference on English Language Teaching, Daegu, Korea.

Vigil, N., & Oller, J. W. (1976). Rule fossilization: A tentative model. *Language Learning, 26*, 281-95.

Vygotsky, L. S. (1978). *Mind in society: The development of higher psychological process.* (M. V. Cole, V. John-Steiner, S. Scribner, & E. Souberman, Eds., Trans.). Cambridge: Harvard University Press.

Wardhaugh, R. (1970). The contrastive analysis hypothesis. *TESOL Quarterly, 4*(2), 123-130.

Warschauer, M. (1996). Computer-assisted language learning: An introduction. In S. Fotos (Ed.), *Multimedia language teaching* (pp. 3-20). Tokyo: Logos International.

Waschull, S. B. (2005). Predicting success in online psychology courses: Self-discipline and motivation. *Teaching of Psychology, 32*(3), 190-192.

Waugh, R. F., & Cavanagh, R. F. (2002). Measuring parent receptivity towards the classroom environment using a Rasch measurement model. *Journal of Learning Environments Research, 5*(3), 329-352.

Werker, J. F., & Tees, R. C. (1984). Cross-language speech perception: Evidence for perceptual reorganization during the first year of life. *Infant Behavior and Development, 7*, 49-63.

Weschler, R. (1997). Uses of Japanese (L1) in the English classroom: Introducing the functional-translation method. *The Internet TESL Journal, 3*(11). Retrieved July 23, 2003 from http://iteslj.org/Articles/Weschler-UsingL1.html.

Wigglesworth, G. (2002). The role of the first language in the second language classroom: Friend or foe. *English Teaching, 57*(1), 17-31.

Williams, P. E., & Hellman, C. M. (2004). Differences in self-regulation for online learning between first- and second-generation college students. *Research in Higher Education, 45*(1), 71-82.

Willis, D. (1990). *The lexical syllabus: The new approach to language teaching*. London: Collins COBUILD.

Windle, S. (2003). Culture in the Korean EFL classroom: A humanizing process. *The English Connection, 7*(1). KOTESOL Newsletter.

Winn, W., & Snyder, D. (1996). Cognitive perspectives in psychology. In D. H. Jonassen (Ed.), *Handbook of research for educational communications in technology* (pp. 112-142). New York: Simon and Schuster Macmillan.

Wittrock, M. C. (1990). Generative process of comprehension. *Educational Psychologist, 24*, 345-376.

Wyatt, D. (1987). Applying pedagogical principles to CALL courseware development. In W. Smith (Ed.), *Modern media in foreign language education: Theory and implementation* (pp. 85-98). Illinois: National Textbook Company.

Yamaguchi, C. (2002). Towards international English in EFL classrooms in Japan. *Internet TESL Journal, 8*(1). Retrieved September 5, 2007, from http://iteslj.org/Articles/Yamaguchi-Language.html.

Yang, H. S. (2002). Learning English songs through notation program. *A new paradigm for innovative multimedia language education in the 21ˢᵗ century* (pp. 299-300). Seoul: Korean Association of Multimedia Assisted Language Learning.

Yip, M (2002). Perceptual influences in Cantonese loanword phonology. *Journal of the Phonetic Society of Japan, 6*, 4-21.

Yoo, H. B. (1996). A constraints based analysis of Korean loanwords. *Studies in Phonetics, Phonology and Morphology, 2*, 147-167.

Yoon, K. E. (2004). CLT theories and practices in EFL curricula a case study of Korea. *Asian EFL Journal, 6*(3), 1-16.

Yoshida, M. (1978). The acquisition of English vocabulary by a Japanese-speaking child. In E. M. Hatch (Ed), *Second language acquisition* (pp. 91-100). New York: Newbury House.

Yu, M. G. (1980). A study on the ways of borrowing and adapting foreign words. (Translation). *Ohak-yonka/Language research, 16*(1), 57-74.

Zimmerman, C. B. (1997). Does reading and interactive vocabulary instruction make a difference? An empirical study. *TESOL Quarterly, 31*, 121-140.

APPENDICES

Appendix One
The Survey

Appendix Two
The Pre- and Post-Test

Appendix Three
The CALL Modules

Appendix Four
The Statistics

Appendix One
THE SURVEY

Appendix One
THE SURVEY

Survey Framework

The survey of student attitudes towards computer assisted language learning in English as a foreign language (SSACAL) was developed to become a measure of student attitudes towards computer assisted instruction in English as a foreign language (EFL). Crucial to development of this measure is student attitudes concerning: (a) disposition towards computer assisted instruction; (b) the Korean learning style; and (c) English as a foreign language learning style. An English version of the survey is included at the end of this Appendix, following the breakdown of the constructs used to develop each item. During the course of the empirical investigation, a Korean translation of the survey was provided to participants for completion.

Section One: Disposition Toward Computer Assisted Instruction

A). Computer Competency

Items 1 and 2 of the survey were created to open a window on the computer experience of students in regards to educational computer use, while items 3 and 4 were developed to highlight student abilities for doing the things, irrespective of the skill level that they believe they maintain, that they would like to do with computers. Item interest thereby lies with student computer assisted instruction (CAI) usage and computer skill levels.

B). Preference for Computer-Based Learning

It was pointed out, particularly around the time the 'media debate' sparked (see Clarke, 1994; and, Kozma, 1994), that computer assisted language learning (CALL) and computer-based learning is only effective because of a novelty factor. Later, researchers like Cuban (2001) illustrated the opposite effect. Young learners with computer access at home become bored and inattentive when using computers at school, and with this factor in mind, items 5 and 6 were created to take into consideration the student use of computers to assist them in learning from within university classes, as well as the use of computers for completion of homework activities. Korea is a collectivist based society, and knowledge of this often sways educator decisions in the assignment of tasks and activities for use with classes (Kent, 2004). As such, items 7 through 12 were established to ask about student use of computers both inside and outside of the classroom, and their use of computers either by themselves, in pairs, or in groups. This maintains and covers, for the items in this section of the survey, a focus on overall interest in CAI usage at university, and working with computers in various collaborative modes.

C). Preference for Learning English through CAI

Items 13 to 36 were written to emphasize the various activities that assist in learning human languages with computers. Items 37 to 40 then subsequently come to ask about the degree to which computers can assist in improving the four English language skills (reading, writing, listening, and speaking). Item 41 then asks about the desirability of computer use for studying English. Following this, items 42 and 43 ask if disc- or web-based deployment of language learning content would provide effective learning. Korean students, although heavily exposed to technology, are not necessarily widely exposed to CAI outside of the school environment, and there is evidence to suggest that students rely more on teacher-directed traditional learning (see Ahn, 2002; Eastmond, 2000; Joo, 1997; Min, et al, 2000) and so students were asked if they would like to combine traditional (i.e. paper-based) learning with computer use in item 44. The remaining items in this section numbered 45 through 53 concentrate on the bilingual functionality of software. This is important as the majority of computer-based instructional material, particularly that produced by commercial software houses, neglects bilingual functionality, whereas the multimedia-based CALL modules, designed for use in the empirical investigation undertaken in this book, were authored to specifically offer various levels of bilingual support and functionality. The fundamental concerns of this survey section can then be seen to be CAI EFL learning activities and CAI EFL software preferences.

Section Two: Korean Learning Style

A). In-Class Relations

This section of the survey consists of items 54 to 57. In the creation and wording of these items, several assumptions were made based upon the 'traditional' view of the Korean cultural identity (see Finch 2000) and the East Asian classroom context (as per Hofstede, 1986; and, Cortazzi, 1990). This view presents Korea as a very collectivist-based society, and therefore collective oriented learning, such as pair and group work, is perceived to be preferred over individual learning. Saving face is important, particularly in public settings such as being called upon by the teacher to speak aloud in class. Items created therefore revolve around the traditional characteristics of student-teacher classroom interaction, and student learning desires.

B). Desired Characteristics of Instructors

This section of the survey (items 58 to 61) focuses on the traditional roles of teachers in Korean society. Questions center on teacher actions and perceived responsibilities such as knowing the subject that they teach (being a 'master'), directing class learning rather than allowing for student suggested activities, and the level of teacher responsibility for the learning of students. Also asked is a question about whether it is important for the English language teacher to be a first language (L1) speaker of English. Aspects of teacher dependency and any changes in Korean cultural assumptions towards educators are thereby considered.

C). View of Education

This survey section, consisting of items 62 to 67, centers on the traditional perceptions of learning, where items are written to take into consideration the importance of class exams, student preferred methods of acquiring knowledge, the level of social status earned by education, and the importance of life-long learning. Central to these items is the view that the Confucian consciousness maintains a stronghold over Korean students, even though a number of traditional cultural notions have been alleviated in the current generation of learners.

Section Three: English as a Foreign Language Learning Style

A) Preference for Cultural Representation

Survey items 68 and 69 are particularly relevant as there has been limited EFL course material available from within Korea that actually comes to represent Korean cultural traits and identity (aside from that developed by the likes of Finch & Hyun, 2000). Korean researchers (such as Ahn, 2002) have recognized this, and have been calling for more Korean cultural representation in the EFL teaching materials of publishing houses (also see Pak, 1999). As a result, it is believed that students wish to see more of their own culture represented in the content of the materials that they use to study English. How the representation of Korean culture in such content impacts student learning with the material is therefore at issue.

B). Loanword Use

This section of the survey examines the ease of learning and using English equivalents of Korean loan terminology when speaking in English. These items, numbered 70 to 73, are significant as these loanword types form the learning content of the multimedia-based CALL modules developed for use in the subsequent empirical investigation. Particularly under consideration is the student perception of the vocabulary applied in the loanword approach, with emphasis on the ease of learning and applying such material.

C). Vocabulary Acquisition Strategies

This survey section takes into account both meaning discovery strategies, and meaning consolidation strategies. Items stem predominantly from a questionnaire undertaken by Park (2001) with Korean EFL students, which follows a study undertaken by Schmitt (1997) with Japanese EFL students. These two studies are based on the creation of a taxonomic framework of vocabulary strategies deriving primarily from the Oxford strategy inventory for language learning (SILL). The meaning discovery strategies include analyzing meaning (items 74 to 77), using aids (items 78 to 81), and help from others (items 82 to 86). The meaning consolidation strategies include social strategy (items 87 and 88), memory strategy (items 89 to 103), cognitive strategy (items 104 to 111), and metacognitive strategy (items 112 to 114). Attention of these survey items thereby resides firmly with vocabulary acquisition strategies, including the usual methods that students rely on for determining the meanings of new words as well as the means employed to remember them.

Computers, Learning and Language Acquisition Survey

	Office Use Only
Student number	
Class number	
Student gender	

INSTRUCTIONS

If you strongly disagree with the statement, please tick SD	SD ✓	D	A	SA
If you disagree with the statement, please tick D	SD	D ✓	A	SA
If you agree with the statement, please tick A	SD	D	A ✓	SA
If you strongly agree with the statement, please tick SA	SD	D	A	SA ✓

A. DISPOSITION TOWARDS COMPUTER ASSISTED INSTRUCTION (CAI)

1. COMPUTER COMPETENCY

(a) CAI usage

1	I use online learning.	SD	D	A	SA
2	I use disc-based (CD/DVD) learning.	SD	D	A	SA

(b) Skill level

3	I am competent in using computers.	SD	D	A	SA
4	I am satisfied with my computer skills.	SD	D	A	SA

2. PREFERENCE FOR COMPUTER-BASED LEARNING

(a) CAI usage

5	Computer technology should be used in my university classes.	SD	D	A	SA
6	Computer technology should be used for university class homework.	SD	D	A	SA

(b) Collaboration

7	I like to work on my own with computers in class.	SD	D	A	SA
8	I like to work in pairs with computers in class.	SD	D	A	SA
9	I like to work in groups with computers in class.	SD	D	A	SA
10	I like to work on my own with computers outside class.	SD	D	A	SA
11	I like to work in pairs with computers outside class.	SD	D	A	SA
12	I like to work in groups with computers outside class.	SD	D	A	SA

3. PREFERENCE FOR LEARNING ENGLISH THROUGH CAI
(a) CAI EFL activities

13	I like to use language games when studying English with computers.	SD	D	A	SA
14	I like to use practice tests (TOEFL / TOEIC / TEPS) when studying English with computers.	SD	D	A	SA
15	I like to use set syllabus modules when studying English with computers.	SD	D	A	SA
16	I like to use grammar exercises when studying English with computers.	SD	D	A	SA
17	I like to use listening tasks when studying English with computers.	SD	D	A	SA
18	I like to use reading comprehension tasks when studying English with computers.	SD	D	A	SA
19	I like to use cloze exercises when studying English with computers.	SD	D	A	SA
20	I like to use matching exercises when studying English with computers.	SD	D	A	SA
21	I like to use writing/typing tasks when studying English with computers.	SD	D	A	SA
22	I like to use crossword puzzles when studying English with computers.	SD	D	A	SA
23	I like to use pronunciation activities when studying English with computers.	SD	D	A	SA
24	I like to use translation tasks when studying English with computers.	SD	D	A	SA
25	I like to use test style exercises when studying English with computers.	SD	D	A	SA
26	I like to use multiple-choice questions when studying English with computers.	SD	D	A	SA
27	I like to use true/false questions when studying English with computers.	SD	D	A	SA
28	I like to use question and answer tasks when studying English with computers.	SD	D	A	SA
29	I like to use clue/guessing activities when studying English with computers.	SD	D	A	SA
30	I like to use word search puzzles when studying English with computers.	SD	D	A	SA
31	I like to use task-based activities when studying English with computers.	SD	D	A	SA
32	I like to use color coding activities when studying English with computers.	SD	D	A	SA
33	I like to use reorganization activities when studying English with computers.	SD	D	A	SA

34	I like to use semantic identification tasks when studying English with computers.	SD	D	A	SA
35	I like to use negotiation exchange tasks when studying English with computers.	SD	D	A	SA
36	I like to use mnemonics/keyword tasks when studying English with computers.	SD	D	A	SA
37	I think computers can help me improve my English reading skills.	SD	D	A	SA
38	I think computers can help me improve my English writing skills.	SD	D	A	SA
39	I think computers can help me improve my English listening skills.	SD	D	A	SA
40	I think computers can help me improve my English speaking skills.	SD	D	A	SA
41	I want to use computers to study English.	SD	D	A	SA

(b) CAI EFL software preferences

42	Using CD/DVD software is an effective way to learn English.	SD	D	A	SA
43	Using the internet is an effective way to learn English.	SD	D	A	SA
44	Learning English with computers is improved when combined with the use of a paper-based workbook.	SD	D	A	SA
45	English language learning software instructions should include only English instructions.	SD	D	A	SA
46	English language learning software instructions should include only instructions in Korean.	SD	D	A	SA
47	English language learning software instructions should include both English and Korean instructions.	SD	D	A	SA
48	English language learning software menu bars should include only English.	SD	D	A	SA
49	English language learning software menu bars should include only Korean.	SD	D	A	SA
50	English language learning software menu bars should include both English and Korean.	SD	D	A	SA
51	English language learning software program icons should include only English.	SD	D	A	SA
52	English language learning software program icons should include only Korean.	SD	D	A	SA
53	English language learning software program icons should include both English and Korean.	SD	D	A	SA

B. KOREAN LEARNING STYLE
1. IN-CLASS RELATIONS

54	I like to learn with a partner.	SD	D	A	SA
55	I like to learn with a group.	SD	D	A	SA

| 56 | I feel nervous or ashamed to speak in class if the teacher calls on me. | SD | D | A | SA |
| 57 | It feels like a test when the teacher calls on me to speak in class. | SD | D | A | SA |

2. DESIRED CHARACTERISTICS OF INSTRUCTORS

58	Teachers should know about the subject they teach.	SD	D	A	SA
59	Teachers should direct the classes.	SD	D	A	SA
60	The teacher is responsible for student's performance.	SD	D	A	SA
61	My English teacher should be a non-native speaker of English.	SD	D	A	SA

3. VIEW OF EDUCATION

62	Class exams are important.	SD	D	A	SA
63	Memorizing knowledge is important.	SD	D	A	SA
64	Practicing skills is important.	SD	D	A	SA
65	Education is a way to achieve higher social status.	SD	D	A	SA
66	The young should learn.	SD	D	A	SA
67	It is important for me to study throughout my life.	SD	D	A	SA

C. ENGLISH AS A FOREIGN LANGUAGE LEARNING STYLE
1. PREFERENCE FOR CULTURAL REPRESENTATION IN EFL LEARNING MATERIAL

| 68 | Seeing Korean culture in English language learning materials gains my interest. | SD | D | A | SA |
| 69 | English language learning material should have more Korean cultural content. | SD | D | A | SA |

2. LOANWORD USE

70	It was easy for me to learn to use direct loanwords (For example, words like 'coffee').	SD	D	A	SA
71	It was easy for me to learn to use the English equivalents of pseudo loanwords (For example, *close physical contact between friends* for *skinship*).	SD	D	A	SA
72	It was easy for me to learn to use the English equivalents of hybrid Korean-English terms (For example, *cherry tomato* for *bangul-tomato*).	SD	D	A	SA
73	It was easy for me to learn to use the English equivalents of truncated loanwords (For example, *remote control* for *remocon*).	SD	D	A	SA

3. VOCABULARY ACQUISITION STRATEGIES
(a) Meaning Discovery Strategies
(i) Analyzing meaning

74	To discover the meaning of unknown English vocabulary, I analyze parts of speech.	SD	D	A	SA
76	To discover the meaning of unknown English vocabulary, I analyze pictures or gestures.	SD	D	A	SA
77	To discover the meaning of unknown English vocabulary, I guess meaning from context.	SD	D	A	SA

(ii) Using aids

78	To discover the meaning of unknown English vocabulary, I use a bilingual dictionary.	SD	D	A	SA
79	To discover the meaning of unknown English vocabulary, I use a monolingual dictionary.	SD	D	A	SA
80	To discover the meaning of unknown English vocabulary, I use word lists.	SD	D	A	SA
81	To discover the meaning of unknown English vocabulary, I use flash cards.	SD	D	A	SA

(iii) Help from others

82	To discover the meaning of unknown English vocabulary, I ask the teacher for the meaning.	SD	D	A	SA
83	To discover the meaning of unknown English. vocabulary, I ask the teacher for a synonym of the word.	SD	D	A	SA
84	To discover the meaning of unknown English vocabulary, I ask the teacher for a sentence containing the word.	SD	D	A	SA
85	To discover the meaning of unknown English vocabulary, I ask classmates or friends for the meaning.	SD	D	A	SA
86	To discover the meaning of unknown English vocabulary, I use group activities to discover the meaning of a new English word.	SD	D	A	SA

(b) Meaning Consolidation Strategies
(i) Social Strategy

87	I remember the meaning of English vocabulary by using the vocabulary with a group of classmates.	SD	D	A	SA
88	I remember the meaning of English vocabulary by using the vocabulary in conversation with a native English speaker.	SD	D	A	SA

(ii) Memory Strategy

89	I remember the meaning of English vocabulary by drawing a pictorial representation of it.	SD	D	A	SA
90	I remember the meaning of English vocabulary by connecting the vocabulary to a personal experience.	SD	D	A	SA

91	I remember the meaning of English vocabulary by connecting the vocabulary to its synonyms and antonyms.	SD	D	A	SA
92	I remember the meaning of English vocabulary by grouping the vocabulary with similar words.	SD	D	A	SA
93	I remember the meaning of English vocabulary by using the vocabulary in a sentence.	SD	D	A	SA
94	I remember the meaning of English vocabulary by spelling the vocabulary.	SD	D	A	SA
95	I remember the meaning of English vocabulary by listening to the sound of the vocabulary.	SD	D	A	SA
96	I remember the meaning of English vocabulary by speaking the vocabulary aloud.	SD	D	A	SA
97	I remember the meaning of English vocabulary by imagining the word forms for the vocabulary.	SD	D	A	SA
98	I remember the meaning of English vocabulary by using keywords.	SD	D	A	SA
99	I remember the meaning of English vocabulary by remembering the word's affixes and roots.	SD	D	A	SA
100	I remember the meaning of English vocabulary by remembering each word's part of speech.	SD	D	A	SA
101	I remember the meaning of English vocabulary by paraphrasing the meaning of the vocabulary.	SD	D	A	SA
102	I learn the words of an idiom together to remember English vocabulary.	SD	D	A	SA
103	I practice words using physical actions to remember English vocabulary.	SD	D	A	SA

(iii) Cognitive Strategy

104	I practice words through verbal repetition to remember English vocabulary.	SD	D	A	SA
105	I write words repeatedly to remember English vocabulary.	SD	D	A	SA
106	I practice words using word lists to remember English vocabulary.	SD	D	A	SA
107	I practice words using flash cards to remember English vocabulary.	SD	D	A	SA
108	I study words by taking notes in class to remember English vocabulary.	SD	D	A	SA
109	I utilize vocabulary sections in textbooks to remember English vocabulary.	SD	D	A	SA
110	I practice words by putting labels on objects to remember English vocabulary.	SD	D	A	SA
111	I keep a vocabulary notebook to remember English vocabulary.	SD	D	A	SA

(iv) Metacognitive Strategy

112	I use English-language media to remember English vocabulary.	SD	D	A	SA
113	I self-test word knowledge to remember English vocabulary.	SD	D	A	SA
114	I continually review the same words over time to remember English vocabulary.	SD	D	A	SA

Appendix Two
THE PRE- AND POST-TEST

Appendix Two
THE PRE- AND POST-TEST

Pre- and Post-test Design and Delivery

The same assessor delivered both the pre- and post-tests to students in the same location and at the same time during the weekly class schedule. The pre-test was delivered in the week following the survey (week five of the sixteen week semester), which was the week preceding the start of treatment. The test of student understanding of pseudo-loanwords (SUPL) was collected immediately, and stored with survey data until being handed over to the researcher.

The post-test was delivered in the same location and at the same time during the weekly class schedule as the pre-test, but it was delivered to all participants in the same week of the completion of treatment (week 12 of the semester). It was collected immediately upon completion, along with the pre-test and the survey, so that data analysis could begin.

Multiple-choice item difficulty was varied by choice of pseudo-loanword, as well as the choice of English words used in test item statements, with particular care not to mix the level of difficulty within single items. By varying the closeness of meaning between distracters and the correct answer, it is easy to modify items to different degrees of difficulty (Nagy, Herman, & Anderson, 1985). When writing test activities, items were checked to ensure that they had only one correct response and were not interdependent. The order of correct responses is randomized so that test wiseness could be reduced. Further, distracters were developed that would be both plausible and equally appealing to students who would not know the correct answer.

It was also important to consider the effect of student exposure to the pre-test when delivering the post-test, and as the period between delivery of each test is two months, it was therefore not perceived necessary to develop a second test instrument for delivery as the post-test. Location threat was diminished as both the pre- and post-test was delivered by the same instructor, in the same location, and at the same time of the weekly class schedule. As with the survey, the test underwent reliability and validity checks by trialing before final deployment, and Rasch analysis before use in hypothesis testing. Trialing assisted in accurately developing a reliable and valid instrument by ensuring that the test was appropriate for deployment. Rasch analysis assisted in determining the reliability of the test in terms of person item difficulty calibration, and validity by ensuring fit of the items to the model and thereby effective measurement of a single trait: student understanding of the English meanings of pseudo-loanwords used in Korean. In this manner, reliable and valid test data was made available for hypothesis testing.

Pre- and Post-Test Instrument

Quiz

Student Number ....
Class Number ....
Gender ....

Test instructions
In each of the sentences below there is an underlined term which is a 'pseudo loanword'. From the four choices provided for each term, select the definition that equals the English meaning for the underlined term.

1. Your neighbor's <u>audio</u> is really loud; someone should complain to the police.

a (1a)	shirt	c (1c)	noise
b (1b)	dog	d (1d)	**stereo**

2. Gangnam is always a good area in Seoul to go <u>hunting</u>.

a (2a)	sleeping	c (2c)	camping
b (2b)	**picking up people**	d (2d)	eating

3. We need to get new batteries for the <u>remocon</u>; it doesn't seem to be working anymore.

a (4a)	brand of batteries	c (4c)	**remote control**
b (4b)	ready mixed concrete	d (4d)	a reverse cycle air conditioner

4. I'd like to <u>Dutch pay</u> tonight.

a (6a)	**pay individually**	c (6c)	pay for everyone
b (6b)	share the cost	d (6d)	use Dutch money

5. What <u>night</u> do you like the best?

a (7a)	**night club**	c (7c)	bar
b (7b)	Saturday	d (7d)	the opposite to day

6. When she fell over, she landed on her <u>hip</u>.
    a (8a)   front   c (8c)   top
    b (8b)   **bottom**   d (8d)   back

7. It is really hot in here; is there something wrong with the <u>steam</u>?
    a (10a)   an angry person   c (10c)   water
    b (10b)   engine   d (10d)   **radiator heater**

8. The <u>sharp</u> is not in your pencil case.
    a (10a)   pen that never runs out of ink   c (10c)   pointed paper
    b (10b)   **mechanical pencil**   d (10d)   knife that can cut well

9. Come in, and take a seat on the <u>sofa</u> over there.
    a (10a)   train station seat   c (10c)   **armchair**
    b (10b)   love seat   d (10d)   place that is not near here

10. I couldn't see anything because I needed a <u>flash</u>.
    a (13a)   **flashlight**   c (13c)   the sound of thunder after lightening
    b (13b)   fresh batteries   4 (13d)   to move like a turtle

11. I had to take good hold of the <u>handle</u> before I could get the car to turn properly.
    a (14a)   part of a machine used to turn it on and off   c (14c)   **steering wheel**
    b (14b)   a person's ability to control a machine   d (14d)   the end of the arm

12. Why do so many people blow their <u>klaxon</u> when driving in Korea?

    a (15a)   **car horn**   c (15c)   boat horn
    b (15b)   siren   d (15d)   alarm

13. He is a <u>talent</u> that is really very well known.

a (16a)	a singer	c (16c)	an actor or actress
b (16b)	**a media celebrity**	d (16d)	an expert

14. Your hands look really nice; you usually don't use <u>manicure</u>.

a (17a)	**nail polish**	c (17c)	hand treatment
b (17b)	hand cream	d (17d)	cut and trimmed toenails

15. I don't like the <u>potato</u> in this store; let's go to another place.

a (18a)	**French fries**	c (18c)	toes
b (18b)	pots	d (18d)	hash browns

16. Oh no, another mistake. I can't see why I just did that. Where's the <u>white</u>?

a (19a)	ball point pen	c (19c)	the person a man marries
b (19b)	eraser	d (19d)	**correction fluid**

17. She always goes on a <u>meeting</u>.

a (21a)	**blind date**	c (21c)	promise
b (21b)	lecture	d (21d)	timetable

18. Don't write with a <u>ball pen</u>, please use a pencil.

a (22a)	sharp	c (22c)	fountain pen
b (22b)	mechanical pencil	d (22d)	**ballpoint pen**

19. Every weekend, my friends and I go out to a <u>hof</u> or two.

a (24a)	amusement park	c (24c)	fast food chain
b (24b)	**bar**	d (24d)	cinema

20. I really enjoyed meeting your boyfriend; he looks very <u>clean</u>.

a (25a)	different from others	c (25c)	well mannered
b (25b)	**clean cut**	d (25d)	short hair cut

21. Plug this into the <u>consent</u> over there.

a (26a)	hole	c (26c)	water outlet
b (26b)	**electrical outlet**	d (26d)	wall

22. If you are going to the store, please get me some more <u>skin</u>.

a (27a)	body covering	c (27c)	body paint
b (27b)	**moisturizer**	d (27d)	shell

23. He's really handsome; I can't believe he's still <u>solo</u>.

a (28a)	a lemon flavored drink	c (28c)	**single**
b (28b)	short	d (28d)	married

24. Everybody was <u>fighting</u> for their team at the soccer game last night.

a (29a)	boxing	c (29c)	**cheering**
b (29b)	rioting	d (29d)	crying

25. I'll need to buy a new <u>spring note</u> after winter because this one will be full.

a (30a)	seasonal message	c (30c)	spring notebook
b (30b)	**spiral bound notebook**	d (30d)	spiral bound note

26. I don't know why the coach hasn't called for a <u>member change</u> yet.

a (31a)	time out	c (31c)	**substitution**
b (31b)	water boy	d (31d)	change of teams

27. Be careful in this area otherwise you'll end up with a <u>punk</u>.

a (32a)	**flat tire**	c (32c)	person with long hair
b (32b)	pumpkin	d (32d)	damage

28. I spend a lot of time training with the <u>sandbag</u>.

a (33a)	plastic bag	c (33c)	bag full of sand
b (33b)	beach bag	d (33d)	**punching bag**

29. That company has an excellent reputation for <u>after service</u>.

a (35a)	**after sales service**	c (35c)	buying things after getting something free
b (35b)	expensive repairs	d (35d)	after selling service

30. I like the <u>sand</u> type biscuits.

a (36a)	gritty textured	c (36c)	fine grained
b (36b)	smooth	d (36d)	**sandwich**

31. I'm just going to the <u>super</u> for a moment.

a (37a)	street market	c (37c)	excellent
b (37b)	gym	d (37d)	**supermarket**

32. Do you want to play a game of <u>pocket ball</u>?

a (38a)	**billiards**	c (38c)	fashionable clothing
b (38b)	ball that you keep in your pocket	d (38d)	game like basketball

33. I'll need to get a <u>driver</u> before I can help you repair it.

a (39a)	spanner	c (39c)	tool
b (39b)	**screwdriver**	d (39d)	shoe

34. Looking at your car, I can see it needs a new <u>wheel cap</u>.

a (41a)	tire	c (41c)	distributor cap
b (41b)	baseball cap	d (41d)	**hub cap**

35. He always wears a fashionable <u>y-shirt</u> when he goes out.

a (43a)	yellow shirt	c (43c)	**dress shirt**
b (43b)	white shirt	d (43d)	business shirt

36. I will need to buy new <u>panties</u> on the way home tomorrow.

a (44a)	shorts	c (44c)	pants
b (44b)	**underpants**	d (44d)	outerwear

37.   Everybody, <u>one shot</u>!
a (45a)   **bottoms up**   c (45c)   taste
b (45b)   cheer   d (45d)   sip

38.   I love going <u>hiking</u> on the weekend.
a (46a)   mountain climbing   c (46c)   **biking**
b (46b)   driving   d (46d)   sailing

39.   I drank too much; I think I'm going to <u>o-bite</u>.
a (49a)   eat more   c (49c)   over bite
b (49b)   over eat   d (49d)   **vomit**

40.   Is your <u>a-pa-teu</u> nearby?
a (50a)   pull apart   c (50c)   put together
b (50b)   house   d (50d)   **apartment**

Note. A bilingual (English and Korean) version of the pre- and post-test instrument was provided to participants of the empirical investigation. A monolingual English version above sees correct responses illustrated in bold.

Appendix Three
THE CALL MODULES

Appendix Three
THE CALL MODULES

Treatment

During the treatment phase of the empirical study, two multimedia-based modules were made available to students through a process of stratified sampling, based on class roll sheet order. The first student on the list was provided with access to Module One, the second with Module Two, the third with Module One, the fourth student with Module Two, and so on for each student in the class and for each of the classes in the study. In this manner, students were assigned to either treatment group one, with use of Module One, or treatment group two with the use of Module Two. Students then used the material as part of normal taught-course procedure over an eight week period (starting in week six of a sixteen week semester). Each module provides around ten hours of learning content, and student progress was checked periodically to confirm scheduled progress and completion of appropriate activities.

The computer assisted language learning (CALL) modules used in the treatment are primarily homework-based so that they would not impinge upon existing syllabus schedules, thereby being less obtrusive and more easily implemented within the existing university English program curriculum. Further, the modules being homework-based assists in minimizing instructor bias as treatment involved measuring performance of student linguistic understanding and development that resulted from completion of material outside the classroom. However, student completion of the modules outside of class time could have led to subject characteristic threats, whereby participants might neglect homework completion or complete materials in one sitting, rather than throughout the semester. These subject characteristic threats were reduced by implementing standard-practice controls (i.e. incremental homework submission due dates – three submissions in total, one every two weeks of treatment). The experiment was also confined to part of a single semester to reduce maturation and mortality, and control of attitudinal effect stemmed from incorporating learning content as part of normal taught-course homework procedure. Through these actions, a course of reliable and valid treatment was provided to students throughout the empirical phase of the research.

Module Design

Characteristic Design Features – Behaviorist-Based Restricted CALL

To incorporate elements of the restricted CALL approach (see Bax, 2003) into a multimedia CALL-based learning system, each module was engineered while keeping five principles in mind. These principles are based on a number of instructional design principles from the behavioristic CALL phase, as presented by Atkins (1993) and Wyatt (1987). The features align with a traditional view of Korean education, a behaviorist-based transmission model, and learner expectations as based on the literature (Cortazzi, 1990; Eastmond, 2000; Finch, 2000; Hofstede, 1986; Joo, 1997; Min, Kim & Jung, 2000; Park & Oxford, 1998). Further, the presentation focus of this module provides vocabulary exercises similar to those found in 'typical' language learning textbooks (refer to Chiquito, Meskill, & Renjilian-Burgy, 1997). The five principles behind this design are:

1. *Small, logically discrete, instructional steps*
   A process of stimulus-response is relied upon to promote learning as students completed tasks; for example, mutually exclusive exercises focusing on single option 'right/wrong' answers.

2. *Rote style learning and memorization*
   To assist with memorization, and to comply with the rote learning strategies of Korean students, tasks are oriented to present the material to be learned by emphasizing question-answer completion over full comprehension; for example, students being focused on answering items correctly. Schmitt (2000) also comments that rote memorization can be effective if this is the vocabulary learning strategy that students are accustomed to using.

3. *Transfer of information*
   The computer takes on the role of an authoritative instructor, and learners are viewed as dependent. For example, applications are used as a medium of information delivery, and students are expected to assimilate this information.

4. *Learning from repetition*
   Students are passive responders as acquisition is based on student activated repetition and not practice. Repetition is the process of repeating the same solution over and over again, as opposed to

practice which is viewed as the completion of an activity through a process of solution (Bernstein, 1967).

5. *Emphasis on content*
Focus remains on completing the task and obtaining the correct answer. For example, students are presented with the information that they need to complete the task and are able to do so in a single step.

Characteristic Design Features – Communicative-Based Open CALL

Not only do elements of the open CALL approach (see Bax, 2003) need to be incorporated within the second module, they also need to contrast the instructional design principles chosen for the first module. As a result, the following five principles, based on aspects of instructional design indicative of the communicative CALL phase were selected (see Underwood, 1984; Raschio, 1986). In this regard, the pedagogical approach behind the module is intended to align with the communicative instructional style advocated by the Seventh National English Curricula and subsequent revisions. Further, the presentation focus of the module provides vocabulary exercises in language puzzle form (see Backer, 1995). The five principles guiding this design (see Alessi & Trollip, 2001; Raschio, 1986; and, Underwood, 1984) are:

1. *Broad all-inclusive instructional steps*
Exercises can be completed by applying cognitive rationalization to a task, with all possible solutions for current tasks self-contained within the presented exercise. For example, choices became evident as students progressed through exercises as a result of the elimination of already used task items.

2. *Application of understanding*
Focus on comprehension over completion; for example, students were expected to utilize cognition to solve puzzles and answer questions rather than just select answers.

3. *Interaction with computer*
The application facilitates learning; for example, students were presented with the information that they needed to know, and the process of arriving at answers to questions involves a multi-step thought process.

4. *Learning from game play*
   Game play is used to motivate students to engage with the material; for example, progress toward learning goals is contingent on progress toward completing the game, or achieving the game's goals.

5. *Emphasis on problem solving*
   Learners are compelled to seek knowledge; for example, exercises are made challenging because information is hidden from the learner, or needs to be discovered.

Common Design Features

The two modules shared several instructional design principles which allow the two systems to facilitate language acquisition, and support learning through use of a multimedia environment. The three common design features are:

1. *Assessment embedded within an activity via immediate and extensive feedback*
   Student responses are always judged, and appropriate response feedback is continuously provided by the system. Extensive feedback is provided through both an auditory comment and a pop-up text balloon. In this manner, the system could illustrate if the answer is correct or not, and explain both the English and Korean usage and definition for the vocabulary item. This allows feedback to relate to learners' previous knowledge and experience, and serves to assist in establishing a mnemonic link between the vocabulary and the definitions in each language. This may have also improved memorability of the content by capitalizing on the organization principle of memory (Alessi & Trollip, 2001).

   The notion of feedback in language learning is based on an evaluation of success that can lead to learner self-correction, and to allow learners to revise their strategies for language comprehension. Speed of feedback provided through computer-based systems is unmatched (Brett, 1995). Davies and Crowther (1995) also state that this kind of feedback can allow for students to understand their errors, develop further understanding from them, and provide "one-to-one tuition" that may not be possible in conventional learner settings. Oxford, Rivera-Costillo, Feyten, and Nutta (1998) also determine feedback to be an important form of learner "consciousness-raising", as do others such as Mayer (2001) and Soper (1997), while Schar, Schluep, and Schierz

(2000) further state that the types of feedback provided through software systems can come to affect the cognitive development of students within multimedia settings, with explicit learning fostered by delaying feedback until actions are completed.

2. *Learner control over pacing and sequence; teacher control of content*
Providing the learner with one-click system control and the ability to control activities establishes a fast pace, and can "appeal to a learner's sense of accomplishment and enhance fluency" (Alessi & Trollip, 2001, p. 187). Yet, Laurillard, Stratfold, and Luckin (2000) along with Schar, Schluep, and Schierz (2000) further make clear that when using computer assisted instruction (CAI), it is the educator who needs to be accountable for establishing an atmosphere that maintains a specific learning focus, clear goals, motivation, and time for reflection so that structured and meaningful learning can occur.

Structured systems promote explicit learning (Schar Schluep, & Schierz, 2000), and structured learning allows for effective learner reflection (Guimaraes, Chambel, & Bidarra, 2000). To maintain the systemic use of language for both modules, it was essential that the learning material be teacher controlled via vocabulary pre-selection. The difficulty level of the content between modules also has to be constant, as the same pre-selected vocabulary items are used in each section and only applied differently based upon the activities found in each module (classify, multiple-choice, identify).

Further, in order to improve vocabulary learning, items are grouped by semantic and situation-specific similarity (see Underwood, Runquist, & Schulz, 1959). That is, financial and banking terminology is placed in the bank unit, restaurant terminology and food vocabulary is grouped within the restaurant unit, and so on. Focus is placed on incorporating six terms per unit within the classify activity, five terms per unit in the multiple-choice activity, and five terms per unit in the identify activity. These vocabulary items are grouped by activity difficulty: the classify section being the easiest; multiple-choice being harder; and, identify being the most difficult.

3. *Proficiency built from the ability to engage in repetitive review*
The limited number of items per activity (five or six) allow for each activity to be completed in a short period of time, and the reason behind this limitation is to create a system in which students can engage in completion of activities quickly and conveniently. Efficient completion of activities also means that

the activity is compact enough for students to approach at any time and repeat for review. The structure of the modules (three activities per unit and twenty units per module) allowes the longest activity to last no more than about five to ten minutes, and it is believed that this helps in avoiding learner fatigue and boredom (Alessi & Trollip, 2001). Once an activity is complete, the score can be recorded. If the student desires, the process can be repeated, scores improved, and then saved. The ability to rework exercises in an attempt to improve upon previous performance provides all learners with the chance to succeed.

Choice of Lexical Content

The lexical content utilized for the purpose of promoting foreign language acquisition through use of the modules was obtained from previous research (see Kent, 1996) and stems from the English inherent within the native vernacular. The core linguistic content of the treatment comprises of a loanword vocabulary base of 220 words: 63 direct loanwords, 13 hybrid terms, 3 substitution terms, 136 pseudo-loanwords (52 truncated terms, 57 false cognates, and 27 fabricated loans), as well as 5 commonly misused English terms such as the direct translation of *hong cha* (*red tea*) for *black tea*, and the reversal of the set phrase *knife and fork* to *fork and knife*. However, it is the 136 terms present in the pseudo-loanword category that is under investigation, and it is student learning gains associated with this category that the one-group pre-test/post-test experiment was designed to assess. A listing of the loanword vocabulary found within the modules are presented by loanword type in Table A3.1.1 (direct, hybrid, substitution, and misused) with Table A3.1.2 presenting a listing of the pseudo-loanwords that became part of the treatment focus. The language learning vocabulary has been sorted into loanword type, with the words in bold font representative of those used in the pre- and post-test. Each module employs the use of the same pseudo-loanword terms in each exercise. The pseudo-loanword terms used in each exercise (classification, multiple-choice, or identification) are illustrated in Table A3.2.1 for units covering the 'university' map, Table A3.2.2 for units covering the 'main street', Table A3.2.3 for units covering the 'underground', and Table A3.2.4 covering units from the 'apartment' map.

Table A3.1.1
Listing of language learning vocabulary, by loanword type, as found in each module

Misused English	Direct Loans	Hybrid Terms	Substitution Words
Fork and knife	Aerobic(s)	Bae-kkob T	A-reu-bai-teu
Play	Airbag	Bang-ul tomato	Hotchkiss
Promise	Announcer	Beef kass	Snack
Red tea	Apple Pie	Com-maeng	
Secret number	ATM	Don kass	
Singing room	Ballad	Jeon-hwa box	
	Band	Jeon-hwa card	
	Brand	Jeon-ja range	
	Buffet	Ot-pin	
	Café	PC bang	
	Cappuccino	Saeng beer	
	Chain	Short dari	
	Cheerleader	Sil-pin	
	Cola		
	Collar		
	Collect call		
	Computer		
	Credit card		
	Cut		
	Date		
	Dance		
	Diet		
	Desk		
	E-Mail		
	Gas range		
	Graph		
	Hair Dryer		
	Hair pin		
	Handout		
	Handsome		
	Interphone		
	Keyboard		
	Menu		
	Message		
	Mixer		
	Napkin		
	Pitcher		

Table A3.1.1 *(continued)*

Misused English	Direct Loans	Hybrid Terms	Substitution Words
	Refill		
	Reporter		
	Restorang		
	(French:		
	Restaurant)		
	Romantic		
	Shampoo		
	Show		
	Sitcom		
	Ski		
	Stress		
	Soda		
	Take out		
	Techno		
	Television		
	Tennis		
	Top ten		
	Tire		
	Tour guide		
	Trousers		
	Tune up		
	Waiter		

Table A3.1.2
Listing of language learning vocabulary, by pseudo-loanword, as found in each module

Pseudo-Loanwords (Treatment Focus)		
Truncated Loans	False Cognates	Fabricated Loans
After (sales) service	**Audio**	A-pull
Aircon(ditioner)	Back number	All back
Ankle (length) boots	Bank	Back mirror
Apart(ment)	Booking	Cash bank
Auto(matic motor)bi(ke)	Check	Cut line
Back(ground)	Chief	**Dutch Pay**
Back(ground) dancer	Cider	Egg fry
Ball(point) pen	Circle	Excellent bus
Can(ed) coffee	Coffee pot	Eye shopping
Cassette (player)	Condition	Gag man
Classic(al music)	Confidence	Goal in
Clean (cut)	**Consent**	Gold collar worker
(paper)clip	Cunning	Home service
(inferiority) complex	Cup	**Hop / hof**
Co(o)rdi(nate)	Dash	**Member Change**
DC (discount)	Dial	**One shot**
Demo(nstration)	Event	Open car
Depart(ment store)	**Fighting**	PC banking
(screw)**Driver**	Fusion	**Pocket ball**
Ex(ample)	Hamburger steak	Prima
Flash(light)	Hair iron	Salary man
Frank(furter) sausage	Hard	Side brake
Free (voltage)	**Handle**	Skin scuba
Fry(ing) pan	Hand phone	Time killer
Hamburg(er)	Health	Tough guy
Infla(tion)	**Hiking**	**Wheel cap**
Kiss(ing) scene	Hint	Vinyl house
N/G (no good)	**Hip**	
Night(club)	Hot dog	
O(ver)-bite	**Hunting**	
O(ver)coat	Interior	
Ome(lete)rice	Jelly	
One piece (dress)	**Klaxon**	
Owner (driver)	Light cable	
Perma(nent)	Maker	
Phone(mee)ting	**Manicure**	
Power (steering) oil(/fluid)	**Meeting**	

Table A3.1.2 *(continued)*

Pseudo-Loanwords (Treatment Focus)		
Truncated Loans	False Cognates	Fabricated Loans
Punc(ture)	Omnibus	
Re(ady)mix(ed)	Parasol	
Remo(te)con(trol)	**Panty**	
Sand(wich)	**Potato**	
Schedule(r)	Remake	
Self(serve)	Report	
Sign(ature)	**Sand bag**	
Sign(ature) pen	Service	
Spring(/spiral bound) Note(book)	Setting	
Super(market)	**Sharp**	
Telemark(et)ing	**Skin**	
Three piece (suit)	Skinship	
Trans(former)	**Sofa**	
VTR	**Solo**	
Whi(te)-shirt	Stand	
	Steam	
	Talent	
	Training	
	Volume	
	White	

Note. Words in bold are those used in the pre- and post-test.

Table A3.2.1
Pseudo-loanword terms employed in each exercise broken down by unit as found on the university map

Unit	Classification	Multiple-Choice	Identification
Career Center	Announcer	Back	Auto-Bai
	Gag Man	Chief	Back Dancer
	Gold Collar Worker	Clean	Driver
	Model	Sign	Gag Man
	Reporter	Skinship	Tour Guide
	Salary Man		
High-Tech Center	Com-Maeng	Audio	Audio
	Consent	Cassette	Com-Maeng
	E-Mail	Consent	PC Bang
	Hacker	Free	Remocon
	Install	Trance	VTR
	Light Cable		
Stadium	Aerobics	Fighting	Back Number
	Cheerleader	Health	Pocket Ball
	Goal In	Hiking	Running Machine
	Member Change	Sand Bag	Sand Bag
	Skin Scuba	Training	Ski
	Tennis		
Student Union Building	Ball Pen	Circle	A-Pull
	Desk	Cunning	Circle
	Graph	Hint	Cunning
	Handout	Report	Cut Line
	Hotchkiss	Sharp	Report
	Spring Note		
Vending Machine	Can Coffee	Cider	After Service
	Cappuccino	Condition	Ex
	Coffee	Confidence	Handle
	Prima	Cup	Note
	Red Tea	Prima	One Piece
	Soda		

Table A3.2.2
Pseudo-loanword terms employed in each exercise broken down by unit as found on the main street map

Unit	Classification	Multiple-Choice	Identification
Bank	365 Cash Bank	Bank	Clip
	ATM	Check	Hotchkiss
	Credit Card	Chief	Sharp
	Inflay	Secret Number	Three Piece
	PC Banking	Sign	White
	Percent		
Bus Terminal	Air Bag	Excellent Bus	Back mirror
	Open Car	Handle	Klaxon
	Power Oil	Klaxon	Mission Oil
	Tire	Owner	Side Brake
	Tune-up	Punk	Room Mirror
	Wheel cap		
Department Store	Ankle Boots	DC	Ankle boots
	Brand	Maker	Bae-kkob T
	Collar	One Piece	De-pa-teu
	Eye Shopping	Over	Museutang
	Trousers	Panty	Y-Shirt
	Y-Shirt		
Night Club	Dance	Booking	Hip
	Date	Dash	Hunting
	Live Beer	Hunting	Night
	One Shot	Meeting	O-bite
	O-bite	Promise	One Shot
	Pitcher		
Restaurant	Buffet	Cider	Beef Kass
	Don Kass	Fusion	Don Kass
	Egg Fry	Interior	Dutch Pay
	Menu	Self	High Rice
	Hamburger Steak	Service	Restorang
	Waiter		

Table A3.2.3
Pseudo-loanword terms employed in each exercise broken down by unit as found on the
underground map

Unit	Classification	Multiple-Choice	Identification
Coffee Shop	Café	Interior	Aircon
	Dutch Pay	Jelly	High-Collar
	Napkin	Prima	Meeting
	Red Tea	Self	Short Da-ri
	Refill	Service	Time Killer
	Service		
Hair Salon	Cut	All Back	Clean
	Hair Dryer	Hair Pin	Hair Iron
	Hair Iron	Manicure	Handsome
	Perma	Setting	Manicure
	Shampoo	Skin	Perma
	Sil Pin		
Macteria	Apple Pie	Chain	A-reu bai-teu
	Cola	Cider	Hamburger Steak
	Hamburg	Hot Dog	Mania
	Home Service	Hamburg	Potato
	Potato	Potato	Punk
	Take Out		
Supermarket	Frank Sausage	Cider	Flash
	Fruit	Hard	Mes
	Remix	Remix	Spring Note
	Sand	Sand	Super
	Snack	Super	Wheel Cap
	Soft Drink		
Video Wall	Back Dancer	Ballad	Headlight
	Band	Classic	Keyboard
	Classic	Omnibus	Romantic
	Singing Room	Remake	Talent
	Techno	Talent	Volume
	Top Ten		

Table A3.2.4

Pseudo-loanword terms employed in each exercise broken down by unit as found on the apartment map

Unit	Classification	Multiple-Choice	Identification
Entertainment	Kiss Scene	Audio	Event
	Performer	Cassette	Eye Shopping
	Play	Event	Hof
	Pocket Ball	Mellow	Human Drama
	Sitcom	No Good (N/G)	Sitcom
	Show		
Family &	Curfew	Back	Bi-nil House
Friends	Roommate	Clean	Cordi
	Short Da-ri	Complex	Ot-pin
	Skinship	Hip	Sign
	Stress	Solo	Sign Pen
	Tough Guy		
Kitchen	Fry Pan	Coffee Pot	Bang-ul Tomato
	Gas Range	Cup	Egg Fry
	Jeon-ja Range	Fork & Knife	Gas Range
	Knife & Fork	Kitchen Towel	Jeon-ja Range
	Mixer	Range	Omu Rice
	Percolator		
Telephone	Collect Call	Dial	A-pa-teu
	Hand Phone	Jeon-hwa Box	Hand Phone
	Interphone	Pon-ting	Menteu
	Jeon-hwa card	Schedule	Promise
	Receiver	Telemarking	Solo
	Message		
The	Computer	Audio	Complex
Household	Remocon	Cassette	Skinship
	Telephone	Flash	Sofa
	Television	Sofa	Stand
	Stand	Stand	Steam
	VTR		

The Shared Interface

Overall interface design is based upon the local cultural and contextual environment of the student, and presented in the form of a map. The initial start screen allows students to select from one of four locations: University, Main Street, Underground, or Apartment. After clicking on one of these options, a map of that location is presented. Each map presents five locations which would form the units of study. This allows the system to bring in realities from outside 'the classroom', and it is from here that the communicative competence of students can begin to be addressed. Support for learning is provided through each module by enhancing motivation, promoting encoding and retention and the use of linguistic knowledge. Motivational factors are bolstered through attention (facilitated through design and selection of media use), confidence (facilitated through navigation and orientation support), and control (facilitated through a user friendly interface) (Alessi & Trollip, 2001). Encoding and retention are promoted through the interactivity of the language tasks available for practice. Learning strategies support is also provided through use of a hypermedia system, mostly through metacognition, which "is our awareness of our own cognitive processes, and includes reflecting, assessing, planning, and intentionally initiating cognitive activities" (Alessi & Trollip, 2001, p. 167).

The Units

A total of twenty units of study were developed for each module. The University section consists of career center, high-tech center, stadium, student union building, and vending machine units. The Main Street section consists of bank, bus terminal, department store, night club, and restaurant units. The Underground section consists of coffee shop, hair salon, macteria, supermarket, and video wall units. The Apartment section consists of entertainment, family and friends, kitchen, telephone, and household units. Each of the four sections is shaded a different color: University is blue, Main Street is maroon, Underground is green, and Apartment is olive.

Each unit page, regardless of section, maintains an identical functional layout. To the top right of the display, there are color coded buttons to take students directly to the 'map' for each of the four sections, and a button to take students to a 'scores' section where they can view their progress and achievement with the material. Below this frame menu is an information panel that displays context sensitive data. This data changes based upon the activity displayed, and at the click of the three buttons next to the panel: 'Overview' for an overview of the current activity; 'Korean' for translation of data displayed in the panel; and, 'Instructions' for information on how to complete the current activity. Below the information panel are buttons that students can select to engage in the linguistic activities of the unit: 'Classify'; 'Multiple choice; and, 'Identify'. Along the bottom of the screen is another frame menu containing seven buttons: 'Help' for context sensitive procedural help for the unit; 'Activity' indicating the current activity; 'Navigation' which jumps to a full-screen menu containing each unit; 'Reset' to reset the activity; 'Grade' to grade and store the score of the currently completed activity; 'Answer' to show the answers for the current activity; and, 'Exit' to close the program. These elements provide a user friendly interface since the buttons contain clear meanings, with appropriate confirmation of selection, and the use of tool tips (Alessi & Trollip, 2001).

Navigation

The central 'Navigation' button at the bottom of each unit page provided students with access to a unit jump point which allows students direct access to any unit of the material, and skips the main section map pages. This full-screen menu then serves as an anchor point, and each unit could also be accessed directly by selecting 'Course maps' from the hierarchical bilingual menu bar, or by selecting one of the map buttons from the top right frame menu. The locus of control was firmly with learners as they were able to select the sequence and pace of their progression. This ease of orientation is not only important for navigation but it is believed that it could have come to promote motivation and assist in promoting higher levels of concentration (Alessi & Trollip, 2001). Access to consistent global control throughout each module also affords students the ability to review material on demand through nonlinear hypermedia navigation. Repeating and reviewing material in this manner can come to aid metacognition and can facilitate encoding, recall, and comprehension (Alessi & Trollip, 2001).

Help

A tutorial for the program exists, and this is accessible from the program menu bar. In addition, a click of the help button on any page would provide learners with context sensitive aid. Depending on the user's system settings, this help would be either in the form of a text balloon pop-up or employ the use of an agent. Merlin is one of four software technology agents produced by Microsoft for use with the Windows operating system. If the operating system has this agent installed, along with the accompanying text-to-speech engine, the help function of the modules would use this facility. In this case, the character Merlin would appear and speak in English, as well as show this speech textually, before moving to different sections of the interface to draw attention to specific areas. In this manner, students can gain access to procedural assistance. Informational help on the content is also consistently provided through the information textbox under the frame menu on the top right of the screen. Further, alongside the informational help textbox are three buttons that provide context sensitive information for the student based upon the activity currently selected.

Bilingual Functionality

Bilingual functionality is provided to students throughout the interface for program usability support, and context sensitive help functions are available to the student in either English or Korean, as are instructions for completing activities. The menu bar is designed so that it would be available in both English and Korean, while icons are constructed so that they would be in English first and auto-translate to Korean upon mouse-over. As a by-product, it is perceived that through the use of such bilingual items in language learning software, students are able to recognize the English associated with common software support functions, and transfer the linguistic assimilation of such vocabulary to any English-only software packages that they may install on their home computer systems, or later utilize within work environments.

Module Assessment

Students are able to keep track of their own progress and levels of achievement by accessing the module's 'Scores' section which consists of color coded areas; one area to track activity completion and the scores for each individual unit, and another area which shows the overall achievement level for activities completed with the program. Information regarding the student is displayed as well, including their name, student number, and class number. A number of buttons are also provided to students in this section; 'Drive' to send data to (for example) a hard disk, 'Erase' to erase the score data (by section or entirely), 'Print' to print the score information (by section or entirely), and 'Device' to import scores to the current computer. To prevent students from copying scores between each other, a mechanism is in place to ensure that only the student registered to use the software imports only their scores and no other. It is this data that was periodically submitted (by email) to verify student completion of the modules throughout treatment.

Submission of Material

To prepare material for submission, students would select 'Export grades' from the 'Scores' section of the menu bar which then sees their scores saved to an encrypted file, which can be verified by selecting 'View exported results'. Alternatively, students can use the buttons found in the 'scores' section of the modules to import and export data to an encrypted file. Students were expected to submit a copy of their grade file every two weeks, and the data on the files were then checked to see if students were on track with completion of activities. A separate utility application was developed specifically to allow the native English speaking instructor deploying the material to parse student grade files to confirm and check student completion of the homework activities. Participating students did not have access to this utility.

Module One Activities

The style of activities designed for Module One is based on those found in typical language learning textbooks and maintain a drill emphasis. Such activities, like those that were selected for Module Two, are ones that students would find familiar. The activities for each module fall into one of three objective-based tasks: classification, multiple-choice, and identification.

Classification

In this section, the aim is to separate presented English direct and pseudo-loanwords by dragging and dropping the terms into one of two different baskets (English and Konglish). Students were presented with a word list, which allowed them to participate in the item selection step and sort through the words that they know. Presenting a complete list of terms is common and useful, particularly for foreign language vocabulary items (Alessi & Trollip, 2001).

Multiple-choice

This activity follows the multiple-choice model closely. A pseudo-loanword vocabulary item was presented along with four choices of definition. One choice is the English dictionary definition, a second embodied the Korean language meaning while the two other choices are distracter definitions. Students were expected to differentiate between the Korean and English meaning for the term, and select the English definition. This type of question allows learners to draw on prior word knowledge, as students tend not to rely on random selection but select answers in vocabulary-based multiple-choice tasks due to association (Paul, Stallman, & O'Rourke, 1990).

Identification
These activities involve the matching of a single pseudo-loanword vocabulary item from a five item word list with a presented English definition. Although perhaps leading to initial errors, recall can be higher when students are presented with the definition, or 'confusable responses', in activities (Alessi & Shih, 1989).

Module Two Activities

The style of activities designed for Module Two are game-based, and like the activities selected for Module One, the language puzzles found in Module Two are of the type students would find familiar. As both modules seek to use the same three objective-based tasks to promote learning, the second module also contains classification, multiple-choice, and identification activities.

Classification
As in Module One, the aim of this activity is to identify direct English loanwords and pseudo-loanwords, and sort them into two categories. Again, as in Module One, students were presented with a word list allowing them to participate in the item selection step and begin classification of the terminology mentally. However, learners using Module Two needed to identify the term in one of two different word search puzzles, one marked 'English' and the other 'Konglish'. Students were engaged with the interactional puzzles in order to classify the terms, and if a term is selected correctly, it is highlighted.

Multiple-choice
This activity follows the model of multiple-choice presented in Module One but extends into a game-based format through the use of scrambled vocabulary. A scrambled pseudo-loanword vocabulary item was presented along with four choices of definition. One choice is an English dictionary definition, a second embodied the Korean language meaning, while the two other choices were distracter definitions. Students needed to differentiate between the Korean and English meanings for the scrambled term, and were then expected to select the English definition. First, however, they must identify the term that they need to select the definition for, as this term is the scrambled word. The aim is for students to unscramble the word based on the definitions presented, and on their prior knowledge, in which case the pseudo-loanword definition assists in their unscrambling of the term so that the English definition can then be selected.

Identification

This activity follows that of the identification task found in Module One, but it was extended into a paired-associate task and made game-based through the use of clues. The activity involves the matching of dual vocabulary items, each from a five item word list, with a presented English definition acting as a clue. Learning from such an exercise occurs in two stages involving response learning, where random errors may occur, and an associative stage in which responses are linked to correct stimuli where discrimination errors are more common (Alessi & Trollip, 2001).

Appendix Four
THE STATISTICS

Tables

Figures

Appendix Four
THE STATISTICS

Tables

Reference to statistics made in the text refers to the tables below.

Table A4.1.1
Breakdown of participant population by gender

Major	Male	Female	Total
Childhood education	3	24	27
Electronics	10	2	12
Elementary education	4	19	23
Pharmacy	8	13	21
Occupational therapy	9	16	25
Total	34	74	108

Table A4.1.2
Breakdown of participant population by major

Major	Population	Percent
Childhood education	27	25
Electronics	12	11
Elementary education	23	21
Pharmacy	21	20
Occupational therapy	25	23
Total	108	100

Table A4.2.1
Summary test-of-fit statistics for 114-item survey

	Item-Person Interaction			
	Items		Persons	
	Location	Fit Residual	Location	Fit Residual
Mean	0.00	0.07	0.10	-0.92
SD	0.71	0.48	0.42	3.82

Item-Trait Interaction		Reliability Indices	
Total Item χ^2	300.61	Separation Index	0.88
Total Deg of Freedom	228.00	Cronbach Alpha	n/a
Total χ^2 Probability	0.00		

Power of Test-of-Fit
Power is EXCELLENT
[Based on Separation Index of 0.88]

Table A4.2.2

Item thresholds for the 114-item survey (centralized)

Item	Thresholds		
	1	2	3
001	-1.26	-0.36	+1.62
002	-1.00	+0.33	+0.66
003	-2.28	-0.29	+2.57
004	-1.53	+0.97	+2.43
005	-1.47	-0.47	+1.93
006	-2.14	-0.58	+2.72
007	-1.84	+0.49	+1.40
008	-1.57	-0.26	+1.82
009	-1.50	-0.26	+1.76
010	-2.09	-0.13	+2.22
011	-2.12	+0.02	+2.10
012	-2.21	-0.15	+2.35
013	-1.53	-0.18	+1.71
014	-1.80	-0.39	+2.19
015	-1.83	-0.61	+2.44
016	-2.29	-0.30	+2.32
017	-1.35	-0.52	+1.87
018	-2.09	-0.13	+2.22
019	-2.35	+0.20	+2.14
020	-1.46	-0.43	+1.89
021	-1.59	0.26	+1.33
022	-1.63	-0.41	+2.04
023	-1.77	-0.26	+2.03
024	-2.13	-0.41	+2.54
025	-2.11	+0.20	+1.92
026	-1.98	+0.10	+1.88
027	-1.93	-0.80	+2.73
028	-2.10	-0.12	+2.22
029	-1.87	-0.29	+2.16
030	-1.83	-0.59	+2.42
031*	-0.75	-0.96	+1.71
032	-0.96	-0.03	+0.99
033	-2.30	-0.45	+2.75
034	-3.77	+0.41	+3.36
035	-2.06	-0.36	+2.42
036	-2.85	-0.05	+2.91
037	-2.45	+0.27	+2.18
038	-2.71	+0.07	+2.64

Table A4.2.2 *(continued)*

Item	Thresholds		
	1	2	3
039	-1.74	-0.18	+1.93
040	-1,88	+0.19	+1.69
041	-1.83	+0.06	+1.77
042	-2.60	+0.03	+2.57
043	-2.51	+0.03	+2.49
044	-1.62	-0.45	+2.07
045	-3.14	-0.28	+3.41
046	-2.63	+0.28	+2.35
047	-2.35	+0.16	+2.19
048	-1.97	+0.47	+1.50
049	-2.49	+0.70	+1.78
050	-1.74	-0.05	+1.79
051	-2.03	+0.13	+1.91
052	-3.22	+0.13	+3.08
053	-1.78	+0.09	+1.69
054	-2.41	+0.06	+2.36
055	-1.45	-0.35	+1.80
056	-0.97	-0.35	+1.32
057	-1.79	+0.02	+1.77
058	-2.14	-0.16	+2.30
059	-1.90	-0.36	+2.26
060	-2.22	-0.34	+2.55
061*	-1.66	+1.00	+0.66
062	-0.93	-0.56	+1.49
063	-1.47	-0.58	+2.06
064	-1.20	-0.80	+1.99
065	-1.28	-0.28	+1.56
066*	-0.29	-1.34	+1.63
067*	+0.44	-2.12	+1.68
068	-2.14	-0.29	+2.43
069	-1.97	-0.27	+2.24
070	-1.00	-0.96	+1.96
071	-3.45	+0.34	+3.10
072	-3.66	+0.44	+3.21
073	-1.41	-0.74	+2.15
074	-2.24	+0.17	+2.07
075	-2.36	+0.68	+1.69
076	2.72	-0.30	+3.02
077	-1.45	-0.88	+2.33

Table A4.2.2 *(continued)*

Item	Thresholds		
	1	2	3
078	-1.32	-0.34	+1.66
079	-1.65	+0.17	+1.48
080	-2.12	+0.06	+2.06
081	-1.96	+0.43	+1.53
082	-1.94	+0.21	+1.73
083	-2.06	+0.29	+1.78
084	-2.55	+0.79	+1.76
085*	-1.20	-1.38	+2.58
086	-2.28	-0.03	+2.31
087	-2.15	-0.07	+2.22
088	-2.22	+0.00	+2.22
089	-2.21	-0.33	+2.55
090	-2.10	-0.50	+2.59
091	-1.91	+0.13	+1.78
092	-2.71	+0.00	+2.71
093	-3.52	+0.09	+3.43
094*	-1.08	-1.15	+2.23
095	-2.72	+0.05	+2.67
096	-2.35	+0.10	+2.25
097	-3.03	+0.46	+2.57
098	-2.89	+0.14	+2.75
099	-2.78	+0.73	+2.05
100	-3.21	+0.15	+3.06
101	-3.09	+0.75	+2.34
102	-2.90	+0.67	+2.23
103	-2.62	-0.09	+2.71
104*	-1.43	-1.49	+2.91
105	-1.58	-0.97	+2.54
106	-1.90	-0.31	+2.21
107	-2.93	-0.06	+2.99
108	-1.93	-0.64	+2.57
109	-2.70	-0.13	+2.83
110	-2.19	+1.26	+0.93
111	-2.21	+0.67	+1.54
112	-2.17	-0.22	+2.39
113	-1.80	-0.11	+1.91
114	-1.85	+0.07	+1.77

*indicates disordered threshold (seven items).

Table A4.2.3
Individual item-fit for the 114-item survey

Item	Location	SE	Residual	DegF	DatPts	χ^2	Prob	degF
001	+0.95	0.12	-0.13	104.03	108	0.17	0.92	2
002	+1.11	0.13	-0.02	104.03	108	0.78	0.68	2
003	-0.09	0.15	+0.17	104.03	108	2.63	0.27	2
004	+0.53	0.13	-0.07	104.03	108	1.34	0.51	2
005	-0.31	0.14	-0.05	104.03	108	0.22	0.90	2
006	-0.06	0.16	+0.24	104.03	108	0.75	0.69	2
007	+0.19	0.13	-0.14	104.03	108	0.56	0.76	2
008	+0.34	0.13	-0.14	104.03	108	0.72	0.70	2
009	+0.42	0.13	+0.03	103.07	107	0.20	0.90	2
010	+0.33	0.14	-0.15	104.03	108	0.40	0.82	2
011	+0.54	0.14	-0.31	104.03	108	9.97	0.14	2
012	+0.91	0.15	-0.17	103.07	107	1.74	0.42	2
013	+0.12	0.13	-0.97	103.07	107	5.87	0.05	2
014	+0.62	0.13	-0.63	104.03	108	3.38	0.18	2
015	+0.32	0.14	-0.63	104.03	108	3.47	0.18	2
016	+0.88	0.15	-0.67	104.03	108	2.28	0.32	2
017*	-0.25	0.14	-0.90	103.07	107	10.92	0.00	2
018	+0.45	0.14	-0.28	103.07	107	2.03	0.36	2
019	+0.21	0.15	-0.15	103.07	107	2.10	0.35	2
020	-0.01	0.13	-0.84	103.07	107	5.22	0.07	2
021	+0.01	0.12	-0.70	103.07	107	4.17	0.12	2
022	+0.01	0.14	-0.15	103.07	107	0.20	0.91	2
023	-0.08	0.14	-0.34	103.07	107	3.35	0.19	2
024	+0.39	0.15	-0.25	102.11	106	1.45	0.49	2
025	+0.00	0.14	+0.06	102.11	106	0.23	0.89	2
026	+0.07	0.14	+0.70	103.07	107	1.57	0.46	2
027	+0.08	0.16	+0.31	103.07	107	3.29	0.19	2
028	+0.05	0.14	-0.33	103.07	107	3.76	0.15	2
029	+0.26	0.14	-0.47	103.07	107	2.83	0.24	2
030	-0.19	0.15	+0.10	102.11	106	0.41	0.81	2
031	-0.71	0.14	-0.68	103.07	107	0.66	0.72	2
032	-0.12	0.11	+0.37	103.07	107	1.55	0.46	2
033	+0.42	0.15	+0.04	103.07	107	1.09	0.58	2
034	-0.47	0.17	+0.14	103.07	107	0.99	0.61	2
035	-0.03	0.15	-0.10	103.07	107	1.20	0.55	2
036	-0.31	0.16	+0.06	103.07	107	4.63	0.10	2
037	+0.57	0.15	-0.52	103.07	107	2.95	0.23	2
038	+1.00	0.16	-0.36	103.07	107	0.14	0.93	2
039	+0.06	0.14	-0.35	103.07	107	3.39	0.18	2
040	+0.29	0.13	+0.56	103.07	107	2.39	0.30	2

Table A4.2.3 *(continued)*

Item	Location	SE	Residual	DegF	DatPts	χ^2	Prob	degF
041	+0.37	0.14	-0.90	102.11	106	5.08	0.08	2
042	+0.23	0.16	-0.37	104.03	108	7.55	0.02	2
043*	-0.34	0.15	-0.47	104.03	108	10.80	0.00*	2
044	-0.14	0.14	-0.45	104.03	108	5.27	0.07	2
045	+1.66	0.17	+0.06	104.03	108	1.62	0.45	2
046	+0.85	0.16	+0.57	104.03	108	4.63	0.10	2
047	-1.75	0.15	-0.72	103.07	107	1.36	0.51	2
048	+0.42	0.14	+0.46	103.07	107	3.13	0.21	2
049	+0.90	0.17	+0.50	103.07	107	4.74	0.09	2
050	-0.83	0.14	+0.17	104.03	108	0.66	0.72	2
051	+0.65	0.14	+0.63	103.07	107	1.53	0.47	2
052	+1.74	0.18	-0.08	103.07	107	1.78	0.41	2
053	-0.84	0.13	+0.30	104.03	108	1.74	0.42	2
054	-0.42	0.15	+0.40	104.03	108	0.06	0.97	2
055	+0.13	0.13	+0.38	104.03	108	0.78	0.68	2
056*	-0.15	0.12	+2.13*	104.03	108	22.77	0.00*	2
057*	+0.05	0.13	+1.54	104.03	108	24.48	0.00*	2
058	-1.69	0.16	-0.15	104.03	108	0.32	0.85	2
059	-0.61	0.15	+0.70	104.03	108	3.18	0.20	2
060	-0.30	0.16	+0.79	103.07	107	0.99	0.61	2
061*	+1.34	0.16	+0.24	104.03	108	9.50	0.01*	2
062	-1.02	0.14	+0.74	104.03	108	0.69	0.71	2
063	-1.09	0.16	+0.34	104.03	108	2.48	0.29	2
064	-1.91	0.17	-0.01	104.03	108	1.19	0.55	2
065	-1.03	0.14	+0.58	104.03	108	1.73	0.42	2
066	-1.19	0.16	-0.11	103.07	107	1.08	0.58	2
067	-1.18	0.17	-0.38	104.03	108	0.10	0.95	2
068	-0.69	0.16	+0.20	104.03	108	3.03	0.22	2
069	-0.55	0.15	+0.34	104.03	108	1.23	0.54	2
070	-1.06	0.16	-0.27	104.03	108	2.77	0.25	2
071	-1.41	0.17	+0.34	102.11	106	0.46	0.79	2
072	-1.39	0.17	+0.07	102.11	106	0.50	0.78	2
073	-0.55	0.15	+0.35	102.11	106	1.36	0.51	2
074	+0.74	0.15	+0.35	102.11	106	2.03	0.36	2
075	+0.63	0.16	-0.12	102.11	106	2.61	0.27	2
076	-0.65	0.17	+0.25	102.11	106	0.95	0.62	2
077	-0.74	0.17	-0.37	102.11	106	0.52	0.77	2
078*	-0.08	0.13	+0.96	102.11	106	10.53	0.01*	2
079*	+0.48	0.13	+0.62	102.11	106	6.92	0.03*	2
080	-0.20	0.14	+0.55	102.11	106	0.16	0.92	2
081	+1.23	0.15	+0.01	102.11	106	1.35	0.51	2

Table A4.2.3 *(continued)*

Item	Location	SE	Residual	DegF	DatPts	χ^2	Prob	degF
082	-0.05	0.13	+0.92	102.11	106	2.41	0.30	2
083	+0.37	0.14	+0.26	102.11	106	1.72	0.42	2
084	+0.49	0.16	-0.19	102.11	106	2.78	0.25	2
085	-0.60	0.18	+0.01	102.11	106	1.03	0.60	2
086	+0.52	0.15	+0.63	102.11	106	2.89	0.24	2
087	+0.52	0.15	+0.49	101.14	105	1.87	0.39	2
088	-0.03	0.15	+0.09	102.11	106	2.11	0.35	2
089	-0.19	0.16	+0.47	102.11	106	2.59	0.27	2
090	-0.25	0.16	+0.04	102.11	106	1.21	0.55	2
091	-0.08	0.14	+0.02	102.11	106	0.56	0.76	2
092	+0.16	0.16	+0.64	104.03	108	2.11	0.35	2
093	-0.40	0.18	-0.15	104.03	108	2.27	0.32	2
094	-0.49	0.16	+0.04	104.03	108	1.23	0.54	2
095	-0.43	0.16	-0.13	103.07	107	1.53	0.47	2
096	-0.16	0.15	+0.16	104.03	108	0.29	0.87	2
097	-0.72	0.15	+0.77	103.07	107	2.38	0.30	2
098	-0.42	0.16	+0.08	104.03	108	2.05	0.36	2
099	+0.42	0.17	+0.05	103.07	107	0.96	0.62	2
100	+0.74	0.17	+0.24	104.03	108	0.55	0.76	2
101	+0.91	0.19	+0.13	104.03	108	0.38	0.83	2
102	+0.17	0.16	-0.06	104.03	108	4.03	0.13	2
103	+0.60	0.16	+0.40	104.03	108	0.14	0.93	2
104	-0.60	0.20	+0.23	104.03	108	0.57	0.75	2
105	-1.01	0.18	-0.23	104.03	108	1.68	0.43	2
106	+0.17	0.14	+0.54	104.03	108	0.40	0.82	2
107	+1.80	0.17	-0.23	104.03	108	0.87	0.65	2
108	-0.60	0.16	-0.09	104.03	108	1.38	0.50	2
109	-0.74	0.17	+0.34	104.03	108	1.73	0.42	2
110	+0.42	0.15	+0.44	104.03	108	4.83	0.09	2
111	+0.33	0.14	+0.26	104.03	108	0.18	0.91	2
112	+0.76	0.14	+0.38	103.07	107	5.78	0.06	2
113	+0.18	0.13	+0.51	104.03	108	2.32	0.31	2
114	+0.05	0.13	+0.06	104.03	108	1.15	0.56	2

Table A4.3.1

Summary test-of-fit statistics for the 95-item refined survey

	Item-Person Interaction				
	Items			Persons	
	Location	Fit Residual		Location	Fit Residual
Mean	0.00	0.11		0.09	-0.79
SD	0.68	0.41		0.44	3.47

Item-Trait Interaction		Reliability Indices	
Total Item χ^2	213.04	Separation Index	0.87
Total Deg of Freedom	190.00	Cronbach Alpha	n/a
Total χ^2 Probability	0.12		

Power of Test-of-Fit
Power is EXCELLENT
[Based on Separation Index of 0.87]

Table A4.3.2
Item thresholds for the 95-item survey (centralized)

Item	Thresholds		
	1	2	3
001	-1.25	-0.36	+1.61
002	-1.00	+0.33	+0.67
003	-2.31	-0.28	+2.58
004	-1.54	+0.10	+1.44
005	-1.49	-0.46	+1.95
006	-2.16	-0.58	+2.74
007	-1.86	-0.45	+1.41
008	-1.57	-0.25	+1.82
009	-1.51	-0.26	+1.77
010	-2.11	-0.13	+2.24
011	-2.13	+0.03	+2.10
012	-2.21	-0.13	+2.35
014	-1.81	-0.39	+2.20
015	-1.84	-0.60	+2.44
016	-2.32	-0.02	+2.34
019	-2.35	+0.21	+2.14
020	-1.47	-0.43	+1.89
021	-1.59	+0.26	+1.33
022	-1.63	-0.41	+2.04
023	-1.78	-0.27	+2.04
024	-2.14	-0.40	+2.53
025	-2.13	+0.20	+1.93
026	-1.99	+0.11	+1.88
027	-1.94	-0.78	+2.72
028	-2.13	-0.11	+2.24
029	-1.87	-0.29	+2.16
030	-1.82	-0.60	+2.42
032	-0.97	-0.03	+1.00
033	-2.32	-0.44	+2.76
034	-3.81	+0.42	+3.39
035	-2.08	-0.37	+2.45
036	-2.89	-0.05	+2.94
037	-2.47	+0.29	+2.19
038	-2.73	+0.09	+2.64
039	-1.76	-0.18	+1.93
040	-1.89	+0.19	+1.70
041	-1.85	+0.07	+1.78
042	-2.61	+0.03	+2.57
044	-1.64	-0.44	+2.08

Table A4.3.2 *(continued)*

Item	Thresholds		
	1	2	3
046	-2.64	+0.28	+2.36
047	-2.35	+0.15	+2.19
048	-1.97	+0.48	+1.50
049	-2.49	+0.72	+1.77
050	-1.74	-0.05	+1.79
051	-2.04	+0.14	+1.91
053	-1.77	+0.08	+1.69
054	-2.44	+0.06	+2.37
055	-1.47	-0.34	+1.80
058	-2.13	-0.18	+2.31
059	-1.90	-0.36	+2.26
060	-2.25	-0.33	+2.58
062	-0.96	-0.56	+1.51
063	-1.51	-0.57	+2.08
064	-1.17	-0.82	+1.99
065	-1.29	-0.28	+1.57
068	-2.18	-0.28	+2.45
069	-1.98	-0.27	+2.25
071	-3.43	+0.33	+3.09
072	-3.66	+0.45	+3.21
073	-1.40	-0.75	+2.14
074	-2.44	+0.18	+2.06
075	-2.37	+0.67	+1.70
076	-2.74	-0.29	+3.03
077	-1.46	-0.88	+2.34
079	-1.68	+0.18	+1.50
080	-2.15	+0.07	+2.08
081	-1.99	+0.43	+1.56
082	-1.95	+0.21	+1.74
083	-2.09	+0.29	+1.79
084	-2.57	+0.80	+1.78
086	-2.31	-0.02	+2.34
087	-2.17	-0.06	+2.23
088	-2.24	+0.01	+2.23
089	-2.24	-0.33	+2.57
090	-2.12	-0.49	+2.61
091	-1.93	+0.14	+1.79
092	-2.72	+0.00	+2.72
093	-3.54	+0.10	+3.44
095	-2.74	+0.07	+2.68

Table A4.3.2 *(continued)*

Item	Thresholds		
	1	2	3
096	-2.36	+0.10	+2.26
097	-3.05	+0.47	+2.58
098	-2.92	+0.15	+2.77
099	-2.81	+0.73	+2.07
100	-3.21	+0.16	+3.05
101	-3.11	+0.76	+2.35
102	-2.91	+0.68	+2.22
103	-2.65	-0.08	+2.73
105	-1.57	-0.98	+2.55
106	-1.92	-2.94	+2.22
107	-2.96	-0.04	+3.00
108	-1.95	-0.64	+2.59
109	-2.73	-0.13	+2.86
111	-2.22	+0.69	+1.54
112	-2.18	-0.22	+2.40
113	-1.81	-0.11	+1.92

Table A4.3.3

Individual item-fit for the 95-item refined survey

Item	Location	SE	Residual	DegF	DatPts	χ^2	Prob	degF
001	+0.95	0.12	+.10	103.84	108	0.05	0.97	2
002	+1.11	0.13	-0.16	103.84	108	0.60	0.74	2
003	-0.10	0.15	+0.18	103.84	108	2.31	0.32	2
004	+0.53	0.13	-0.02	103.84	108	0.31	0.85	2
005	-0.32	0.14	+0.04	103.84	108	0.16	0.92	2
006	-0.07	0.16	+0.24	103.84	108	0.15	0.93	2
007	+0.19	0.13	-0.11	103.84	108	1.29	0.52	2
008	+0.33	0.13	-0.07	103.84	108	0.41	0.82	2
009	+0.42	0.13	+0.04	102.88	107	1.18	0.55	2
010	+0.33	0.14	-0.08	103.84	108	0.79	0.67	2
011	+0.53	0.14	-0.26	103.84	108	3.56	0.17	2
012	+0.90	0.15	-0.20	102.88	107	0.91	0.63	2
014	+0.62	0.14	-0.57	103.84	108	2.32	0.31	2
015	+0.30	0.14	-0.61	103.84	108	3.16	0.21	2
016	+0.88	0.15	-0.71	103.84	108	3.86	0.15	2
019	+0.20	0.15	-0.01	102.88	107	3.33	0.19	2
020	-0.01	0.13	-0.72	102.88	107	4.15	0.13	2
021	+0.00	0.12	-0.57	102.88	107	5.91	0.05	2
022	+0.01	0.14	+0.07	102.88	107	1.11	0.57	2
023	-0.08	0.14	-0.31	102.88	107	1.31	0.52	2
024	+0.38	0.15	-0.21	101.92	106	1.60	0.45	2
025	-0.01	0.14	+0.14	101.92	106	0.59	0.74	2
026	+0.05	0.14	+0.80	102.88	107	2.72	0.26	2
027	+0.06	0.16	+0.39	102.88	107	3.30	0.19	2
028	+0.04	0.15	-0.28	102.88	107	1.72	0.42	2
029	+0.25	0.14	-0.51	102.88	107	3.52	0.17	2
030	-0.20	0.15	+0.22	101.92	106	1.43	0.49	2
032	-0.12	0.11	+0.47	102.88	107	0.84	0.66	2
033	+0.41	0.15	+0.02	102.88	107	2.61	0.27	2
034	-0.49	0.17	+0.12	102.88	107	1.10	0.58	2
035	-0.04	0.15	-0.16	102.88	107	1.12	0.57	2
036	-0.32	0.17	+0.02	102.88	107	5.18	0.07	2
037	+0.56	0.16	-0.54	102.88	107	3.29	0.19	2
038	+0.99	0.16	-0.35	102.88	107	0.22	0.89	2
039	+0.05	0.14	-0.34	102.88	107	2.02	0.36	2
040	+0.28	0.14	-0.56	102.88	107	1.74	0.42	2
041	+0.37	0.14	-0.91	101.92	106	5.72	0.06	2
042	+0.22	0.16	-0.35	103.84	108	4.22	0.12	2
044	-0.15	0.14	-0.50	103.84	108	5.79	0.06	2
046	+0.86	0.16	+0.62	103.84	108	4.17	0.12	2

Table A4.3.3 *(continued)*

Item	Location	SE	Residual	DegF	DatPts	χ^2	Prob	degF
047	-1.75	0.15	-0.52	102.88	107	6.71	0.03	2
048	+0.41	0.14	+0.53	102.88	107	3.81	0.15	2
049	+0.88	0.17	+0.54	102.88	107	5.25	0.07	2
050	-0.83	0.14	+0.35	103.84	108	1.67	0.43	2
051	+0.65	0.14	+0.67	102.88	107	1.80	0.41	2
053	-0.84	0.13	+0.51	103.84	108	2.30	0.32	2
054	-0.43	0.15	+0.46	103.84	108	0.88	0.65	2
055	+0.12	0.13	+0.38	103.84	108	3.74	0.15	2
058	-1.70	0.16	-0.09	103.84	108	2.35	0.31	2
059	-0.62	0.15	+0.80	103.84	108	6.13	0.05	2
060	-0.31	0.16	+0.79	102.88	107	0.79	0.67	2
062	-1.04	0.14	+0.89	103.84	108	3.31	0.19	2
063	-1.11	0.16	+0.44	103.84	108	5.68	0.06	2
064	-1.91	0.17	+0.16	103.84	108	8.31	0.02	2
065	-1.04	0.14	+0.81	103.84	108	4.80	0.09	2
068	-0.71	0.16	+0.19	103.84	108	0.72	0.70	2
069	-0.56	0.15	+0.39	103.84	108	0.72	0.70	2
071	-1.40	0.17	+0.50	101.92	106	1.15	0.56	2
072	-1.40	0.17	+0.14	101.92	106	0.55	0.76	2
073	-0.55	0.15	+0.44	101.92	106	2.89	0.24	2
074	+0.72	0.15	+0.46	101.92	106	1.88	0.39	2
075	+0.63	0.16	-0.09	101.92	106	1.24	0.54	2
076	-0.67	0.18	+0.26	101.92	106	1.98	0.37	2
077	-0.76	0.17	-0.33	101.92	106	0.08	0.96	2
079	+0.47	0.13	+0.54	101.92	106	5.31	0.07	2
080	-0.21	0.14	+0.54	101.92	106	0.01	0.99	2
081	+1.24	0.15	-0.05	101.92	106	1.14	0.57	2
082	-0.06	0.14	+0.95	101.92	106	4.65	0.10	2
083	+0.37	0.14	+0.24	101.92	106	0.97	0.62	2
084	+0.49	0.16	-0.19	101.92	106	2.46	0.29	2
086	+0.52	0.15	+0.55	101.92	106	2.89	0.24	2
087	+0.51	0.15	+0.47	100.96	105	0.50	0.78	2
088	-0.04	0.15	+0.02	101.92	106	0.08	0.96	2
089	-0.20	0.16	+0.42	101.92	106	1.91	0.38	2
090	-0.26	0.16	-0.04	101.92	106	0.33	0.85	2
091	-0.09	0.14	+0.05	101.92	106	0.34	0.85	2
092	+0.15	0.16	+0.70	103.84	108	2.13	0.34	2
093	-0.41	0.18	-0.09	103.84	108	1.51	0.47	2
095	-0.45	0.16	0.11	102.88	107	1.56	0.46	2
096	-0.17	0.15	+0.18	103.84	108	0.66	0.72	2
097	-0.73	0.15	+0.76	102.88	107	3.33	0.19	2

Table A4.3.3 *(continued)*

Item	Location	SE	Residual	DegF	DatPts	χ^2	Prob	degF
098	-0.43	0.16	+0.02	103.84	108	2.17	0.34	2
099	+0.42	0.17	+0.02	102.88	107	0.13	0.94	2
100	+0.72	0.17	+0.30	103.84	108	0.55	0.76	2
101	+0.91	0.19	+0.18	103.84	108	1.53	0.47	2
102	+0.16	0.16	+0.07	103.84	108	1.57	0.46	2
103	+0.60	0.16	+0.31	103.84	108	0.03	0.98	2
105	-1.02	0.18	-0.10	103.84	108	6.02	0.05	2
106	+0.16	0.14	+0.53	103.84	108	0.73	0.69	2
107	+1.80	0.17	-0.25	103.84	108	1.89	0.39	2
108	-0.61	0.17	-0.10	103.84	108	1.51	0.47	2
109	-0.75	0.17	+0.30	103.84	108	0.10	0.95	2
111	+0.32	0.14	+0.32	103.84	108	1.56	0.46	2
112	+0.75	0.15	+0.45	102.88	107	5.70	0.06	2
113	+0.17	0.13	+0.60	103.84	108	1.27	0.53	2

Table A4.4.1
Summary test-of-fit statistics for the 40-item test

	Item-Person Interaction				
	Items			Persons	
	Location	Fit Residual		Location	Fit Residual
Mean	0.00	0.04		-1.21	-0.16
SD	1.47	1.59		1.09	0.88

Item-Trait Interaction		Reliability Indices	
Total Item χ^2	207.55	Separation Index	0.83
Total Deg of Freedom	80.00	Cronbach Alpha	0.84
Total χ^2 Probability	0.00		

Power of Test-of-Fit
Power is GOOD
[Based on Separation Index of 0.83]

Table A4.4.2
Individual item fit for the 40-item test data

Item	Location	SE	Residual	DegF	DatPts	χ^2	Prob	degF
01	+0.79	0.20	+0.06	208.65	215	0.99	0.61	2
02	+2.45	0.36	-0.50	208.65	215	0.60	0.74	2
03	+2.37	0.35	-0.09	208.65	215	0.51	0.77	2
04*	-0.74	0.15	+4.22*	208.65	215	17.99	0.00*	2
05	+0.04	0.17	-0.61	208.65	215	1.51	0.47	2
06	-0.84	0.15	-2.20	208.65	215	3.92	0.14	2
07	+0.82	0.20	-1.43	208.65	215	5.32	0.07	2
08	+0.70	0.19	+0.18	208.65	215	0.62	0.73	2
09	+0.02	0.17	+0.21	208.65	215	0.73	0.70	2
10	+0.64	0.19	-0.93	208.65	215	1.52	0.47	2
11	-0.55	0.16	+0.95	208.65	215	2.94	0.23	2
12	+0.53	0.18	-0.12	208.65	215	0.16	0.92	2
13	-2.26	0.17	-1.28	208.65	215	7.93	0.02	2
14	+0.75	0.19	+1.71	208.65	215	7.55	0.02	2
15	+1.42	0.24	-1.25	208.65	215	4.38	0.11	2
16	-0.83	0.15	-2.12	208.65	215	5.81	0.05	2
17	-0.43	0.16	-0.61	208.65	215	4.52	0.10	2
18	+1.08	0.21	+1.41	208.65	215	9.01	0.01	2
19	+2.86	0.43	-0.70	208.65	215	0.84	0.66	2
20*	-2.59	0.18	-0.35	208.65	215	11.15	0.00*	2
21	+1.07	0.21	-0.43	208.65	215	1.37	0.50	2
22*	-0.31	0.16	+3.29*	208.65	215	34.59	0.00*	2
23	+2.96	0.45	-0.58	208.65	215	2.28	0.32	2
24	+0.31	0.18	+0.20	208.65	215	1.12	0.57	2
25	-0.96	0.15	-0.48	208.65	215	0.87	0.65	2
26	-1.24	0.15	+2.00	208.65	215	1.83	0.40	2
27	+0.17	0.17	+1.43	208.65	215	6.13	0.05	2
28	+0.12	0.17	+1.66	208.65	215	2.34	0.31	2
29	-1.89	0.16	-1.62	208.65	215	2.12	0.35	2
30	-0.79	0.15	+1.61	208.65	215	4.53	0.10	2
31	+1.41	0.24	+1.12	208.65	215	4.64	0.10	2
32	-0.51	0.16	-1.99	208.65	215	3.31	0.19	2
33	+0.18	0.17	-0.34	208.65	215	1.19	0.55	2
34*	-1.51	0.16	-1.62	208.65	215	11.60	0.00*	2
35*	-1.51	0.16	-2.34*	208.65	215	11.19	0.00*	2
36*	-0.62	0.15	+3.91	208.65	215	12.91	0.00*	2
37	-0.91	0.15	+0.17	208.65	215	2.69	0.26	2
38*	-3.18	0.20	+0.98	208.65	215	9.00	0.01*	2
39	-1.50	0.15	-1.10	208.65	215	3.39	0.18	2
40	+2.51	0.37	-0.95	208.65	215	2.40	0.30	2

*indicates items with high residuals and/or low chi-square probability values.

Table A4.5.1
Summary test-of-fit statistics for the 33-item test data

	Item-Person Interaction			
	Items		Persons	
	Location	Fit Residual	Location	Fit Residual
Mean	0.00	0.13	-1.55	-0.14
SD	1.35	1.42	1.20	0.79

Item-Trait Interaction		Reliability Indices	
Total Item χ^2	137.78	Separation Index	0.82
Total Deg of Freedom	68.00	Cronbach Alpha	0.81
Total χ^2 Probability	0.00		

Power of Test-of-Fit
Power is GOOD
[Based on Separation Index of 0.82]

Table A4.5.2
Individual item-fit for the 33-item test

Item	Location	SE	Residual	DegF	DatPts	ChiSq	Prob	degF
01	+0.52	0.20	+0.54	204.79	212	0.52	0.77	2
02	+2.20	0.36	-0.58	204.79	212	0.58	0.75	2
03	+2.11	0.35	-0.16	204.79	212	0.55	0.76	2
05	-0.25	0.17	-0.60	204.79	212	2.29	0.32	2
06	-1.14	0.15	-1.84	204.79	212	5.29	0.07	2
07	+0.51	0.20	-1.14	204.79	212	2.64	0.27	2
08	+0.41	0.19	+0.38	204.79	212	0.97	0.62	2
09	-0.27	0.17	+0.48	204.79	212	3.88	0.14	2
10	+0.37	0.19	-0.76	204.79	212	0.97	0.62	2
11	-0.84	0.16	+0.75	204.79	212	1.47	0.48	2
12	+0.24	0.19	-0.02	204.79	212	0.26	0.88	2
13	-2.59	0.17	-0.70	204.79	212	5.97	0.05	2
14	+0.48	0.20	+1.44	204.79	212	3.58	0.17	2
15	+1.15	0.24	-1.26	204.79	212	3.18	0.20	2
16	-1.17	0.15	-1.71	204.79	212	6.80	0.03	2
17	-0.73	0.16	-0.36	204.79	212	3.12	0.21	2
18	+0.80	0.22	+1.83	204.79	212	14.99	0.00	2
19	+2.57	0.43	-0.62	204.79	212	0.56	0.76	2
21	+0.80	0.22	-0.22	204.79	212	4.65	0.10	2
23	+2.71	0.46	-0.58	204.79	212	2.36	0.31	2
24	+0.04	0.18	+0.54	204.79	212	5.59	0.06	2
25	-1.25	0.15	-0.20	204.79	212	0.72	0.70	2
26	-1.53	0.16	+3.00	204.79	212	2.33	0.31	2
27	-0.10	0.17	+1.95	204.79	212	8.83	0.01	2
28	-0.16	0.17	+1.77	204.79	212	3.00	0.22	2
29	-2.23	0.16	-1.89	204.79	212	4.04	0.13	2
30	-1.07	0.16	+1.84	204.79	212	5.31	0.07	2
31	+1.14	0.24	+1.23	204.79	212	5.81	0.05	2
32	-0.82	0.16	-1.69	204.79	212	8.89	0.01	2
33	-0.12	0.17	-0.45	204.79	212	2.40	0.30	2
37	-1.21	0.15	+0.81	204.79	212	0.66	0.72	2
39	-1.80	0.16	-0.64	204.79	212	4.49	0.11	2
40	+2.23	0.37	-1.02	204.79	212	2.46	0.29	2

Table A4.6.1

Pearson correlation of independent variables with the dependent variable (n = 108)

Independent Variables	Correlation (r)
A1. COMPUTER COMPETENCY	
(a) CAI usage	-0.04
1 I use online learning.	0.04
2 I use disk-based (CD/DVD) learning.	-0.12
(b) Skill level	-0.11
3 I am competent in using computers.	-0.12
4 I am satisfied with my computer skills.	-0.07
A2. PREFERENCE FOR COMPUTER-BASED LEARNING	
(a) CAI usage	-0.01
5 Computer technology should be used in my university classes.	-0.05
6 Computer technology should be used for university class homework.	-0.13
(b) Collaboration	-0.18
7 I like to work on my own with computers in class.	-0.14
8 I like to work in pairs with computers in class.	-0.12
9 I like to work in groups with computers in class.	-0.24*
10 I like to work on my own with computers outside class.	-0.14
11 I like to work in pairs with computers outside class.	-0.13
12 I like to work in groups with computers outside class.	-0.07
A3. PREFERENCE FOR LEARNING ENGLISH THROUGH CAI	
(a) CAI EFL activities	-0.03
14 I like to use practice tests (TOEFL / TOEIC / TEPS) when studying English with computers.	0.06
15 I like to use set syllabus modules when studying English with computers.	0.06
16 I like to use grammar exercises when studying English with computers.	0.00
19 I like to use cloze exercises when studying English with computers.	0.10
20 I like to use matching exercises when studying English with computers.	0.09
21 I like to use writing/typing tasks when studying English with computers.	-0.10

Table A4.6.1 *(continued)*

	Independent Variables	Correlation (r)
22	I like to use crossword puzzles when studying English with computers.	0.22*
23	I like to use pronunciation activities when studying English with computers.	0.00
24	I like to use translation tasks when studying English with computers.	0.03
25	I like to use test style exercises when studying English with computers.	0.07
26	I like to use multiple-choice questions when studying English with computers.	0.06
27	I like to use true/false questions when studying English with computers.	-0.03
28	I like to use question and answer tasks when studying English with computers.	0.11
29	I like to use clue/guessing activities when studying English with computers.	-0.10
30	I like to use word search puzzles when studying English with computers.	0.01
32	I like to use color coding activities when studying English with computers.	0.00
33	I like to use reorganization activities when studying English with computers.	0.12
34	I like to use semantic identification tasks when studying English with computers.	-0.17
35	I like to use negotiation exchange tasks when studying English with computers.	-0.21*
36	I like to use mnemonics/keyword tasks when studying English with computers.	-0.22*
37	I think computers can help me improve my English reading skills.	-0.16
38	I think computers can help me improve my English writing skills.	-0.03
39	I think computers can help me improve my English listening skills.	-0.06
40	I think computers can help me improve my English speaking skills.	-0.11
41	I want to use computers to study English.	-0.10

Table A4.6.1 *(continued)*

Independent Variables	Correlation (r)
(b) CAI EFL software preferences	-0.15
42 Using CD / DVD software is an effective way to learn English.	-0.19*
44 Learning English with computers is improved when combined with the use of a paper-based workbook.	-0.12
46 English language learning software instructions should include only instructions in Korean.	-0.14
47 English language learning software instructions should include both English and Korean instructions.	-0.04
48 English language learning software menu bars should include only English.	0.06
49 English language learning software menu bars should include only Korean.	-0.07
50 English language learning software menu bars should include both English and Korean.	-0.07
51 English language learning software program icons should include only English.	0.08
53 English language learning software program icons should include both English and Korean.	-0.13
B1. IN-CLASS RELATIONS	-0.08
54 I like to learn with a partner.	-0.08
55 I like to learn with a group.	-0.06
B2. DESIRED CHARACTERISTICS OF INSTRUCTORS	0.05
58 Teachers should know about the subject they teach.	0.03
59 Teachers should direct the classes.	-0.04
60 The teacher is responsible for student's performance.	0.12
B3. VIEW OF EDUCATION	0.04
62 Class exams are important.	-0.00
63 Memorizing knowledge is important.	-0.11
64 Practicing skills is important.	0.02
65 Education is a way to achieve higher social status.	0.20*

Table A4.6.1 *(continued)*

Independent Variables	Correlation (r)
C1. PREFERENCE FOR CULTURAL REPRESENTATION IN EFL LEARNING MATERIAL	0.19
68 Seeing Korean culture in English language learning materials gains my interest.	0.18
69 English language learning material should have more Korean cultural content.	0.15
C2. LOANWORD USE	0.00
71 It was easy for me to learn to use the English equivalents of pseudo loanwords (For example, *close physical contact between friends* for *skinship*).	0.01
72 It was easy for me to learn to use the English equivalents of hybrid Korean-English terms (For example, *cherry tomato* for *bangul-tomato*).	-0.06
C3. VOCABULARY ACQUISITION STRATEGIES	
(a) Meaning Discovery Strategies	
(i) Analyzing meaning	0.02
74 To discover the meaning of unknown English vocabulary, I analyze parts of speech.	-0.02
75 To discover the meaning of unknown English vocabulary, I analyze affixes and roots.	0.02
76 To discover the meaning of unknown English vocabulary, I analyze pictures or gestures.	-0.10
77 To discover the meaning of unknown English vocabulary, I guess meaning from context.	0.12
(ii) Using aids	-0.13
79 To discover the meaning of unknown English vocabulary, I use a monolingual dictionary.	-0.03
80 To discover the meaning of unknown English vocabulary, I use word lists.	0.01
81 To discover the meaning of unknown English vocabulary, I use flash cards.	-0.25*
(iii) Help from others.	-0.19
82 To discover the meaning of unknown English vocabulary, I ask the teacher for the meaning.	-0.16
83 To discover the meaning of unknown English vocabulary, I ask the teacher for a synonym of the word.	-0.13

Table A4.6.1 *(continued)*

Independent Variables		Correlation (r)
84	To discover the meaning of unknown English vocabulary, I ask the teacher for a sentence containing the word.	-0.02
86	To discover the meaning of unknown English vocabulary, I use group activities to discover the meaning of a new English word.	-0.21*
(b) Meaning Consolidation Strategies		
(i) Social Strategy		-0.25**
87	I remember the meaning of English vocabulary by using the vocabulary with a group of classmates.	-0.24*
88	I remember the meaning of English vocabulary by using the vocabulary in conversation with a native English speaker.	-0.16
(ii) Memory Strategy		-0.09
89	I remember the meaning of English vocabulary by drawing a pictorial representation of it.	-0.22*
90	I remember the meaning of English vocabulary by connecting the vocabulary to a personal experience.	0.05
91	I remember the meaning of English vocabulary by connecting the vocabulary to its synonyms and antonyms.	-0.07
92	I remember the meaning of English vocabulary by grouping the vocabulary with similar words.	-0.03
93	I remember the meaning of English vocabulary by using the vocabulary in a sentence.	-0.01
95	I remember the meaning of English vocabulary by listening to the sound of the vocabulary.	-0.00
96	I remember the meaning of English vocabulary by speaking the vocabulary aloud.	0.06
97	I remember the meaning of English vocabulary by imagining the word forms for the vocabulary.	-0.02
98	I remember the meaning of English vocabulary by using keywords.	-0.30**
99	I remember the meaning of English vocabulary by remembering the word's affixes and roots.	0.05
100	I remember the meaning of English vocabulary by remembering each word's part of speech.	0.04
101	I remember the meaning of English vocabulary by paraphrasing the meaning of the vocabulary.	-0.16

Table A4.6.1 *(continued)*

Independent Variables		Correlation (r)
102	I learn the words of an idiom together to remember English vocabulary.	0.00
103	I practice words using physical actions to remember English vocabulary.	-0.04
(iii) Cognitive Strategy		-0.16
105	I write words repeatedly to remember English vocabulary.	-0.03
106	I practice words using word lists to remember English vocabulary.	-0.11
107	I practice words using flash cards to remember English vocabulary.	-0.27**
108	I study words by taking notes in class to remember English vocabulary.	-0.11
109	I utilize vocabulary sections in textbooks to remember English vocabulary.	0.03
111	I keep a vocabulary notebook to remember English vocabulary.	0.07
(iv) Metacognitive Strategy		
112	I use English-language media to remember English vocabulary.	-0.10
113	I self-test word knowledge to remember English vocabulary.	0.02

Table A4.7.1
Model Summary

R	R^2	Adjusted R^2	Std. Error of the Estimate
0.44(a)	0.19	0.03	0.83

a Predictors: (Constant), C3(b)(iv), A2(b), B2, C3(a)(ii), A1(b), C3(a)(i), C3(b)(i), C2, A1(a), A2(a), C1, A3(b), B3, C3(b)(iii), B1, A3(a), C3(a)(iii), C3(b)(ii).

Table A4.8.1

Treatment group one RUMM ANOVA output for each item

Item	Test F-Ratio	Prob
1	0.50	0.48
2	1.62	0.21
3	0.15	0.70
5	0.53	0.47
6	1.04	0.31
7	3.00	0.09
8	0.00	0.98
9	0.17	0.68
10	0.29	0.59
11	0.14	0.71
12	0.39	0.53
13	2.95	0.09
14	3.40	0.07
15	0.97	0.33
16	0.19	0.66
17	0.02	0.89
18	0.85	0.36
19	0.14	0.71
21	1.94	0.17
23	0.44	0.51
24	0.33	0.57
25	0.08	0.78
26	0.01	0.93
27	0.00	0.95
28	0.23	0.63
29	1.14	0.29
30	1.19	0.28
31	1.09	0.30
32	0.04	0.84
33	0.00	0.99
37	0.24	0.63
39	7.97	0.01*
40	0.06	0.80

* Indicates $p < 0.05$

Table A4.8.2
Treatment group two RUMM ANOVA output for each item

Item	Test F-Ratio	Prob
1	0.39	0.53
2	1.18	0.28
3	0.18	0.67
5	1.51	0.22
6	8.65	0.00*
7	0.80	0.37
8	1.04	0.31
9	0.20	0.66
10	0.06	0.81
11	0.02	0.89
12	0.08	0.77
13	7.71	0.01*
14	2.61	0.11
15	0.07	0.79
16	0.63	0.43
17	1.33	0.25
18	3.41	0.07
19	0.69	0.41
21	0.07	0.79
23	0.42	0.52
24	1.92	0.17
25	0.08	0.78
26	4.00	0.05*
27	3.37	0.07
28	0.00	0.97
29	4.43	0.04*
30	0.33	0.57
31	0.02	0.90
32	1.62	0.21
33	1.48	0.23
37	0.51	0.48
39	1.44	0.23
40	1.95	0.17

* Indicates $p < 0.05$

Figures

Reference to figures made in the text refers to these below.

I0066 Descriptor for Item 66   Location = -1.185   Residual = -0.111   Chi Sq Prob = 0.582

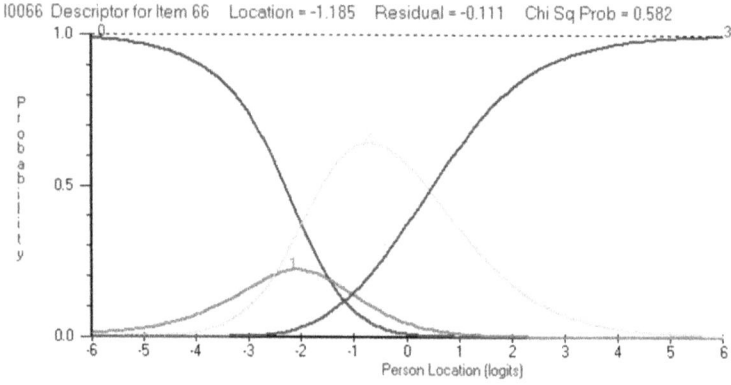

Figure A4.1.1 *Item with disordered thresholds (uncentralized)*

I0001 Descriptor for Item 1   Location = 0.945   Residual = 0.099   Chi Sq Prob = 0.973

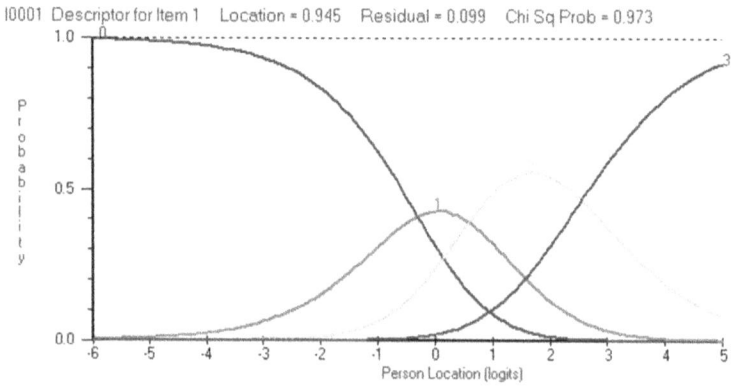

Figure A4.1.2 *Item with ordered thresholds (uncentralized)*

Location	Persons	Items [location]
2.0		107
	X	081
1.0	X	002
	XX	046 016 049 012 101 001 038 086 004 011 037 103
	XX	014 075 051 074 100 112 008 041 083 024
	XXXXX	048 033 099 009 079 084 092 106 102 113 007
	XXXXXXXXXXX	019 042 029 040 015 111 006 082 088 035 020 025
0.0	XXXXXXXXXX	021 022 028 039 026 027 023
	XXXXXXXXXX	030 096 044 032 003 091
	XXXXXXXX	005 036 060 090 080 089
	XXXX	069 073 034 095 098 054 093
	XX	077 109 097 068 076 059 108
-1.0		053 050
		063 062 065 105
		072
	X	071
-2.0		047 058
		064

X = 2 persons

Figure A4.2.1 Person-item map for the 95-item refined survey

Location	Persons		Items [uncentralized thresholds]			
3.0						
			23			
			19			
			40			
2.0			03	02		
1.0			31	15		
			18			
		XX	21			
		X	08	14	07	01
		XX	12	10		
0.0		XXX	24			
		XXXX	28	33	27	
		XXXXX	09	05		
		XXXXXX				
		XXXX	17			
-1.0		XXXXXXXXXXX	11	32		
	XXXXXXXXXXXXXXXXXXX		16	06	30	
		XXXXXXXXXX	25	37		
		XXXXXX	26			
		XXXX				
-2.0			39			
		XXXXXXX				
		XXXX	29			
		XXXXX	13			
-3.0		XXXXXXXXXXXXX				
		XXXXX				
-4.0						
		XXXX				
-5.0						
		XX				
-6.0						

X = 2 persons

Figure A4.2.2 *Person-item map for the 33-item test*

GLOSSARY

ANOVA	Analysis of Variance
EFL	English as a Foreign Language
EIL	English as an International Language
ELF	English as a Lingua Franca
CA	Comparative Analysis
CAI	Computer Assisted Instruction
CALL	Computer Assisted Language Learning
CLI	Cross Linguistic Influence
CLT	Communicative Language Teaching
CSAT	College Scholastic Ability Test
ICT	Information Communication Technology
IL	Interlanguage
L1	First Language
L2	Second Language
L_b	Borrowing Language
OT	Optimality Theory
RUMM	Rasch Unidimensional Measurement Models
SILL	Strategy Inventory for Language Learning
SLA	Second Language Acquisition
SPSS	Statistical Package for the Social Sciences
SSACAL	Survey of Student Attitudes towards Computer Assisted Language Learning in EFL
SUPL	Test of Student Understanding of Pseudo-Loanwords
TOEFL	Test of English as a Foreign Language
TOEIC	Test of English for International Communication
UG	Universal Grammar

ABOUT THE BOOK

Of all the approaches to the teaching of English to speakers of other languages (TESOL), the loanword approach is mindful of the English words found within students' native languages, and seeks to apply these in the learning process for positive transfer. Taking into account research and implementation going back to and prior to the last millennium, here is a study of such a use in the Korean context. As focus is on implementing the loanword approach from multimedia-based learning materials, the Korean cultural influences on computer assisted language learning (CALL) of English as a foreign language (EFL) are explored. The advantages and difficulties associated with implementing the approach are outlined, as is the place of EFL and the application of computer technology in the Korean education system. Focus then turns to investigating the efficacy behind deployment of the approach coupled with a multimedia-based curriculum grounded on culturally constructed methods of learning and teaching.

A loanword approach to the teaching of EFL in Korea deserves not only consideration by teachers but also further study. The book is well-resourced and comes to provide an in-depth examination of just one of many practical ways for implementing such an approach in the Korean context.

ABOUT THE AUTHOR

David Kent is an Assistant Professor at the Graduate School of TESOL-MALL at Woosong University in the Republic of Korea. He has been working and teaching in Korea since 1995, and with a doctorate from Curtin University in Australia, he is a specialist in computer assisted language learning (CALL) and the teaching of English to speakers of other languages (TESOL). He has presented at international conferences, as well as published a number of peer-reviewed journal articles, books, and book chapters in his areas of specialization.

www.ingramcontent.com/pod-product-compliance
Lightning Source LLC
Chambersburg PA
CBHW021224090426
42740CB00006B/373